GOAL DUST

GOAL DUST

An Autobiography by
WOODY STRODE
and
SAM YOUNG

Madison Books
Lanham • New York • London

Published by Madison Books
4720 Boston Way
Lanham, Maryland 20706

3 Henrietta Street
London WC2E 8LU England

Distributed by National Book Network

The paper used in this publication meets the minimum
requirements of American National Standard for
Information Sciences—Permanence of Paper for
Printed Library Materials, ANSI Z39.48–1984. ∞™
Manufactured in the United States of America.

5   4   3   2   1

Library of Congress Cataloging-in-Publication Data

Strode, Woody.
Goal dust : an autobiography / by Woody Strode and Sam Young.
p.   cm.
1. Strode, Woody.   2. Motion picture actors and actresses–United
States–Biography.   3. Afro-Americans–Biography.   I. Young, Sam.
II. Title.
PN2287.S787A3   1990   791.43'028'092—dc20   90–33330
CIP

ISBN 0–8191–7680–X (alk. paper)

British Cataloging in Publication Information Available

Contents

Twenty-four pages of photographs follow page 124.

Dedicated to
the Kingfish, Papa, the Princess,
and the proposition that
all men are created equal

CHAPTER ONE

Mixed Breed

My daddy smoked cigars and when he'd step off the street car, I could smell him coming a block away. That's how clean the air was in the City of Los Angeles when I was growing up. I was born there in 1914. They named me Woodrow Wilson Woolwine Strode. My daddy admired the President and Woolwine, who was the District Attorney of Los Angeles. Well, I had to get rid of that title. "And now, ladies and gentlemen, Woodrow Wilson Woolwine Strode!" It was like a goddamned announcement. So I cut it down to Woody Strode.

My great-grandfather was the first of my line to reach freedom in this country. His heritage was in Africa, but those people were captured and sold into slavery. He was a warrior, a rebellious person, and this made him dangerous to his owners. But he was too good an African to kill, so they decided to teach him something. They taught him how to drive the sugarcane train through the fields of the big plantation. His rebellious nature led him to escape, and he reached safety with a wild tribe of Creek Indians. He married one of their squaws, and they had a son. Their son, my grandfather, eventually took off and married a full-blood Blackfoot Indian.

I forget the exact age I found out I was a mixed breed. I

1

thought we were all colored and everybody was similar. Nobody looked at your skin to see if you were a little bit brown or a little bit black. I looked like a Blackfoot and didn't know it. I've got the Plains Indian look from my high cheek bones. I have a picture of John Grass, the Blackfoot Chief; I look just like him. But as strange as I looked, I never thought I was different from any other Negro. My daddy said I looked like an uncle who was six-feet-five and weighed 230 pounds. He worked on the wharf in New Orleans and could buck 300-pound bales of cotton. I grew to be six-feet-four, 210 pounds, so I was a throwback, just on a smaller scale.

I didn't find out about my Indian blood until I got into college. I knew something had to be different because I had such a physical nature. I figured it out when the doctors started talking about me.

"You are the most physical person that has ever come through the gates of UCLA. What type of racial background do you have?"

"I don' know, I'se colored."

I went home, told my daddy what happened. He got a little indignant. He said, "You can tell them your great-grandmother was a Creek and your grandmother was a full-blood Blackfoot Indian!"

See, race was a very touchy subject for the Southerner who migrated. My daddy came to Los Angeles in 1900 to escape the racial pressure in Washington, Louisiana. I remember he had a trunk full of guns and thirty-ought-six bullets; that was based on his Southern background, fear. But he saw the white people out here were different from the white people where he came from. He wanted me to fall into their path. That's why he never talked about race.

My daddy was a brick mason; his daddy taught him how to lay brick at the age of fourteen. There was no schooling then. My father got all his schooling after he moved out here to California. He got a high school education at night at Jefferson High School. But he knew construction. He helped build the City of Los Angeles. A lot of the old brick buildings downtown have my daddy's bricks in them. The faster you laid brick, the better you were. My daddy set a record, 2,500 bricks a day.

He had huge corns on his knuckles from handling all the brick and mud. If he hit you, he might as well have hit you with brass knuckles, it'd cut you. He was very strong and pretty beat up physically. He wouldn't teach me to lay brick. He was against me learning a trade. When I was a child he would say to me, "Daddy don't want you to do this. He wants you to go to school. He wants you to get educated."

He was smart enough to realize the importance of an education. So when I got into UCLA based on my athletic ability and became famous as an athlete, he was proud. He didn't know I was going to become a professional athlete; that was the furthest thing from his mind. But I'm glad I became an athlete; it gave me better insight and helped integrate me into society. Only the white world was involved in athletics in my generation, and I got headlined by the white press. That was unusual. You were a special Negro if they let you play.

My mother was much closer to the slave scene than my father. She was from New Orleans, Louisiana. Her mother was a slave, a servant in the master's house. The house servants were the best-looking slaves, and my mama was a beautiful woman. And she must have had some good people behind her because she went to school; she graduated from college. But even with that background, my mother was part Cherokee. That's how close the Indians and the slaves were in those days; they were both downtrodden in America.

My mama told me that when slavery first started we were compared to the animals. The first hundred years they wouldn't teach us religion. That's how they kept us down. The slaves had to hide under tubs and pray. But how do you read the Bible? You read about Moses and the brotherhood of man. So the white man began to let us sit in the back of the church, and the American Negro became a Christian. I used to wonder why the slaves would want their master's religion. I figure it this way: if I was a witch doctor and I'm going to fight you, and I go in and make all my medicine and I still get my ass kicked, then I'm going to believe in *your* God.

The Western Negro wasn't as close to the church as the Southern Negro was. My mother, with her Southern background, was always searching for God. She started with the Seventh Day Adventists. Part of my grade school education came from that

3

church. I have a lot of rules in my head based on what we read in the Bible every day. There's hardly a scripture in there I don't know. I wasn't going to be a preacher, but you have to live by some civilized rule.

This helped me when they recruited me to play football at UCLA because they put me in class with the rich kids like Douglas Fairbanks' niece and Joe E. Brown's son. I didn't have an educated background, so when they had me up quoting French you can imagine the floundering. It was the funniest thing. I would sit and watch the white kids and I'd imitate them. That's what exposure did for me. I was a nice person, so if you were my white friend you'd say, "Woody, don't use that fork, use this one." And slowly, I learned.

I didn't have anything going in my head like, this guy's Chinese or this guy's Italian. The Jewish kids went to their synagogues, but I never thought about it. As far as I was concerned they were just going to church. So when it came time for me to integrate the National Football League in 1946 with my best friend Kenny Washington, our Western upbringing made it possible. And the same was true of Jackie Robinson, who played football with Kenny and me at UCLA and went on to integrate Major League Baseball in 1947.

We were hanging loose out here in Southern California; we thought we were equals. I didn't want to be a doctor or a lawyer anyway; I wanted to play football. I didn't know I'd get out of school and make a living at it. No blacks played in the NFL during my college days. But the Hollywood Bears showed up, and they paid me $1,800 for half a year of semi-pro football. We'd play for six months and then basketball would push us right off the sheet.

World War II came along and I started playing football for an integrated service team on a segregated field down at March Field Air Force base in Riverside, California. I lived in the gym with all the other football players. Somehow, I've always found someone that said, "Come here Woody, you don't have to take that shit." Like when the Rams dropped me after the 1946 season: I was contacted by the Calgary Stampeders football team up in Canada. They gave me $500 a week to play football; I was getting only

4

$350 a week from the Rams. We won their national championship, the Grey Cup, in 1947. After that, the millionaires came up to me and asked, "What do you want, Woody?" I could have asked for anything; I could have become a Canadian, but I was too embarrassed to ask.

When my kids came along, I had to get another job because of inflation. That's when I began to wrestle in the off-season. Then I broke my ankle, separated my shoulder, and broke two ribs up in Canada, and I had to quit football. I went to wrestling full-time. I learned to wrestle at the Olympic Auditorium in downtown Los Angeles. On Wednesday nights we'd wrestle in front of 10,000 people. I wrestled Gorgeous George and Barone Leone, the most glamorous of the old-time wrestlers. My whole life was nothing but exposure to crowds. So when the motion picture industry saw me wrestling on the tube and pulled me into the movies, I had no fear. I said, "Why do you want me? I don't know how to act."

They said, "Well, you don't look like you came from New York City. All we're going to do is shave your head, give you this loin cloth to wear and put this spear in your hand." When they did that, boy, primitive I was. But I made a living, and I was very lucky for that.

Hollywood loved physical actors. When I first worked for John Ford, he said, "Can you ride a horse, shoot a gun? Can you fight?"

"Yes, sir!"

I developed a personal relationship with him because I was tough, and he respected toughness. I made four pictures for him because there was no other actor in Hollywood physical enough to play the roles. My first Ford picture was *Sergeant Rutledge,* a major role for a black actor at that time. That one gave me dignity. After the fourth picture I was on the world market. I didn't realize until later, when I moved to Italy and became a true star, what John Ford had done for me. I could step off a plane anywhere in the world and people would recognize me.

John Ford made me a character actor because there wasn't any work for black stars. And because of my mixed background I could play anyone from the third world. I played natives in the old jungle pictures; I fought Tarzan to the death. They stuck a pigtail on me for *Genghis Khan,* and slanted my eyes and made me Chinese in *Seven Women,* and I could play all the Indians. I never played myself, a Negro-Indian breed, until I did *The Professionals* with Lee Marvin and Burt Lancaster.

So it was always my look and my physical nature that got me the jobs. I remember the first time I became really conscious of it was when I was working on *Spartacus.* I was standing with Kirk Douglas in the Roman arena. We were getting ready to fight to the death. I was standing with my head dropped and Sir Laurence Olivier, who was watching us said, "Woody Strode!"

"Yes, sir?"

"I'm a fan of yours and Kenny Washington."

I said, "I don't know what I'm doing here in your business."

He looked down in the arena and said, "What you're about to do, I could never do."

Well, that gave me all the confidence I needed. See, I could fight.

CHAPTER TWO

A History Lesson

I was born in bed in a three-bedroom house near the corner of Fifty-First Street and Holmes Avenue in an area we called Furlong Tract. It was a predominantly black neighborhood, but we had some Germans, Italians, and Mexicans living there. All the kids would play together in the street. We didn't have any problems like they have now. When they integrate now, they start a big fight. We fought some, but then we'd back off, shake hands and go eat at the other guy's house.

Today, that area would be called South-Central Los Angeles. My daddy owned a half-acre of land there. He didn't build the house: it was wood frame. And it stood twenty or thirty years before they tore it down. I lived there with my parents and my brother, Baylous Strode, Junior. He was two years older than me.

For some reason my brother inherited all my mother's side. He wasn't very physical; he was all up in his head. He was all ribs and no shoulders. He had to wear suspenders and a belt to keep his knickers up. When we'd go to the playground, he preferred to sit by himself and read a book. That made him pretty attractive to the bullies.

One day we were on the playground. Baylous was sitting in the bleachers behind the baseball diamond; I was across the field playing marbles with some friends. I looked up just in time to see some big kids throw my brother to the ground, getting ready to kick his brains out. I lost my clear blue aggie when I ran over there to help him out. There were some loose bats lying by home plate and I picked one up. I couldn't have been more than six years old and I ran over and hit this big kid right across the head with the bat. I laid him out, completely unconscious. The playground director came and carried me away, but I was exonerated because I was defending my brother. That's when Mama pulled me into church to try and teach me some rules.

My mother was like a protective old hen. That's the Louisiana attitude. She used to dress me up in Buster Brown collars with the coat, short pants, and string tie. And some big, hard, black shoes. I was a nice-looking kid anyway and after she dressed me up, I looked like a mama's boy. I used to get teased a lot for that.

If you looked too smooth, you were a marked man. But inside I had the gorilla, so I ended up fighting a lot. I could always fight well. When I got mad, I'd just black out and go. I had all my father's fire. After I got to high school he told me how glad he was my mother raised me in the church. As delicate as I looked, I had a tiger inside. That's why I excelled at football, because I had no fear. Of course we were all like that; I wasn't unusual. Everybody came off the earth and our education was kind of crude.

We used to salt meat; that shows you how old I am. There was no refrigeration. Everybody had iceboxes, and the iceman would come twice a week with a big block of ice. There was no freezing until I got to high school. Then they discovered dry ice. That was a whole program by itself. We grew our own vegetables. Potatoes we'd buy because they took up too much ground. My daddy would buy a hundred pound sack of potatoes and Mama would bury them in the ground so they wouldn't rot. I don't know how they learned that stuff. It was part of their generation; they brought the earth to us.

I lived on beefsteak; I grew up on it. It was nothing for us to have it on the table every night. I used to eat a dozen raw eggs every morning. That gave me the strength to play sixty minutes of football. We raised our own chickens; the beef we had to buy. Pork we bought. For New Year's, Mama would serve us hog's head and black-eyed peas. The hog's head we got in Chinatown for a dime. We had chitlins and hog maws, the lining of the stomach. I ate a southern diet, and because my mother was from Louisiana, she knew how to season the fish. Nobody cooks as good as the Louisiana people.

My mama made soap out of lye and lard that she would boil and cook. That's why we didn't get infections. In my day you were either a strong son of a bitch or you died. Of course in those days they had just come out of bloodletting. Anytime the doctors showed up you had the right to be a little bit scared.

Imagine how they would amputate in the old days. They had no idea of infection. The doctor would put on an apron that was covered with the blood and gore of a hundred other patients; he wouldn't wash his hands until after the operation. They'd set you up on the kitchen table and lay a box underneath to catch the blood. They'd get you drunk, cut the limb off with a saw, and use a hot iron poker to seal the wound. It's hard to believe anyone could survive something like that.

You see, civilization, let me tell you about the disease scene. When the bubonic plague hit in Europe, only the strongest people survived. The plague spread based on the open sewage, the rats, and the filth. One-third of the population died. They found out that the cheese eaters, the ones who ate the moldy cheese, survived because of the penicillin formed in the mold. It was antibiotics in a crude form.

Now, the Indians and the Hawaiians were wiped out by small pox. Same with the Eskimos. They were all disease-free until the white man showed up. They didn't know about tuberculosis or consumption. The early tribal people lived by the rivers. They'd stay so many months, then they'd move on. I imagine they would just squat down to take a crap. Even if they dumped their waste into the rivers, the rocks and the natural purification process would clean the water before it hit the next tribe.

This is how California was originally: different tribes living up and down the state. There was so much distance between them they didn't know what the other was doing. Then the Spanish came, and they rounded up the Indians and taught them Christianity. They put the Indians to work building their missions and tending their fields and orchards.

By the time I was born this whole structure of missions and priests had disintegrated and all the fruit was growing wild. We used to have white peaches that you don't see any more. Old man Burbank crossed the peaches and made them all big and beautiful and all different colors. The white peaches were flat, they got about normal peach size, but flat. And boy, were those things sweet and tasty. We all had them growing in our backyards. We had white figs, too, and that was the sweetest fruit I've ever eaten.

After the Spanish system broke down, the Mexicans took over. Then came the migration of the American white man and the Negroes followed him. They were both crude farmers and ranchers; they were both downtrodden on the earth. They were sharecroppers. Imagine that scene. I'd be farming and the owner would say, "Woodrow, I'm going to let you keep this little bit of your crop." They never got off the hook, so they loaded up the wagons and they moved to California.

The Negroes who migrated came out here to escape the hate scene down South. To them, the Far West was just like the promised land. That's why my parents moved out here. I remember when Mayor Shaw was running for re-election. He used to walk through Furlong Tract, knock on doors and say, "Don't vote for so-and-so because he belongs to the Ku Klux Klan." They tried to scare us, but we didn't believe it; we had just left that in the South.

They had a Klan out here, but they were passive. They read books, talked and all that but they never put on the hoods or got involved with any of the terrorism. They did no parading because we weren't afraid of them. We all had guns—who's going to try and pull you out of your house when they know you've got guns? White, black, Mexican, or Indian, we were all armed. "That's my land; don't you walk across that son of a bitch!"

But if you said, "Hey Woody, you know that back pasture of yours, may I come across it and put my horse down there?"

"Sure, go ahead. I don't want nobody else in there, but you

can." That was the kind of law and order we had out here. "Excuse me," instead of, "Get the hell out of the way!"

See, from the time I was born until the 1960's and the Watts riots, racial tension actually got worse in the city of Los Angeles. First off, when I was growing up there just weren't that many blacks out here. There was no tension because there were enough menial jobs to keep us happy. Jobs like janitor, street sweeper, or dishwasher. (We used to call the dishwashers, pearl divers.) Or you were a cook or a garbage man. The best job a black man could have was policeman or fireman—which were very limited in number— or work in the post office. Most of them weren't carrying mail, they were clerks. Or you could be a chauffeur. That was a good job: wear a cap and uniform and drive a big Packard or Rolls Royce. But basically, we were never a factor economically. We weren't in competition for the good jobs, so no one paid much attention to us.

The racism out here was very subtle. A restaurant wouldn't have a sign saying, "Whites Only," like they would in the South. They'd have a sign saying, "We reserve the right to refuse service to anyone." That was their loophole. We knew where we weren't wanted, and we didn't go to those places. Why would I want to go somewhere and have the door slammed in my face? But normally, they were very high class about it. If I made the mistake of going to a restricted club, they'd say, "It'll cost you $100 to come in." Well, they knew I couldn't afford to pay that.

You could get a feel for the racial situation riding the street car. The street car would travel east on Fifth Street and then turn and go down Central Avenue. When it got down on East Fifth Street, all of a sudden all the people would be black. Then going west on Fifth, when it got past Hill Street, all of a sudden all the people would be white.

Some communities were more prejudiced than others. Up through the 1940's a black man couldn't walk through Inglewood after dark. They had a sign posted: "NO JEWS AND NO CO-LOREDS ARE WELCOME IN THIS TOWN!" Today, Inglewood is primarily a black neighborhood. And Pasadena was a prejudiced area; that's where most of the rich white people lived.

That's where Jackie Robinson was from; I think that's why Jackie had a little more hate going than the rest of us. But in the local sports they never held any grudges, especially between the players.

I remember when Moselle Elerby from Tuskegee came out here in 1938. He was one of the greatest runners we had. He came out here with a bottle of whiskey and set a record in the 100-yard dash. We were together in the Coliseum and I said, "Moselle, why in the hell are you drinking?"

He said, "This is the first time I've ever run against a white man." I nearly fell over. That shows you how ignorant I was; I didn't know what it was like in the rest of the country. I got slapped in the face once in a while, but race never deterred me. Out here, if a kid had the ability he could play.

I didn't realize that going to UCLA was a rare step for a black kid. I started out there in 1934. Smokey Joe Lillard had already been to Oregon ten years before me. Iowa had Duke Slater, the first black All-American football player. He later became a judge. Fritz Pollard played for Brown; Paul Robeson played for Rutgers. And I can't leave out Ralph Bunche, who preceded Kenny Washington, Jackie Robinson, and me out at UCLA. He graduated in 1927.

Ralph worked his way through school as a janitor in the men's gym. The average Negro didn't know anything about Ralph Bunche. Not until he went over to the Middle East and sat down talking peace. He won the Nobel Peace Prize. But Kenny, Jackie, and I, we came in the so-called modern era; that was the big deal.

California schools had been integrated as far back as the late 1800's. I started my schooling right across the street at the Holmes Avenue Grammar School. We had a black principal, Mrs. Bessie Burke. She graduated from the University of Southern California in 1910. She was the first black teacher in the Los Angeles school system. And while I was there she was the only black principal.

I remember my teacher, Mrs. Snow, had jet black hair. I thought she was an Indian because we all grew up with westerns, playing cowboys and Indians. And right behind my parents' house lived this old Indian named Harry. I loved to go see Harry; I had a friendship going with him. In my day, Indians were as strange and exciting as you could get.

12

I don't know what Harry saw in me. But it wasn't my brother; I was the one he put his hand on. He used to bring me a bag of candy every weekend. And we had a signal. Saturday night he'd go get really drunk and start war dancing. He'd start whooping and hollering and I'd come running. Normally he was sort of withdrawn; that was an Indian quality. He put on the white man's clothes and tried to conform to society, but every Saturday night he'd go on the war path.

I remember so clearly the first time I heard him, I was sitting in the kitchen watching my mama work the old wood stove. I heard this yelling and I snuck out in the backyard to see what it was. We had an old white picket fence that separated the two properties. I crawled up to it and watched Harry from between the slats. He had a face that was older than dirt, all ruddy looking. His face had more lines and wrinkles than a dried-up old prune. But his eyes were wild and bright, like two headlights on a dark country road.

He was dancing in a circle, doing some sort of one-legged stomp. He still had a suit of clothes on, but he had ditched his shoes for a pair of moccasins. He had a bottle of whiskey in his right hand, and he was waving it in the air as he howled at the moon. The moon lit him up so he was nothing but a silhouette and his shadow flowed across the ground until it piled up against the fence. As he circled around in my direction, he saw me peering through the slats.

I wanted to run right then, but my body was frozen, and we stood there and stared at each other. He motioned me over, and despite the fear I crawled through the fence. We had some kind of understanding, Harry and me, and it was there right from the beginning. And that was the beginning of our friendship.

I was about Harry's only friend. The worst thing to be in 1900 was an Indian; that's a historical fact. Harry told me, "After Custer, the American government hunted Indians with the intent of wiping them out all together." The massacre at the Little Bighorn really shook up the United States. So if someone were to ask me if I was part Indian, I'd answer, "No, I'm a mulatto." If I said Indian, they'd hate me even worse.

General George Custer wanted to be President of the United

States. He was a great general in the Civil War; hardly anyone knows that. He did something and they broke him, sent him out West. He was going to regain his position fighting the Indians.

Did you know he had an Indian son? Regardless of hate you might look at Woody Strode and think, "I hate that son of a bitch," but look at my wife and say, "Yeah, I'm going to take her to bed."

It was Custer's ego that led those men to their deaths. The Cheyenne and Sioux wiped out over 200 men, June 25, 1876. Custer came to destroy the Indian villages, but the Indians knew, and they hid, waiting for him behind a hill near the Little Bighorn. That was the 7th Cavalry that got destroyed, and the first ones on the scene after the battle were the squaws. They cut the testicles off the men; some were still alive. Then the warriors cut off the soldiers' legs. They did that in case they met the same enemy in the afterworld.

Harry taught me all this stuff about the Indians. Like the Blackfeet got their name from dancing in the wood ash and coal dust. They were the most powerful Indians because they controlled the buffalo. They followed the buffalo. When it got cold, the buffalo would move out of the mountains and cross the plains. In those days, you could measure the herds by the square mile. When they came out of the mountains, it was like tipping over a can of paint. They just flowed across the landscape. But the American government decided to destroy the kitchen table. In ten years they hunted and killed ten million buffalo. And that's how they conquered the Indian, because the buffalo created food, clothing, shelter, weapons, everything in the Indian's life.

The Cheyenne were the best-looking of all the Indian people and some of the fiercest warriors. The Crows were the "Uncle Toms." Just about every Indian scout the white man used was a Crow. But when it came to reservation time, they were forced off to the badlands anyway; they didn't gain anything by that. Now, can you believe the Plains Indians hadn't seen a white man until the 1850s? And the Apaches, to get moisture, would cut a small hole in a horse's neck and drink the blood through a straw?

Today we have *Star Wars,* but in my generation it was all cowboys and Indians. As young as seven years old I used to ride

14

the streetcar downtown to see the picture shows. Nobody molested kids in my generation. I'd see three Westerns at ten cents apiece. I'd watch them until my head hurt.

I loved the old-time cowboys, Tom Mix, Ken Maynard, and William S. Hart. I always thought William S. Hart was part Indian because he had the look: dark hair, a thin, beaky nose, dark, wary eyes, and he could speak the Sioux language. He'd pull his hat way down over his eyes until the shadow crossed his lips. When he got ready to pull his guns, he'd bite his lower lip. When he started firing, the whole street would light up; he'd kill everybody.

I'd get so worked up watching these guys that I'd come home and hang all the chickens and the ducks. And when my mama saw all these birds hanging by their necks, she'd whip my butt with a peach switch. Boy, those things really hurt. A peach switch is soft and flexible and my mama could make one of those things sing. She'd make me go out in the yard and choose the switch. If I grabbed a small one, she'd send me back after the tree.

In my day, whatever your mama or daddy said, you did; I don't care if you were a grown man. That's the kind of family we had then. We were taught to honor our mothers and fathers. Everybody was taught that, white, black, Mexican, or Indian. And you don't have to beat a kid to death. Just make them get a peach switch and hit them across the back of the legs; they'll behave.

CHAPTER THREE

City of the Angels

We had electric trolley cars out here and that system had to be one of the best in the world at the time. We called the trolleys Red Cars and they were owned by the Pacific Electric Company. I could leave home, walk two blocks, and pick up the Red Car. It would travel down to Sixth and Main, and from there I could go anywhere.

The reason Los Angeles grew the way it did, with all the communities spread around, was based on the good transportation we had. There must have been a thousand miles of track. They'd go as far south as Long Beach, as far east as Riverside and San Bernardino, which was about sixty miles, and they hit all the beaches, Santa Monica to Redondo Beach.

In those days you could pitch a tent and sleep right on the beach. My daddy would carry the whole family down there for a weekend. It was like a vacation. We cooked on an open fire. There was a pier that had a Ferris wheel and a merry-go-round; it was like an amusement park. We used to fish right off the side of the pier. I was about eight years old when we first went down there. I remember when I first saw the ocean; I just stood there in shock. I never dreamed a body of water could be so big.

Back when I was a kid the Los Angeles River was our close

beach. I used to walk there, three miles from my backyard, down an old dusty road that cut through the middle of Furlong Tract. In the summers I used to take my shoes off so I could feel that soft dusty dirt creep up between my toes; what a good feeling that was.

Today the river's just a concrete runway, but in my day it was still running wild. I can remember getting all scraped up fighting through the bushes and the brambles that lined the river's edge. When I broke through, I'd just run and plop in that old lazy river. We could swim there and go fishing, too. It was full of crawdads. They were so soft and tender you could put the whole thing in your mouth, eat the meat and spit out the shell. I never went through that fancy peeling. There was a place on the map we used to go, Nigger Slew, and that place was just full of crawdads.

In the summer the river would dry up a little, and a bunch of us would go down into the river bed where you didn't have to hunt for rocks. You could just reach down and pick one up. We'd hunt for the nice, smooth ones that would throw true. Ones you could put a little twist on, and we'd have a rock fight. If a kid came out bleeding, holding his head, we usually didn't throw any more rocks at him. And when the fight was over, we'd decide who'd won and go on about our business.

Our business was on the playgrounds. That's where we grew up; we were never into school. You don't see kids monkeyin' around on the playgrounds today like we used to. After school, during the summers and practically every night of the year, all the neighborhood kids would gather. At that time, there was a Pacific Electric shop nearby and every night they'd blow the whistle at nine o'clock. That meant it was time for us to head home. If I wasn't home ten minutes after the whistle blew, I was off choosing a peach switch.

Los Angeles was the first city to form a department to develop the parks and playgrounds. That happened to keep the kids from playing in the streets. I remember when I was six years old I got hit and run by a horse-and-buggy. I was out in the road fooling around and the horse sideswiped me, knocked me down and the wagon wheel rolled right over my head. Lucky for me it was one of those light surreys with the fringe on top or I would have been killed. And when the automobiles took over, it became that much more

18

dangerous. We had so much land out here there was no reason for the kids to play in the street.

In New York City, they didn't have that luxury. The kids back East developed games like stickball because they didn't have room for a regular baseball game. Stickball they play with a broomstick and a Spaulding handball, a "spauldeen." By sticking your thumb in that soft ball just as you're releasing it, you can get it to take a crazy hop. I imagine a guy could develop a pretty good eye hitting a small handball with a broom stick. That's how Willie Mays became a great hitter. And Duke Snider used to play with the kids on his way home from Ebbetts Field. Stickball was the street kid's game; they controlled it.

Out here, the playground director controlled everything. He was like a chaperon for the kids. Our parents could dump us at the playground and know the director would look after us. He taught us the games, and we played all the major sports: baseball, basketball, and football. And we had horseshoes and croquet. I was into tennis for just a little bit; that was too high class a sport for me.

Football was the main sport; baseball and basketball were nothin' compared to football. See, baseball you need at least one ball, a bat, and nine gloves. That was too expensive for most kids. One time they had a benefit show, raised a little money, and donated four fielder's gloves to the playground. Somebody stole two of them right away and for years those other two gloves were the only two we had on the playground. The catcher wore one and the first baseman wore one; everyone else was out there barehanded.

Basketball only takes one ball, but we didn't have any good courts. I played my basketball on an old asphalt tennis court with a hoop on one end. In the summertime it would get all soft and sticky. The tar would come up and get all over the ball, your hands, and clothes. I'd scratch my head and have tar in my hair for a week. It was a mess. Then in the winter, the ground would get wet and we couldn't play. It was a hard game for us to get into.

With football, all we needed was a ball and a field. Weather didn't matter, and it was hard to lose a football. We used the old footballs that were fatter, more like a rugby ball. You can imagine a

young kid trying to throw a ball like that. We had to balance it on
our hand, throw it like a shot put, and hope the trajectory would
cause it to turn around in a spiral. Those old footballs were really
unwieldy. It reminds me of a quote from John Heisman, who was
the football coach at Georgia Tech. They named the Heisman
trophy after him. Before each season, he would describe a football
to his team:

> A prolate spheroid, that is, an elongated sphere, in which the outer
> leather casing is drawn tightly over a somewhat smaller rubber tubing
> . . . Better to have died as a small boy than to fumble this.

Because the ball was so big, we didn't throw much. Of course,
in those days the forward pass was still something new in football.
It was still a running game, so all the glamor positions were in the
backfield. Three or four guys, the ball handlers, would form the
nucleus of a team. The best guy would play halfback. Whoever else
was around, the lesser-thans, the uncleans, the gorillas, played line.

I was one of the gorillas. My athletic ability didn't begin to
show up until I hit McKinley Junior High School; I was thirteen,
fourteen, fifteen years old. We didn't have organized teams, but
every lunchtime we were out in the yard playing. I had fun in
school based on the recreation. All the kids were the same; we were
all poor; we all had holes in our jeans that were patched up. Those
were the years of the Great Depression.

I remember when the Depression hit in 1929, when the stock
market crashed and everyone lost their jobs. People were jumping
from the skyscrapers in New York. The Depression hit hard in Los
Angeles, but I don't think people could have asked for a better
place to starve. At least out here they were sleeping in the sun. The
Depression actually brought people together because everybody
was poor. It may sound strange, but I don't even remember the
Depression as a mark. It wasn't like we were ever without food.
Maybe it wasn't steak, but we ate.

Thank God for Roosevelt or we would have starved to death.
At fourteen, fifteen years of age I worked for the WPA building the
roads through Griffith Park. That was my introduction to a pick
and shovel. The WPA was a government-sponsored work program.

20

They'd pay us off with some money and some food. I'd go down to 54th Street and Fourth Avenue to pick up the food; the county had a station down there. You'd be entitled to so much depending on the size of your family. Canned goods, milk, cheese, vegetables, they even had reindeer meat in the can. They gave us everything we needed to keep healthy.

Those were the years when the Communists really had a chance to gain control by enlisting support from the minorities. That's when our way of life was most vulnerable. But for some reason the Communists couldn't recruit the blacks. It must have been based on our education, our belief in the American ideal.

The Communist party used to have mixed dances for us with white girls. That was the first stage. "We have a white girl here for you. See what we've done for you; you're free!" I saw through that even as a teenager. Because every day in the black newspapers, like the *Los Angeles Sentinel* or the *Pittsburgh Courier,* I read about one of us getting lynched somewhere in the United States. They were still hanging us by the neck. Well, I wasn't going to go through that, not for a piece of ass. Kenny Washington and I used to kid each other about that. If I saw Kenny looking at a white girl, I'd yell out, "TO THE TREES!"

Well, because of the Depression, my daddy couldn't find work, couldn't pay his mortgage, and we lost the house in Furlong Tract. We moved over to what was basically a one-room house at 34th Street and Central Avenue. That was a move to the city for my family, and that hurt my mama, having to make that move. Mama cried for days over that, but for me, that was the most exciting move.

At that time most of the black people in Los Angeles lived in the Central Avenue area. It was no ghetto like it is today; today it's Skid Row. Back then it was really plush. It had the best nightclubs and after-hours spots. And the greatest barbecue stands, where you could get soul food before anyone knew what soul food was. The smell of ribs and chops was always in the air. You could have blindfolded me and I would have known where I was by the smell of the barbecue. Redd Foxx, the comedian, had a place down there

21

called the Hog Hut. He used to say, "We sell all of the hog but the grunt!"

Central Avenue was brightly lit up like a Hollywood Boulevard would be today. There was foot traffic all night long, and there was always some guy standing in the shadows trying to sell fake jewelry or phony watches. You could hitch-hike anywhere on the Avenue. And, when the sun set, all the Hollywood producers and directors would come down to soak up the atmosphere. Even the glamorous movie stars like Ginger Rogers, Cary Grant, Lana Turner, and Bing Crosby would show up.

The clubs and hotels on Central Avenue were developed by our professional people, the doctors and lawyers. The most famous hotel was the old Dunbar down at 42nd and Central; it's a historical landmark today. A Dr. Sommerville built the hotel and named it after himself. During the Depression, he got a little desperate and had to sell it. That's when it got renamed the Dunbar, after Paul Laurence Dunbar, the famous black poet.

The Dunbar was the finest Negro hotel west of the Mississippi; it was all warm glows and velvet. It was just as plush as anything they had up in Hollywood. You could buy the best meal in town at the Dunbar, and the area was surrounded by the hottest night spots in Los Angeles: the Turban Room, the Last Word, the Orpheum, Club Nemo, and the Club Alabam', which was like the Cotton Club in New York City. People traveled to Los Angeles for the climate and to go to Central Avenue for the best entertainment in the world. The Ellington boys, Nat King Cole, Bill "Bojangles" Robinson, Louis Armstrong, Lena Horne, all the big names played down there.

Lena Horne: there wasn't a black man alive that didn't dream of a night with Lena. She had a kind of smart sophistication that went along with a creamy smooth complexion and small powerful features that made her irresistible. But Lena wasn't just beautiful by herself; that's how the whole chorus line used to look. The women would try and lighten up their skin with bleaching creams. The men straightened their hair; kinky hair was not the vogue. We called it "gassing your hair." Gassing, because they put it to sleep. I did it, and I had soft hair, but I wanted that whole modern scene.

The first time I had it done was before a UCLA game. I took my helmet off in the Coliseum and my hair was shinning like gold. I felt so pretty.

Well, you can imagine what a great place Central Avenue was; we had so much freedom compared to any other area in the country. That's how I got my liberated attitude. And I thank God for that because it's helped me every step of the way. Here's a little story that Ralph Bunche tells that explains what Central Avenue was like:

> The young voting Negro of today might well be likened to the Texas colored man who had been in a virtual state of slavery to his southern boss. But by careful saving he was able to take a short trip to Los Angeles and partake of the freedom and grandeur of the Southland, and more particularly, the pure liberty inspiring atmosphere of our own Central Avenue.
>
> Needless to relate, the Texas colored man returned home truant and rebellious. He didn't try to regain his old job. But his southern master finally came to him and said, "Sam, you'd better come on back to the job. We've just killed a new batch of hogs, and I've got some mighty fine hog jowls for you."
>
> But Sam just shook his kinky head wisely and with a superior air told the white man, "Uh uh, boss. You ain't talkin' to me, no suh. I've been to Los Angeles and I don' want you' old hog-jowls, cuz I'm eating' high up on de hog now."

I moved to Central Avenue the year I started high school. That was 1930; I was sixteen years old. I stood six-feet-one, weighed 130 pounds. I looked like a toothpick. The speed and strength hadn't shown up yet. I ran the 100-yard dash in fourteen flat, any woman could have outrun me. That was the awkward stage I was in.

The school put up a big sign for all those that wanted to come out for football. A couple hundred kids showed up and whatever I had to do, I passed the test. I may have been skinny, but I wanted one of those uniforms. That was the first time I had a uniform.

I was so skinny the only thing that stayed on me good was the helmet. I think they gave us the shoes. That's when I started to go through the taping scene; we used to tape our ankles. During my

23

college years I started shaving my legs. As a high school kid I didn't have much hair on my body. Nobody did except for the Italians; that was really a shaving job.

We had a Jewish coach who was born back in the Middle East and migrated out here. His name was Harry Eadleson. Harry played football for the University of Southern California and almost made All-American. He was a member of the famous USC backfield that included Russ Saunders, Jim Musick, and Ernie Pinkart. Pinkart is still a legend out here; he was the Kingpin. They beat Pittsburgh 47–14 in the 1930 Rose Bowl, the same year Harry graduated and came over to coach at Jefferson. So we both arrived the same year.

As tall and skinny as I was starting high school, I had to play end. I didn't have the weight to be on the interior line. I didn't have the quickness to play in the backfield. The first year I sat on the bench for two or three ball games until the first-string end got injured. Harry stuck me in there, and I played the whole second half. I was like a wild man, hitting anything that came my way. When I got off the field, Harry said, "My God, Woody, I thought you were going to get broke in half."

I looked like a broomstick running around out there. But I was like a piece of wire; I just didn't have the weight. I impressed him so much that I took over the first-string job. And that was when they began to recognize me.

Harry Eadleson taught me everything about playing the end, I played that position for the rest of my career. Maxwell Stiles wrote in the *Los Angeles Examiner:*

> The big boy has always played at end. He is, of course, "a natural for that position." He haunts his end like a departed spirit, taking out four men on one play if need be.

Harry taught me how to block the tackle. In those days the end blocked the tackle either inside or out, depending on which way we were going to run. After the games my cheekbones would be black and blue from banging them against those old canvas pants. They were really rough. But by the time I got to UCLA I was so well prepared that I didn't need a halfback to help me block the tackle. I could handle him by myself.

24

At Jefferson we played a formation known as the Notre Dame box. That formation was made famous by the Four Horseman of Notre Dame back in 1924. Maybe you've read the famous lines written by Grantland Rice:

> Outlined against a blue-gray October sky, the Four Horseman rode again. In dramatic lore they are known as Famine, Pestilence, Destruction and Death. These are only aliases. Their real names are Stuhldreher, Miller, Crowley and Layden. They formed the crest of the South Bend Cyclone before which another fighting Army football team was swept over the precipice at the Polo Grounds yesterday afternoon as 55,000 spectators peered down on the bewildering panorama spread on the green plain below.

Notre Dame played pure rock 'em sock 'em football. For the guys in the backfield it was one-two-three: boom, one-two-three: boom; inside tackle, outside tackle. If you were on the line it was just sheer strength and power. We ran plays where the whole left side of the line would pull out to the right to run interference. We had to be involved in every play.

In those days we didn't platoon offense and defense; we played both ways. If they took you out in one quarter, you couldn't come back until the next. If you were good, you'd play the whole game. I'd play fifty, fifty-five minutes of a sixty-minute game. I'd play until my tongue was scraping on the ground, until every muscle in my body was on fire. It'd take me fifteen minutes after a game just to get enough breath to speak. We had no oxygen tanks on the sidelines; we had to breathe normally. One play you're running away from a guy, the next play you're trying to catch him. There's no doubt in my mind that we were in better shape than the football players of today.

Once I got into high school I'd leave the football for football season. Most of my time before football season I'd spend on the track field rehearsing. I used the track to keep me in shape for football; that was like a tune-up. I did four events: the shot put, high jump, and high and low hurdles. We didn't have the javelin or discus in high school because they were too dangerous; they might end up in the stands.

Shot putting, I started with the twelve pound shot and moved up to the sixteen; you had to graduate. It took me two years to learn to throw the sixteen pounder over fifty feet. I high-jumped over six feet. And at one meet out at Belmont High, I ran the 120 yard low hurdles in thirteen flat. Somewhere it's documented: I won the city high hurdles and was all-state in the low hurdles. By the time I was a senior I was all-state in everything.

I was so into athletics that my body was always doing something. It was great for me because by the time I got to be a senior, I had really matured. I grew from six-feet-one to six-feet-three. I went from 135 pounds to 175 pounds. The speed, strength, the coordination all showed up.

My senior year I made the all-city football team; I was selected captain. That meant you got every vote. Based on that and my all-state in track, I got five scholarship offers. That was a big deal because before my time at Jefferson, there were no athletes that went anywhere. The only one I can remember is Al Duval, who went to Loyola. We were prepared to leave high school and go to work. They taught us things like shop, printing, industrial math, things you could go out and get a job with.

So when they offered the scholarships no one was more surprised than me. I got one from Cal, Washington, Oregon, Loyola, and UCLA. I never did go to see Cal, Washington, or Oregon; they didn't ship us around in those days.

The people at Jefferson wanted me to go to Loyola; they figured the Fathers would be able to teach me something out there. But Loyola didn't have the exposure of the other schools. That left UCLA, which I barely knew existed. They had just built a beautiful new campus in Westwood, and they were looking to compete in athletics on a national level.

They wanted to compete with USC for the local football dollar. Back then it was always USC; they were the machine. USC and Notre Dame had the best teams every year. But USC and Notre Dame didn't give the black athletes a chance to play at that time. So I ended up at UCLA, and that turned out to be one of the best things that ever happened to me.

26

CHAPTER FOUR

Genesis

As a kid, I followed USC football because they had the only football team that amounted to anything. There were no major league professional sports in Los Angeles until the Rams moved out from Cleveland in 1946. As a kid, I used to sneak onto Bovard Field and watch the Trojans practice. I saw Ernie Pinkart and Harry Eadleson play.

Their biggest game of the year was against Notre Dame. The whole town would shut down. Anyone that couldn't go to the game would listen on the radio; it would go national. The biggest game I remember was in 1931. Notre Dame had won 26 straight and the Trojans went back to South Bend to play them for the National Championship. USC was down 14–0 in the fourth quarter and scored 16 points to win. Johnny Baker kicked a field goal in the last minute to win the game.

When the Trojans got home the city gave them a ticker-tape parade downtown. Three hundred thousand people turned out; you can imagine the following they had. MGM filmed the game, and it opened as a second feature at the Loew's State Theater. The crowds got so big, they pulled the feature and ran the game film continuously. It broke all the house records at Loew's State.

USC was the biggest, richest, most popular school. All the

movie stars turned out for USC. Mary Pickford, Gary Cooper, Ronald Colman, all the big names. USC and Notre Dame were the two biggest recruiting schools in the country at that time. They were both private schools, so for a kid to go there he had to have either parents with a lot of money or tremendous athletic ability.

USC used their money and influence to get the best athletes, and they could get just about anybody they wanted. They wanted the glassy-eyed boys. The kind of athlete where if the sun hit their smiles, it'd blind you for a second. Cotton Warburton and a lot of the early USC stars would get brand-new Fords. I remember USC bought a house for one kid's parents, and he became a star running back and an All-American.

Howard Jones was the coach who brought USC into big time football. People have forgotten about him today, but he and Knute Rockne were the two greatest coaches of my generation. From 1929 through 1933 the Trojans won 48 games, lost six and tied one. They won three Rose Bowls, and one season they only allowed thirteen points to be scored on them. They were the Thundering Herd; their teams were so deep they had three complete ball clubs.

Howard Jones was a clean-shaven, steely-jawed, man's man. He looked like a Marine drill sergeant; he had a high, tight haircut and two big ears that stuck straight out. He was very strict, and about his only vice was cigarettes, which he chain-smoked. He was a confirmed bachelor, never known to consort with women. He was tough and hard core; I'm sure many people wondered if Howard Jones had a heart.

He taught fundamental football, blocking and tackling. Nothing fancy, just straight-ahead, power football. I'll show you how tough a coach Howard Jones was. I found this article in the newspaper, quoting Howard Jones:

> When a player is injured, he should say so but not until then. Nothing is more harmful to the morale of the squad while scrimmaging than the agonizing cry of an injured man. A good rule to follow is to keep still until one is sure he's hurt, and then not yell the information from the house tops but to report quietly to the physician in charge.

Howard Jones was the type of guy who could walk into a drug store, run into two or three of his players and not recognize one of them. But he coached nineteen All-Americans in his fifteen years at USC. The first was a kid named Bryce Taylor in 1925.

Bryce was black and just about the only one they ever had in those days. He was a tackle and a damn good one. He only had one hand; the other one was a nub. He was a backfield man in high school, but when he got to college and the kids got a little bigger, started hitting a little harder, Bryce couldn't hold onto the ball and he fumbled a lot. They moved him up to tackle and that's where he won All-American.

Well, to be one of the eleven best footballers in the country and be black was quite an accomplishment. The white men used to talk about how great Bryce Taylor was. In those days for that type of conversation to come out, well, that Negro had to be a good athlete. It was the old supposition; if I was going to play on your team, then I had to be twice as good as everybody else.

There was another black kid on that team named Bert Richie; he played in the backfield. After Bryce Taylor and Bert Richie, the black kids that ended up at USC never got a chance to play. It was rumored that Bert Richie got involved in some sort of scandal involving a white woman and Howard Jones vowed he would never let another black kid play on his team. I don't know if that's true, but I can't remember another during my time in college.

The black ballplayer was just not popular in the United States at that time. At USC, the Alumni Association was very powerful, and they didn't seek us out. It's not like USC was the only one; Notre Dame didn't have any black players either. And the few schools that did give us a break, like Cal and Oregon, you'd never see more than one black kid playing.

The white world didn't pay to see the black athlete. That situation didn't change until Jesse Owens won four gold medals in the 1936 Berlin Olympics, and Joe Louis won the world heavyweight championship in 1937 and later beat the German, Max Schmeling.

By the time I came along in 1934, USC's football reputation

had begun to slip. Howard Jones and his staff got to riding on their oars, figuring every great high school star would want to be part of the Thundering Herd. But, a lot of those kids realized that if they went to USC they'd only sit on the bench, while at one of the other schools they might get a chance to play. This is when UCLA stuck their foot in the door.

The quality players started getting divided up between all the schools in the Pacific Coast Conference. Cal was getting them, Stanford was getting them, and UCLA was getting them. But UCLA was just getting started in football. They were still a relatively new school. It'd only been a few years since they were over on Vermont Avenue and playing schools like Pomona, Occidental, and Whittier State School, which was a reform school.

UCLA made the big athletic push when they moved out to Westwood. Dr. Bourne, Regent Dixon, and communities like Santa Monica raised the money for the new campus through a bond issue. They started offering scholarships and doing the things that USC had been doing all along. Then in 1927 Stanford introduced them into the Pacific Coast Conference, and that put them in a position to compete.

The Bruins struggled through those beginning years. I remember in a game against Oregon UCLA set a record by kicking from their own end zone twenty-three times. They said practice consisted of ten minutes of workouts and fifty minutes of practicing goal line stands. What they lacked in size they made up in slowness.

Bill Ackerman was the graduate manager at that time and his goal was making UCLA a national name. Bill was a tall, handsome guy who grew up down near Western and Sixth. He attended UCLA while the school was still over on Vermont. After he graduated, he stayed with the school and helped engineer the move to Westwood. Bill's father was a civil engineer, and his family made no distinction over color. As far as Bill was concerned we were all Christian, all went to church on Sundays, and took our baths on Saturday.

In 1940 he was manager of the track team that went back to the Midwest for the NCAA's. Jackie Robinson was a member of that track team. He was the best all-around athlete UCLA ever had.

30

The people back there wanted Jackie to sleep somewhere else. Bill said, "No soap, you treat him just like the white boys or I'll take the team home. You won't have a track meet." They weren't too happy about it, but they finally agreed to let Jackie sleep in their hotel.

Bill Ackerman was the Godfather; he helped integrate us into society. He provided us with a cultural education, so that if we were to go to the White House, we'd know how to dress and how to act. When we got to places like Oregon or Washington we never had any problems staying with the team because Bill had made all the arrangements. And there was no discrimination at UCLA; the students would bend over backwards to have it equal for everybody. Whenever they had anything involving discrimination, Kenny Washington would handle it. He was on the student council; he'd be a committee of one.

One of the racial incidents I remember happened during a game against Washington State. Kenny had the ball, and he was running. The Washington State coach was so frustrated that he swore at Kenny as Kenny was running by. He called Kenny a nigger; you didn't call Kenny Washington a nigger without a reaction. We were nice, affable people but we'd react to that. Kenny stopped the whole proceedings and went after the coach. Kenny swung on him, and it sort of went into fisticuffs. But that's how we were taught, to defend ourselves.

Now I'm trying to remember who actually came and got me out of high school. I don't think UCLA made a conscious effort to bring some black kids into the program; the effort was to bring in some top-notch athletes. And when you've got a Kenny Washington or Jackie Robinson, people who were proving themselves, then you're going to go after them. We were the leaders. We paved the way for all those that followed. Jackie broke the color barrier in baseball; Kenny and I did it in football. How many blacks do they have in professional sports now?

The coaches did all the recruiting; in this case it was a guy named Bill Spaulding. He came from Minnesota. Bill Ackerman needed somebody to take over the football program that was really good. Bill Spaulding had been coaching back in the Big Ten and had done very well stopping Red Grange. That's when Grange was running wild at Illinois. In one game against Michigan, Red Grange got the ball five times in the first quarter and scored four touchdowns. Any coach that could stop him was pretty good. So they brought Spaulding out here to coach the Bruins.

Bill Spaulding was a farm boy. His body was hard as nails, but he had sort of an oval face with soft features and kind eyes. He wasn't really sophisticated; he was the type to take out a knife and clean his teeth on the sidelines. What he lacked as a coach was discipline, which you have to have in athletics. He was more a friend to the players than a coach. Like if a kid wasn't in bed on time, Spaulding wouldn't make a big deal out of it. We took advantage of that like most kids would, but Bill Spaulding was a pretty good coach; he won a lot of ball games for UCLA.

Bill Spaulding had an assistant named Cliff Simpson. He had a good eye for talent, and he was the one who actually went out and made contact with the high school players. We had letters of intent at that time; if you signed the letter you could get your room and board paid for by the school. That's how USC existed; how else could they get the athletes into a school that charged $25 a unit? UCLA was not expensive, only twenty-five dollars a quarter. Of course, the big enticement was a chance to play on a good team. I mean, the alternative was getting a job.

UCLA ended up taking care of me and my whole family while I was in school. They gave me one hundred dollars a month and an eleven-dollar meal ticket. Every week they gave me twenty bucks under the table so I could pay the bills at home. They gave Kenny Washington and me a car, all my books free from Campbell's book store and all my clothes free from Desmond's. They gave us tickets to the home games which I would sell. I was always after Bill Ackerman to give me more tickets, but he always said no. And Bill had my daddy do some brick work out at his house; he was always looking out for us. Well, you can imagine what a candy store that was for me.

Guys like Joe E. Brown and Ed Janss would donate money to the school, and the school would pass it out in the form of scholarships. Ed Janss owned all the property in Westwood. He made a fortune selling lots to the fraternities and sororities. Joe E. Brown was an actor and comedian. I think he got involved with UCLA because of Mike Frankovich. He sort of adopted Mike because Mike didn't have any parents. Mike eventually became famous as a movie producer but back then he was a great football player for UCLA.

They called him "Miracle Mike" because he threw a blind, 50-yard pass in the fog at Oregon that was caught for the winning touchdown. I ended up working for Mike in the movies, but he was always really involved with the school. He used to get Joe E. to do yells at the games because Joe E. had a real big mouth and could really ham it up.

Joe E. Brown was a real sports fan. He had a trophy room with the greatest souvenirs like James Braddock's boxing shoes and Babe Ruth's bats. He had been a pretty good baseball player himself, and one of his sons was the manager of the Pittsburgh Pirates baseball team. His other son played second-string end behind me at UCLA; he's the one who taught me how to bowl, so you know there was no jealousy. And when it came to talking an athlete into coming to UCLA, Joe E. Brown was a good one to have around.

Well, when they took me out to Westwood for the first time it was like taking a young boy to Disneyland. You can't believe how nice it was before it got all cluttered up. The buildings were all brick and stone; the windows were all leaded glass, and they were set like an English castle in the middle of some rolling green hills. I took one look at this place and said, "This is where I want to be. Tell me what I have to do."

They said, "You'll have to take all your high school courses over again."

"Where?"

"Right out here at our extension school."

And that's where I labored for two-and-a-half years trying to get into the University. Bill Ackerman used to kid me: "Woody, the trees," meaning the players, "are getting bigger and bigger."

But UCLA was tough; you had to have the units to get in. There was no bullshit from upstairs; we had to work to get our grades before we could play football. Normally the school would have taken an athlete like me and stuck him into one of the military academies, either Black Fox Military or Urban Military Academy. The colonels saw to it that the kids got their grades and units. Well, because I'm black, I couldn't attend those schools. So UCLA put me under an umbrella and hid me out in Bel Air.

The school owned a house in Bel Air that was donated by Ed Janss. That was before all the mansions were built and the rich people moved into Bel Air. We used to see deer and coyotes out there. The school moved me in with a bunch of Jewish kids who were on the football team: Verdie Boyer, Jake Cohen and Izzy Cantor.

Izzy and I became pretty good friends. Izzy was quite a character, and he could talk a blue streak. I think he saw himself as somewhat of a confidence man. He was always trying to sell the other students something. For a while it was neckties, which he'd bring to class in a suitcase. After class he'd set up a little stand out in the common area and pitch his ties. Izzy was a one-man carnival. It's no surprise he thought he was a better football player than he really was. Spend a few minutes with Iz and you'd think you were talking to Red Grange.

I was raised with Jewish kids whose families had left Poland and Russia under the pressures of the czars and all that royal blood. The Germans would not let them own land. When I first became aware of the Jewish people, they were the junk men, poor immigrants that could barely speak the language. They'd ride down the street in a horse-drawn wagon and pick up all the sacks and bottles. I watched the next generation start climbing. By the time I got to college, Nate Sugarman owned the biggest fixture business in Los Angeles. His grandfather was a junk man. But that was the kind of opportunity we had out here; that's why the immigrants poured into Southern California.

So the Jewish kids had been through some racial abuse, and they were aware of some of the problems confronting the black kids. We were both from the same side of town. The Jewish community was called Boyle Heights; it was east of Central Avenue on the other side of the Los Angeles River. Izzy and the guys used to take me out to Brooklyn Avenue, where all the bakeries and delicatessens were. We ate pastrami and bagels.

All the synagogues were out there, because a Jew's got to be able to walk to his temple. That's part of their religion. Izzy and the boys taught me their customs, like wearing the little hats at the synagogue. One of the guys got married and I said, "Izzy, what in the hell are they doing with those hats on?" That stuff was a completely different world for me.

So, whatever racial pressure was coming down in the City of Los Angeles, the pressure was not on me in Westwood. All the kids on campus enjoyed a good relation. We had the whole melting pot, and it was an education for all of us. As far as the people that supported me were concerned, I was just like any other athlete. And I worked hard because there was always the overriding feeling the UCLA really wanted me.

CHAPTER FIVE

The Real Heroes

Well, you talk about getting roughed up: they gave me Spanish, Geometry, Physics and Algebra and I flunked them all. I remember sitting in Algebra class thinking I was flunking Spanish. In high school the longest essay I had ever written was 350 words, now they wanted me to write a ten thousand word thesis for History, on Martin Luther and the religious revolution. So I sat with the Wonder Books and copied. I got it all together and turned the whole mess into Dr. Melvin Koontz. He looked at my work and said, "Woody, how did you do in your other classes?"

"I flunked everything."

He said, "Well this isn't quite up to par, but you did so much work, I'm going to give you a C."

I needed a C average to get into the university, and I was far away from that. Cliff Simpson came to see me; the school was worried about their investment. He said, "Why don't you go down to San Diego this weekend and compete in the National AAU Track Meet? Compete against somebody with a reputation and get yourself a headline."

Well, I realized what he was trying to do. He was trying to keep me in school.

That was 1934. I got down to San Diego and all the universities were there. Jesse Owens was there; he got beat in the 100-yard dash by Eulace Peacock. Eulace was the only guy who could beat Jesse. Slinger Dunn was there from Stanford. He was the best in the world shot putting, doing about fifty-five feet. I got in there behind him and threw over fifty feet, but that wasn't good enough.

Ken Carpenter, the great discus thrower from USC, came over and started talking to me. "Woody, how do you expect to compete with all these universities when you're just out of high school? Why don't you compete against some of the junior colleges; the competition's not as tough. What else can you do?"

"I can high-jump a little, but I don't have any shoes."

He said, "Well here, take mine."

I took the shoes, got up to 6 feet 2 inches and broke the shoes. They moved the bar up to 6 feet 4 inches. I jumped that in my bare feet and won the event. That's how bad I wanted to go to UCLA.

I got my headline and went back to school. I was sitting in Bill Ackerman's office and he said, "How'd you do in your studies, Woody?" He acted like he didn't know.

"I flunked everything but History."

He said, "Son, you aren't discouraged, are you? You just weren't familiar with the courses. Don't worry, just keep going to class."

The next semester they switched my Spanish to French. Every Sunday I would go to the French teacher's house, and she would rehearse me so I could get up and speak in front of the class. I had Dr. Kaplan for Physics; he had to put me on crutches. I'll always remember him saying, "The only thing we will never do is split the atom."

But I had good teachers, like Dr. Koontz. One day I was sitting in the back of his class trying to disappear when I heard my name called. The Doctor wanted me to get up and read to the class. I started reading, "So and so were migrating and Strode migrated to England from Germany to escape religious persecution." Everyone in the class started laughing, "Woody's a German." I got a little embarrassed because in 1934 Germans were not popular. Hitler was on the prowl and the Nazis were turning out.

The Olympic Games were scheduled for Berlin in 1936. Hitler hoped to use the Olympics as a showcase for his master race. But

38

instead those games became the greatest showcase for the American Negro athlete.

In 1936 the best sprinters and jumpers in the world were black Americans. At the Olympics, Cornelius Johnson won the high jump, Archie Williams won the 400 meters and John Woodruff won the 800 meters. Jesse Owens won the long jump and the 100 meters with Ralph Metcalfe finishing second. Jesse set a world record in the 200 meters with Mack Robinson, Jackie's brother, finishing second. And Jesse won a fourth gold medal with the 400 meter relay team.

When these black athletes went over to Germany and won all those gold medals in Hitler's backyard, white Americans began to take notice. The more conservative whites had to give us recognition for our ability and the more liberal-minded whites began to give us a break. Because the American philosophy was totally different from what Hitler was trying to do in Germany. The extermination camps are well-documented. Negroes were no threat to Hitler because we had no economic power, but athletically, losing to a Negro was like losing to a Jew.

The Nazis were interested in me because I was a mixed breed. Somewhere they saw a photograph of me, and they came over to do some paintings for their Olympic Art Show. I used to pick up a lot of dough by modeling, and I was ashamed of that. I'd hide but they'd come around and find me. They'd pay me twenty-five dollars a week to stand around and pose.

I was contacted by Leni Riefenstahl. She was a beautiful, intelligent German who was also a great athlete. She was famous as a filmmaker; her film *Olympia,* a documentary on the 1936 Olympics, is possibly the greatest sports film ever made. She contacted me and asked me to meet her at this club down in the Wilshire District. She had an artist with her, a little man that stood about as tall as her shoulder. A studious-looking fella with a full beard and glasses. He wore a powder-blue smock that almost touched the ground.

They pulled me into a small, curtained-off room. I stripped until I had nothing on but my jockey shorts. I crouched down and the German artist walked around me, eyeballing me and tugging on his beard. Leni Riefenstahl was standing in the corner. She said, "We saw your picture but we couldn't believe it. You have the greatest physique of any athlete we have ever seen."

Then the artist went to measuring me, every detail. I'd flex and he'd get out the calipers and measure and paint. He stood on a stool to measure my face, right down to my eye lashes. They wanted to do five paintings of me, but I was too lazy. They ended up with two; one doing the shot put and one doing the discus. They won second prize in the show.

When Hitler saw my pictures he couldn't believe how I looked. He sent Leni Riefenstahl back here to shoot some film on me. She said, "We'd like to take you up to Carmel and film you against all that beautiful white scenery."

I was ready to go, but people started whispering, "Don't you know who she is? Don't you know what's happening over there in Europe?"

I said to myself, "No. No, I can't be part of that." I called her back and apologized and said, "Sorry, I can't do it."

You can imagine the heat in those years and I was a goddamned innocent. I've often thought that if Hitler had won the war, they would have picked me up and either bred me or dissected me.

I was actually in training for the 1936 Olympics. They trained me right up until cutoff time, but I never did go to the Olympic trials at Randall's Island, New York. The school said I needed another half-unit to maintain my eligibility. So I took a shop class, and I never went to the Olympics.

I don't know if I could have won a gold medal, but I had become a pretty good all-around track man. I learned to throw the discus and javelin after I got out to UCLA. I could already throw the shot, high-jump and run, so they moved me into the decathlon. I trained with Glenn Morris, who won the gold medal in Berlin. He could beat me in all the running events; mile, 440, 100 and the high hurdles. But I was stronger than Glenn, and I could high-jump, broad-jump, throw the shot, discus and javelin farther than he could. The only event I had trouble with was the pole vault, and I learned to pole vault eleven feet.

By training together, Glenn Morris and I became great friends.

He was like my superior; I learned to do what he could do. I didn't care about beating him; we didn't have that going. We just felt we were two Americans that were going to go over there and kick Hitler's ass. But when I saw what happened to Jesse Owens, I'm glad I didn't go. When Jesse got home they made a circus out of him. First he went on a tour, tap dancing his way across the country with Eddie Cantor. Then he became a sideshow, racing against horses and trains. It was disgraceful and pretty soon Jesse Owens disappeared.

Well, years later, I was at the Mint Hotel acting in *The Professionals* for Richard Brooks. I met Glenn Morris at the bar. I didn't recognize him because he had aged so. But he recognized me from the movies and he said, "Woody Strode!"

I said, "You know who I tried to find over in Germany?" I had just done a picture over there. "Leni Riefensthal!"

I was about fifty years old, but I still had the body. I said, "Yeah, I was in this old-fashioned club, a key club, nothing but doctors and lawyers, nothing but high-class Germans. I wanted the German lady to see me now; I wanted the super race to take a look at me. So I stood up and yelled, 'Does anyone know where I can find Leni Riefensthal?' Well, they jumped back like there was a rattlesnake in the room!"

That's the last time I saw Glenn Morris. He died shortly after that. Shows you how fast life goes by. He thought I was going to be with him in Berlin. We were going to be one-two. I think maybe I could have beaten him in the Olympics. I don't know, but I do have this little write-up by Erwin Baker that shows how close Glenn and I were in ability.

BRUIN MENTOR SEES NEW WORLD RECORD

"I frankly think Woody can break the world decathlon record now held by Glenn Morris." With that candid observation, varsity coach Harry Trotter disclosed what has been nearest to his heart for a long, long time, the coaching of Woodrow Wilson Strode to the world's decathlon championship in the 1940 Olympic games.

Continued the enthusiastic Bruin mentor, "I have seen and I know what Strode can do. Competing in the Junior National AAU in 1934, Woody jumped 6'4" in bare feet. Of course I realize that he has put on 15 or 20 pounds since 1934."

I picked up twenty pounds by doing one thousand push-ups a day. The school wouldn't allow us to lift weights. The coaches thought weight lifting would slow you down. So I developed natural strength from working out with my own body weight. I got so I could do a thousand push-ups, a thousand sit-ups and a thousand knee-squats every day. With the push-ups I'd have to rest after every hundred. The others I could do without stopping. I got into the knee-squats because of a wrestler named Ghama. He was an Indian wrestler who built this tremendous body by doing five thousand knee-squats continuously. It would go on so long they would serve him tea.

When I became a professional wrestler, they used to announce me at 230 pounds, even though I weighed 210. That's because my upper body was so well-developed. I got this whole look a weight lifter would get, only without the bulk. I was as strong as a guy who weighed 250 pounds. Because the big guys in my generation weren't weight lifters, that was just natural strength and fat. They used to ask me, "Woody, how can you play against such big men?"

I said, "Hell, the way you guys write you'd think this guy was a gorilla."

I always thought if a guy weights 250, he's just human. He can become only so strong.

As big as I was, I could do an iron cross on the rings because of all those push-ups. That went on until I was forty years old, then I began to taper off and cut down. But I still do push-ups to this day. I don't have to do as many; I just maintain by keeping myself lean and wiry. And I owe this whole look to Johnny Weissmuller, who played Tarzan in the movies. I wanted to be Tarzan; I saw every movie. I'd look at him and I'd want to be out in the jungle swinging from the trees and fighting alongside Tarzan.

In my day you either had to know how to fight or you had to be a hell of a track man. The worst thing you could call a kid was yellow. He'd be scared to death, wouldn't want to fight, but he'd better fight or he'd be yellow. If we got in a fight on the playground the director made us come into the gym and put the gloves on so that nobody would really get hurt.

I used to hang out around the old Main Street Gym; that's where I got introduced to boxing. When you're young, you stand and watch and eventually you start imitating. The boxers who were in training used to run over Silverwood's Hill, where Dodger Stadium is today. We called it Silverwood's Hill because there was a big sign up there like the Hollywood sign that advertised the clothing store.

I remember the fighters would always run with a broomstick they carried in both hands across their bodies. I don't know what that was supposed to do but every kid in the neighborhood had a broomstick, and we'd run after them as long as we could keep up.

We used to watch them fight out at the Naud Junction Pavilion, up where the railroad changed lines. It was near East Alameda Street and North Main. They had fights there every Saturday night. The place was a big tent, like a circus, with bleachers and sawdust on the floor. We used to sneak in through a break in the tent.

The men that went there got drunk watching fights. When they reached into their pockets for some money to pay for a beer, some change would fall out and drop in the sawdust. After the fights there would be a jillion kids digging through the sawdust looking for the loose change. You'd be surprised how much money all of us would pick up out of that stuff. It was all change, but in those days you could buy a lot of food for fifteen cents.

I saw the greatest fighters, like Nebraska Wildcat, Dynamite Jackson, and Ace Hudkins. Max Baer was my favorite fighter. He was a Californian and one of the first to break into the East Coast boxing syndicate without a promoter. He used to train in my neighborhood, and all the kids would show up. He had the most beautiful body of any heavyweight we ever had. They made a movie star out of him after he was through fighting.

I used to look at him like I looked at Johnny Weissmuller. He was tall, six-feet-four-inches, which was unusual, because there never really had been a tall boxing champion. The greatest fighters were six feet, 190 pounds like Joe Louis. Max Baer was my favorite fighter until Joe Louis came along.

43

I think Joe Louis was the greatest boxer of all times. Of course that's only my opinion, but I like what Red Smith, the great sportswriter, had to say about Joe:

> Joe Louis may very well have been the greatest fighter who ever lived. Comparisons with Jack Dempsey and Gene Tunney and others are foolish, though there is no shadow of doubt here that he would have caught and destroyed Muhammad Ali as he caught Billy Conn and other skillful boxers.
>
> Early in Muhammad Ali's splendacious reign as heavyweight champion, he hired Joe as an "advisor" and they appeared on television together.
>
> "Joe, you really think you coulda whupped me?" Ali said.
>
> "When I had the title," Joe said, "I went on what they called a bum-of-the-month tour."
>
> Ali's voice rose three octaves. "You mean I'm a bum?"
>
> "You would have been on the tour," Joe told his new employer.

But Joe was more than a great boxer. He'd knock a guy out in one round and say, "I's lucky I's wins."

He did more for the black people than any man before him because every time he opened his mouth he said the right words. In Bert Randolph Sugar's book, *The 100 Greatest Boxers of All Time,* Sugar wrote:

> Joe Louis used his words, as he did his punches, with a commendable economy of effort, saying a surprising number of things, and saying them in a way we wish we had. There was his evaluation of his country's chances in the global confrontation with the Axis powers: "We'll win 'cause we're on God's side." Dignity. And there was his enunciation of his opponent's chances in the second Conn fight: "He can run, but he can't hide." Honesty.
>
> But Joe Louis' place in the pantheon of greats doesn't rest on his using his words, but on his using his body—and the bodies of his collective, and soon to-be collected opponents. He drove Max Baer to the canvas like a nail, straightly driven, his body almost flush to the surface. He hit leading contender Eddie Sims so hard with his first punch that the beclouded Sims walked over to the referee and asked "to take a little walk around the roof."

Joe's fight against Max Baer only went four rounds. Max took the count on one knee. After the fight somebody said to me, "Your fighter quit on you."

I said, "Well, both of my favorites were in the ring."

But I don't blame Max; he took enough of a beating. He never denied he could have gotten up, but after the fight Max said, "If they want to see the execution of Max Baer it'll cost them more than twenty-five dollars a seat."

Joe Louis wasn't the first black heavyweight champion; he was the second. The first was Jack Johnson; he won the title in 1908. The white people hated Jack Johnson because he was smart and arrogant. He messed with white women; he had three white wives. And he consistently beat white fighters. This is where the term "Great White Hope" started, because the white world searched desperately for a white fighter that could beat Jack Johnson. Finally Jess Willard beat him in 1915, and from that time until Joe Louis beat James Braddock in 1937 there were no black heavyweight champions.

Joe Louis was the first popular black heavyweight champion. Joe was quiet, reserved, shy—everything Jack Johnson wasn't. He married a beautiful black society girl. He did everything right. He was humble; he never taunted his opponents. But Joe had the gorilla heart. You hit him, he'd come after you. Joe Louis stalked his opponents like an animal. If Joe hit you in the arm, it'd hurt you. He was a perfect physical specimen, and he never dissipated throughout his entire career. He was the perfect fighting machine. He threw the quickest, most powerful punches of any fighter I had ever seen.

I met Joe when he was nineteen; we were the same age. He came out here to fight Lee Ramage. They had me pick him up and take him out to UCLA with me, to keep the hustlers and the pimps off him. Joe had a baby face; he was better looking than his sister, who must have looked more like their father. You would have never known by looking at Joe that he was one of the greatest fighters who ever lived.

They had Joe training down in the Main Street Gym. I asked him how much they were paying for sparring partners.

"Twenty-five dollars a round."

That was like a million dollars back then. I said, "Well, hell, I'd like to go two or three rounds with you."

But UCLA wouldn't let me do it, because it would have hurt my athletic eligibility. So I never did fight with Joe, so I've never had the honor of saying I was knocked out by Joe Louis. But he did get me some seats to his fight against Lee Ramage. I was sitting in the fourth row. Joe had his back to me; Ramage was facing me. All I saw was Joe's shoulder drop and Ramage hit the canvas. Nobody saw the punch; we had to watch the newsreels to see what happened.

Here's how Chris Mead describes the fight and Joe Louis in his book, *Champion: Joe Louis:*

> This time Louis knocked Ramage out in the second round. Joe Louis was now the best fighter in the world, a once-in-a-generation talent, and he must have been electrifying to watch for the first time. His shoulders and back were massive, his chest and stomach flat. His muscles were solid but deeply buried. In the ring Louis's legs moved slowly, cautiously, and his feet were always planted. But his hands were incredibly fast. He threw short, jolting punches with both hands in quick sequences. In a fight, Louis always seemed to occupy the center of the action.

What really made Joe Louis were his two fights against a German heavyweight named Max Schmeling. Schmeling was the former champion and the most popular Nazi athlete. He was very strong; he knocked guys out with a powerful right hand. Their first fight was in 1936. At that point Joe had done a lot of fighting, had won every bout, and was considered the best boxer in the world. Joe was favored 8–1 to beat Schemling. He was so overconfident that he didn't train for the fight.

Joe paid for that.

In the fourth round, Schmeling stepped across Joe's left-hand jab and nailed him with a short right. That punch almost ended the fight. I watched the egg form on Joe's cheekbone. From that point on, Joe was walking around in limbo. For the next ten rounds Joe took an awful beating. They took his mama out of the arena after the sixth round; that's how bad it was. I sat in that theater watching Joe get beat and I cried because Joe was our boy.

After that fight people started doubting Joe's ability. In the meantime, Schmeling was boasting and strutting. He called Joe yellow. That's the only time we ever saw Joe mad. He said, "You say Smellin' calls me a quitter? I'll tell you something, when we meet again, he'll only go one round. That's all—just one!"

They fought again in 1938, in New York. Joe had won all eleven fights between the two Schmeling fights, including the heavyweight championship. There was no clowning around before the second fight. This time Joe was out for blood. Of course by 1938, stories about the German persecution of the Jews were coming out. America was alarmed. The country rallied around Joe Louis as a symbol of American tolerance. And we looked at Max Schmeling as a symbol of all Nazis. Chris Mead wrote:

> The 1936 Olympics in Berlin added to the impression that the Nazis viewed sports as a test of their racist and nationalistic ideology. The performance of Jesse Owens and a host of other black track-and-field athletes highlighted the symbolic aspects of contest between American blacks and Germans. Now a German boxer was sailing to America for a fight with the black heavyweight champion of the world. The swastika hugged Schmeling like flypaper.

It was a war in the ring between Germany and the United States. There were 70,000 people in Yankee Stadium to see the fight; the rest of the world was listening on the radio. Joe didn't waste any time; he went right after Schmeling. Two minutes and forty seconds later it was over.

It was the most brutal three minutes in ring history. Schmeling would have gone down at the minute mark if Joe hadn't held him up with punches. The last punch was a body shot to Schmeling's side. Joe hit him so hard it broke vertebrae in Schmeling's back. Usually, the referee would walk in and stop it, but hell no, we're fighting the Germans, kill the son of a bitch. And Joe nearly did. The Germans were so embarrassed that they cut the radio wires and stopped the transmission.

And to think Joe Louis left the ring broke, drunk, and beaten up: it's shameful. Joe earned five million dollars during his career. To make five million dollars in eleven years, with no inflation, that was unheard of.

He was so generous that he'd give the entire purse from a fight to charity. And to think that years later the IRS hit up a penniless, broken-down Joe Louis for $300,000 in back taxes. It got so disgraceful the government had its head down. The Mafia bailed him out, and they took care of Joe until he died. I'll never forget Joe looking so pitiful in his wheelchair, sick from all the punches he took and thinking how great this man was; the biggest star.

Today, every black athlete, whether he knows it or not, owes his success to Joe Louis and Jesse Owens. They were the real pioneers. Jackie, Kenny, myself, and everyone that followed, only capitalized on their success.

CHAPTER SIX

He Wore Number 13

I've often made the comment that I was one of the few athletes that actually had to study in order to get into school. I appreciate that; I'm not an intellectual, but I'm a well-rounded citizen. My first semester in the extension school was like reckless shooting. When I came back the next semester, I said to myself, "I won't do it like that; I'll do it like this." And slowly I learned by trial and error.

I concentrated hard and somehow I maintained a C average. When I got through the extension school two-and-a-half years later, I told my parents, "I think I'll quit."

I was exhausted. I felt like I had now accomplished something. But my parents said, "No, you can't quit now. You're going to college."

So in 1936 I became a freshman at UCLA. I was twenty-one years old and fully matured. Well, all this time I didn't know it, but I'd been waiting for Kenny Washington to come to me. I met him for the first time when he was seventeen years old. We hit it off right away because I needed a running mate, and we became very close, like brothers. We were always together on the field and socially.

Kenny was from Lincoln Heights, up off North Broadway.

That was a big Italian community with a few Irish mixed in. All of his old buddies that I met were either of Italian or Irish descent. Originally, Lincoln Heights was a middle-class white neighborhood. Most of the people out there worked on the railroad as engineers, firemen, or brakemen, and switchmen. At that time the Italians lived east of Main Street, but gradually the more affluent people migrated west towards the ocean, and the Italians started moving in.

To the best of my knowledge, the Washington family was the only black family in that neighborhood. When I met Kenny, I swear he was nothing but a nice Italian kid. He couldn't speak good English; he had an accent that was half-Italian. I used to make fun of him because I couldn't understand him. At the training table at UCLA he used to trade me his steak for my ice cream, then afterwards we'd go down to North Broadway and he'd eat ravioli and pasta. But Kenny was well-educated; he could go into the classes and get all his grades.

Kenny wasn't baptized Catholic, but the first church Kenny saw was the Catholic church. There was nowhere else for him to go. An old Italian woman lived next door to the Washingtons and she'd take Kenny with her to the early morning mass. He was only five or six years old and half the time the priest would be mumbling in Latin that no one could understand. But he learned to cross himself, take communion, say a little prayer before he sat down, all that stuff. He was on the fence, never baptized Catholic, but he knew his catechism. And every once in a while, before a big game, I'd catch Kenny crossing himself.

Kenny introduced me to the Italian people. He'd take me to dinner with him when he went visiting friends in the old neighborhood. And when these Italians got to eating they'd have a spread that included everything from soup to nuts. They'd start eating at six o'clock and go all night. And my wine glass was never less than half-full. They considered it an insult for you not to drink. They weren't trying to get me drunk; it's just that the Italians drink wine as a beverage, like we drink coffee or tea.

This is how Kenny got even with me for making fun of his Italian way of speaking. The first time he carried me out to Lincoln

Heights he said, "Woody, when you get into their home, you can't turn nothin' down. They would be highly insulted. They're going to be offering you wine and you have to accept."

So we went to four or five houses, and at every house they said, "Here Woody, try some of our home-made wine."

Well, my body was pure; I had never drank alcohol. By the time we cleared out of that fifth house, I was in the fourth dimension. And we had to go out to football practice. Because it was summer, and it was hot, we were practicing at night.

Kenny carried me to the field, and I had such a buzz on that I could barely stand up. Kenny let the other players in on what he had done and to them it was the biggest joke. But luckily they protected me from the coaches. They said, "Woody's sick, coach; he's got a stomachache."

"Okay, you boys take care of Woody." And they led me to the locker room and left me in front of the toilet. I was mad at Kenny for a while after that, but in the long run it's those kinds of things that really make you close friends.

Kenny Washington was such a star coming out of high school that he was taken care of a little better than the rest of us. The school gave him a car, an old Model T Ford that Bill Ackerman picked up for twenty-five bucks. Kenny was only seventeen so they put the car in my name. We were both living at home at that point, and we used the car for transportation to and from school.

We'd ride out Wilshire Boulevard and it'd take us an hour, hour-and-a-half to get out there. We'd listen to Al Jarvis on the radio and sometimes the music would be so good we'd stop the car and do a jitterbug right in the middle of the street. Every morning I'd swing by Lincoln Heights and pick him up. That's how I got introduced to the whole Washington family.

Kenny's grandfather was a cook on the railroad, which is how the Washingtons happened to settle in Lincoln Heights. When they settled out here, the old man started to work out at the mining camps. He had a mess wagon and he would cook for the men. He taught his wife how to cook and you had never really eaten until you ate some of Susie Washington's cooking. She could take a couple of napkins, a little wine and make a meal out of it.

51

Kenny owed a lot to his grandma Susie and he'd be the first to tell you. She's the one that really raised him, sponsored him, encouraged him. If Kenny needed baseball shoes or a glove or something, she'd call Bill Goodman at W. A. Goodman and Sons— that was the athletic supply store. She'd tell Bill to give Kenny anything he wanted and she would pay for it and Bill did. They never met, Bill and Susie, but they had this telephonic acquaintance; Bill came to refer to her as Grandma. There was always that association between Kenny and Grandma.

Grandma Susie worked as a janitor at the Avenue 19 Grammar School. But she was more like a supervisor for the kids. She was better with the kids than the teachers. Any time a kid would come in off the playground dirtied up, she'd make them go down and take a shower. At first the kids would be kind of bashful, but she wouldn't stand for that. She'd throw them in there and soak their backs and these little kids would be standing around buck naked. She really cared about the kids and they got to the point where they just loved her.

I guess in her way Susie Washington was a philosopher. She could size a person up in a minute. She dropped out of school in the sixth grade, but she was well-read. Every morning she would get the *Examiner* and read the paper to her kids. She was very wise and she passed this on. She came to be known as the Mother Superior of Avenue 19. If one of those Italians out in Lincoln Heights wanted to marry someone's daughter, they would bring him to talk to Mrs. Washington. If she said, "No good," well then, they could just forget it.

Susie Washington had three sons; Julius, Rocky, and Edgar. Edgar was Kenny's father. He married Marione Lanone when he was eighteen and she was sixteen. They were much too young but Marione was pregnant. Edgar took up with another woman and Marione separated from him. That's when Kenny moved in with the rest of the Washington clan while they were all living over on Avenue 19. Kenny was probably two or three years old when he started in over there.

Everyone knew Edgar Washington as Blue, but the family called him Biscuits. Whoever got home first from school would get the old wood stove going and run the pan of biscuits in the oven, cook them and have them for lunch. The pan held four biscuits across and six biscuits the other way. Twenty-four biscuits. As the story goes, Edgar got home first one day and by the time the other two boys and their sister Becky got home, all the biscuits were gone. They accused him of eating the whole pan, and I wouldn't have been surprised because he was capable of doing it. He was only twelve, thirteen years old, but he already had a big appetite.

Blue was a playboy, for want of a better name. He liked the girls, the bright lights, and so forth and he really put his heart and soul into it. He got lucky and landed a few parts in the movies. He played sidekick to Ken Maynard and Tom Mix. He had a part in *Gone With the Wind*. He's the one who saves Scarlett from harm when a gang of bad guys tries to attack her.

Blue was making seventy-five dollars a day when guys were making ten, fifteen dollars a week. He'd get four or five days in, have $300 in his pocket and nobody would see him again until the money was gone. The Washington family was constantly looking for Blue because some director was holding up a production until he could be found.

Blue could have been a star. At one point they gave him his own dressing room. They made a picture in which he was the star but they never did release it because towards the end Blue screwed up and disappeared. It was called *Ormsby the Faithful Servant*. Blue played Ormsby. They shot the last scenes out on the Santa Cruz Island and Blue never showed up. They spent a lot of money on that picture; Blue alone was getting $750 a week. I've never forgotten that; that was a fortune. And it was that production that pretty much ended his career in the movies.

Athletically, Blue had the ability to do just about any damn thing he wanted. He was a hell of a baseball player, playing outfield and first base. He played against Bob Feller back in the days of barnstorming. They say he hit one off Feller that cleared railroad tracks and everything else. Blue was a big powerful man; he went about six-feet-five and weighed well over 200 pounds.

He started his so-called professional baseball career with the Kansas City Monarchs of the Negro National League. And he played briefly for the Chicago Americans, Rube Foster's team. Rube Foster was the father of black baseball and the Chicago Americans were like the Yankees as far as the average black kid was concerned. So between baseball, the movies, and the women, Blue wasn't home very much.

He used to show up at some of our home games at the Coliseum. He'd stand outside the Peristyle end and tell stories about how great his son was. Or he'd tell stories about funny things that happened to him in the movies. Or stories about how great an athlete he was. The crowds would gather around this big noisy guy until everyone thought we were having a riot. Bill Ackerman would have to go down there and pull him inside the stadium. That's how Blue got into the games free, because Kenny didn't want to have anything to do with him.

Kenny's Uncle Rocky was really the father. Kenny made no bones about it; he'd tell people it was between Grandma Susie and Uncle Rocky that accounted for his success. Rocky was about fourteen, fifteen years older than Kenny. If Kenny got into trouble, Rocky would carry out the orders, which usually came down from Grandma. He'd whip Kenny's butt.

Rocky was a cop. He was the only black officer of any rank on the Los Angeles Police Department. There were a couple of black men in the detective bureau who had the rank of detective lieutenant. That was the plainclothes detail, but Rocky was the first black uniformed officer to make the rank of lieutenant.

He was in charge of the Central Division which took care of downtown Los Angeles. At that time, the Central Division had 450 men, which was larger than 90 percent of the police departments in the United States. When he first got over there, the whole department was buzzing, "If you send that nigger over here, everybody in the station will be asking for a transfer out."

By the time Christmas came around those guys brought him so much booze and whiskey that his basement was full, his back porch was full, and he had whiskey all over the place. When they found out what kind of guy he was, every guy on the force wanted to be on the night shift with Lieutenant Washington. That's the kind of friendship the officers developed with him.

During his early years on the force, Rocky was in charge of the Junior Auxiliary Police, which was a youth program. He didn't have much to do but keep an eye on the kids and attend a lot of local high school games. He worked out of the Chief's office and his big assignment was to watch the gang activities among the kids. The only time he got mad was when there were no high school events going on. Usually you'd find him at a football or basketball game. Off-days he'd spend out at the race track. They didn't dare blow the bugle out at Santa Anita unless Roscoe Washington was there.

Rocky became sort of a self-appointed guardian to make sure the kids behaved themselves. He didn't want the kids to get in trouble; if you got a police record, you were zilch. Well, because of his relationship with the kids, Rocky came to acquire quite a few nephews. Policemen would come up to him and say, "You know, we stopped your nephew last night."

"Who?"

"Oh, some kid named James O'Neill."

And Rocky'd say, "Oh, oh yeah," not knowing who the hell that was. Kenny and I used that all the time, "Hey, you know my uncle, Lieutenant Washington?" We'd get out from under a lot of tickets that way.

Rocky never missed one of our games, and you know what a thrill it is for a player to have a relative show up at a game. He always dressed up in a suit and tie, and we were all proud to know him. Rocky was a real class person. He was like a role model for us, and we had a tremendous respect for him. If he told us to do something, we did it.

At halftime he'd be waiting for us at the goal post. He'd follow us right into the locker room, tell us what we were doing right, what we were doing wrong, what was working, what wasn't. Rocky knew the game pretty well. Bill Spaulding used to talk to Rocky, ask him advice, and Spaulding listened. Of course Rocky was never paid by the school, but I'm sure he was more than paid back through the accomplishments of Kenny's career.

Kenny wouldn't do anything without consulting his Uncle Rocky first, even after he got out of school. Rocky was level-headed, the kind of guy that always had his feet on the ground. He'd look

55

things over for Kenny, tell him what he thought the good side and the bad side was. Kenny always flipped the coin but Rocky had an influence. Ultimately, Rocky got a lot of praise for the way he brought up Kenny.

Kenny's athletic career began at the Downey Avenue Playground. North Broadway was named Downey Avenue in those days. The Washingtons lived two blocks away. The Lincoln Heights Merchants played out at Downey; they were a semi-pro baseball team. Kenny was interested in baseball because of his father, and the Merchants attracted him to the playground. Of course they had football, basketball, boxing, and all that stuff.

Kenny was quite a boxer. I remember when the boxing team came down from Cal. When their heavyweight found out he had to fight Kenny, he wouldn't get in the ring. But Kenny didn't particularly like to hurt people. If Kenny knocked a guy down, he'd go over and pick him up after the play was over. He'd hit you; he had no compunction about hitting you; he'd knock you on your ass but then he'd pick you up.

Anyway, Kenny got involved in playground sports just like the rest of us. The coach of the Lincoln Heights Merchants was a guy named Dutch Schultz. His real name was Paul, but everyone called him Dutch. He was a bricklayer like my father. He sort of adopted Kenny. The team liked to have kids around to shag balls and do odd jobs and Kenny was it. They made Kenny their mascot. Kenny showed me a team picture with him sitting on the ground in front of the players. It was quite cute, this little black kid with this white baseball team. He had his overalls on, one strap dangling, no shirt and the sole of one shoe was coming off.

Kenny was a natural athlete: he played baseball and football, he ran a little track and put the shot a bit. He played basketball, but not too much. Football and baseball, these were his two main loves. If a kid had his ability today, they'd be waving million-dollar contracts in his face. But back then, in the thirties and early forties, the hurdles were just too great for a black kid to make the major leagues.

I found this article written by Jackie Robinson for *Gridiron* in 1971; here's what Jackie had to say about Kenny's ability.

56

A lot has been written about my accomplishments in various sports. Besides playing football and baseball at UCLA and elsewhere, I won an NCAA long-jump championship and was the leading scorer on the Pacific Coast during my two years of varsity basketball. But Kenny was an equally exceptional athlete. In fact, Kenny's future in baseball, the sport everyone considers my best, seemed much brighter after his brief exposure to the college game than did mine. Because of our athletic commitments, each of us played only one season of baseball at UCLA. In 1937 Kenny batted .454, one of the highest averages ever compiled by an undergraduate. In 1940 I got off to a good start as a shortstop, getting four hits and stealing four bases, including home twice, in my first game. But I went into an awful slump after that, the worst of my entire baseball career, and batted only .063 for the rest of the season to finish with a final average of .097.

Kenny was a damn good baseball player. Jackie had more speed than Kenny as far as running the bases, but Kenny could throw, and he could hit. He and Joe DiMaggio were the only two guys to hit one over the centerfield fence at St. Mary's College up in Northern California.

He also had a remarkable arm. He could throw a baseball just as well as he could throw a football. He could throw sixty yards on the fly consistently. We used to have contests in the Coliseum to see if anybody could throw a football clear out of the bowl. We'd bet to see who could throw the farthest. Kenny got seventy-eight rows; there are about eighty rows altogether. Try that with a baseball sometime; I'll bet you only get halfway.

As a runner Kenny was more of the fullback type. He was very powerful. He had broad, thick muscles. He was a well-proportioned six-feet-one, and he weighed about 195 pounds, which was big for those days. He wasn't a scatback, but he was capable of making the long runs. I think he still holds the record for the longest run from scrimmage as a Los Angeles Ram, 91 yards against the Chicago Cardinals. And by then he'd been under the knife five times for knee operations.

People thought his knee problems came from playing football, but his biggest injury came sliding into second base. It happened out at Roosevelt High School. His spikes caught in the old, ragged, torn-up base and ripped his knee up. He limped off the field; he even finished the game, but that was the beginning of the real injuries to his legs.

Kenny Washington had some funny legs. They looked like an X crossed at the knees. Kenny was the original "Crazy Legs." He ran kind of knock-kneed. You didn't realize it so much coming to you, but going away you'd see the way his feet would fly out to the side. Because of that, Kenny could run almost as fast sideways as he could straight ahead. That's part of the reason he was such an elusive runner. Sometimes I would be forty yards downfield, watching him fake out guys on his way to me. His legs would go one way and he'd go another. They'd try to tackle him and all of a sudden he'd relax, the tackler would give up and off he'd go, seventy yards to a touchdown. I asked him, "What do you see when you cut back?"

"I see alleys."

This is how all the great runners see the field. And Kenny had a funny habit that used to drive opponents crazy. Every time he came out of the huddle, he'd just drag himself out. You'd have thought he was going to collapse, he'd look so tired and near death, but as soon as he touched that ball he was gone.

Kenny had deceptive speed for a big man. I remember an official commented after one of our games, "A lot of people don't realize how fast Kenny is, but you ought to run behind him and try to catch him, then you'd realize how fast he really is!" Kenny could run 100 yards in ten flat in full uniform. For that era and for his size that was good running.

Kenny played left halfback in the single-wing formation. Today he would have been a quarterback, but in the single wing the left halfback received the snap and did ninety percent of the ball handling. The quarterback called the signals but was used as a blocking back. If the quarterback ever handled the ball it was handed off to him. So from his position, Kenny pretty much controlled the offense.

On defense Kenny played a position similar to strong safety, but actually it was more of a linebacker position. And he was equally as good on defense as he was on offense. However, I do think that if Kenny had been able to concentrate solely on offense like today's players, he'd be better remembered.

I've talked to quite a few of my old teammates from UCLA as a result of writing this book and any one of them will tell you that Kenny Washington was one of the greatest football players that ever lived. But I particularly like what Ned Mathews had to say. Ned was our quarterback. He's the one who called the plays and laid the blocks that sprung Kenny into the open. Ned went on to have quite a fine professional career in the NFL. He said, "The two finest football players as backs that I ever had the pleasure of playing with were Kenny Washington and Whizzer White. This is based on all-around ability to play defense, block a tackle, run with the ball, and pass the ball. And Kenny could kick; he was a pretty fair placekicker, although we never used him. And as the years have gone by and I got into coaching that opinion has never changed."

And Bill Ackerman, who is eighty-five years old today and has seen and known every athlete to play at UCLA, told me, "I think Kenny Washington, to me, and I saw 'em all play, was one of the greatest football players ever to play on this coast."

Kenny Washington was the man. As far as the general public was concerned, I mean the local yokels, Kenny was it. He was the main drawing card. He became quite a celebrity; people would stop him on the street to say hello. He was a handsome, clean-cut kid. He had a broad nose, warm, kind eyes and a smile that lit up his whole face. He had a really good sense of humor. People loved to hang out with the guy. Kenny was a real class guy.

He got so he felt very comfortable in front of a crowd; he grew to it. And he became a pretty good ad-lib speaker. He wasn't one to brag about his ability; he wasn't cocky, but he had a belief in himself and that with a good team behind him, they could beat anybody. Of course it wasn't that way in the beginning at UCLA. We started from zero and worked our way up. But whatever success we achieved at UCLA we owe to Kenny. His was the first uniform number to be retired at the university. Kenny wore number 13.

CHAPTER SEVEN

Black Lightning Strikes

Kenny Washington went to Lincoln High School. The team was a contender, and Kenny was the kid getting them there. The kids on that team loved him, and they took care of him. If Kenny pulled a muscle, hurt his knee or something, the whole football team would come over to his house, put hot packs on him, rub him down and make sure he was all right. It was no baloney; they were sincere. Joe Garrafolo, Pete Torreano, Ralph Stanley, and an Irish kid—I think his name was Joe Greene—were the main guys. Even after Kenny got to UCLA the kids from Lincoln Heights would come to the campus and bring Kenny his lunch. And Kenny would give his football tickets to the kids.

It was at Lincoln High where Kenny's legend as a runner and a passer began. In a game against Garfield in 1935, Kenny threw his first sixty-yard pass, to Pete Torreano. Lincoln went on to win the city championship that year. I think they beat either Hollywood or Fairfax in the Coliseum. Bill Spaulding and Bill Ackerman went to the game, took one look at Kenny Washington, and said, "Yeah, he's good enough."

Kenny really wanted to go to Notre Dame, but Notre Dame didn't want him. His second choice was USC and USC was interested. They were interested in sitting him on the bench so none of the other schools could have him. The choice came down to UCLA and Loyola.

Jim Tunney was the coach out at Lincoln; his son, Jim Junior, is a referee in the NFL. Jim Senior was a great football man, and he helped develop Kenny's career as much as any one man. Tunney graduated from Loyola; he was a star out there. The people at Loyola tried to prevail upon Tunney to persuade Kenny Washington to come to their school. But Jim told Kenny, "Loyola is my school and they want me to get you to go there. But look, go to a big school so that when you graduate you can get national recognition. At a small school, who cares if you ran 100 yards against Pomona? But at a big school you can get national recognition and capitalize on that."

Of course, Jim Tunney was right. And at UCLA Kenny knew he would get his chance to play.

Well, because of Kenny's high school performance, by the time he got to UCLA the crowds kept coming. All the minorities followed UCLA because they were the first school to really give the minority athlete a chance to play. If we drew 100,000 people to the Coliseum, 40,000 of them would be black; that was just about every black person in the city of Los Angeles.

They came to see Kenny and me play. We received a lot of attention from the press and that added to our exposure. It was unusual for a black athlete to get featured in the white press, but they had a special way of writing about us. I have this article written by Melvin Durslag of the *Herald-Examiner* that explains the journalistic style of that time:

THE CLIMATE OF WASHINGTON'S ERA

As a running mate of Jackie Robinson in the UCLA backfield, Kenny Washington rose to a place of prominence during a curious time in sports.

It was a period in which the black athlete was applauded, but not yet admitted to the main stream of athletics.

You didn't see Negroes playing at Notre Dame, or USC, or Stanford, or Yale, or a number of other schools.

Nor did you see them in professional baseball or football.

Their place in the press was interesting, too. In the sports journalism practiced at the time, it was normal, if not fashionable, to patronize the black athlete in a way that would upset stomachs today.

Washington, for instance was known as "Kingfish," from the Amos and Andy character of the same name.

Together, he and Robinson were called the "Gold Dust Twins," a mocking appellation that might have been given a pair of black tap dancers working a nightclub in Reno.

You reflect on the routine language in the journalism of that period and you tend to wince. It wasn't uncommon to see a black runner described as a "sepia sprinter."

Nor did you blanch when you read about a "Senegambian speed merchant."

Another beauty was "dusky speedster."

Such was the climate during the time that Kenny Washington and Jackie Robinson romped up and down the lawn in college football, forming the best backfield twosome of that era.

Actually, we were called the "Goal Dust Twins." Bob Hunter of the *Los Angeles Examiner* started that, and he first used it as a reference to Kenny and me prior to Jackie Robinson joining us at UCLA. We were a running team, but when Kenny couldn't find room to maneuver he'd look for me downfield; I was his battery-mate. We didn't throw too many short passes, mostly forty yards going away. And I could outrun everybody. We started hooking up on a lot of those passes and that's when Bob Hunter came up with the name.

He got the idea from a box of soap powder, Fairbank's Gold Dust, that used a picture of two coal-black kids on the cover. They were the "Gold Dust Twins." It was quite a popular advertising slogan at that time; we heard it on the radio every day. So that was just a play on words; Bob Hunter changed it to the "Goal Dust Twins" and hung that label on us. After Jackie arrived in 1939, Bob Hunter just kept it going.

Kenny and I didn't really pay any attention to it. We were always a little late because of the way we were raised. We were naive; maybe that's why we were compatible with the white people. Hell, judging from the names we had for each other you would have thought we were the racists. This guy was a dago; that guy was a mick.

There was no enjoyment for the racists because Kenny and I had no fear of them. You call me a son of a bitch, that's fine; say the wrong thing and we are going to fight. I used to tell Kenny when we were playing for the Rams, "Thank God we thought we were equal."

We were out there knocking down people like we thought we were white. We had to have that attitude to play football in my generation; if we had felt the least bit inferior, we wouldn't have made it. We were lucky we came up on the West Coast.

I'll tell you how I was introduced to the Southern mentality. In 1936 Kenny and I were playing on the freshman team; in those days freshman couldn't play with the varsity. We started to hear some whispering among our teammates, "There are some players on the varsity saying they don't want to play with any niggers."

We came to learn that most of the talk was coming from a kid named Celestine Moses Wyrick. They called him Slats. A six-foot-four-inch, 212-pound, blond-haired, blue-eyed farm boy from Oklahoma, Slats played tackle. I played end and we figured to play next to one another on the varsity. Some of my teammates told me, "Slats ain't going to play with you, Woody. He called you a nigger, Woody."

The next year we were bound for a confrontation. We started scrimmaging and every time Spaudling put me in, Slats backed out and walked off the field. Finally, Bill Spaulding stepped in and said, "This can't go on. I'm the coach, Slats. If I put you in, you stay out there and play. Woody is a good ballplayer; he might make you an All-American."

But Slats wouldn't budge in his beliefs. He said, "I can't play next to a nigger because my folks would disown me."

Well, Spaulding was smart; he moved me onto the red team, the defensive squad. When we lined up, this put me right across the line from Slats. The whistle blew, the scrimmage started, I threw a block and Slats went down. He said, "You black son of a bitch."

The bulldog came out of me. I climbed on top of Slats and started punching. The coaches stood around and watched for a

64

little while. Finally they said, "That's enough, Woody!" and they came and pulled me off.

Slats and I became good friends after that. He thought I was chicken. In Oklahoma, no black man would have had the nerve to stand up to him like that. He didn't know what kind of guts we had. He had no respect for Negroes, but I stood up for myself and he respected that. He had to learn.

We played Oklahoma that year. Before the game, Slats went over to talk to the Oklahoma players; he knew them all. He said, "Kenny Washington and Woody Strode are my friends. They may whip you, but you'd better respect them for the good players they are!"

Well, Oklahoma ended up putting Kenny on their all-opponent team. See, sometimes a person like Slats who you know for just a short while can make the biggest influence on your life. He died on his way home from the second world war. He was riding on top of a box car and got electrocuted by some high tension wires. I felt so bad.

My run-in with Slats was the only racial problem I had with the team at UCLA. But we ran into a few problems on the road. I don't want to name any names now, not at this late date. But I remember they used to mark the field in lime and sometimes when they had Kenny down they'd try to rub that stuff in his eyes. Kenny would come back to the huddle and say, "That son of a bitch tried to hurt me."

The lineman would say, "Who was it?"

On the next play, seven guys would go after him. We fought for Kenny because we loved him. The only way a running back can survive in football is having some lineman that loves him.

Some players would insult me. They'd call me a nigger and I'd fight over that. I got kicked out of a few ball games based on that name-calling. Teams knew I'd fight and it got so they would think, what can I say to this nigger to get him kicked out of the game?

It didn't matter. If they hit Kenny, if they called me a nigger, then they were going to sleep. We had white kids on our team that would react to nigger just like I did. We got so beat up, but it was like a badge of honor.

We fought a lot, and we lost a lot of ball games. In 1937 we only won two ball games and finished in last place. I remember when we'd go up against Stanford, Mladin Zarubica, one of our tackles, saw Norm Standlee running at him and he just laid down. Standlee was the Stanford fullback, and he was as big as the Lord made 'em in those days. You knew where he was going, either inside tackle or outside tackle. The whole Stanford line would pull out and Norm would point and run over you. Those Stanford guys were big, and they hit pretty hard. So when they snapped the ball, Mladin would just lie down and get out of the way. Mladin, he was the crazy Serbian. He smoked cigars and walked around like he was the most sophisticated man on earth. He figured he was the big "I am" in football at UCLA. But we liked him, and he played tackle pretty well.

Our biggest game of the 1937 season was our finale against USC. Bill Ackerman first tried to develop the rivalry right after Stanford introduced UCLA into the Pacific Coast Conference in 1927. The first argument was over who'd get the Saturday games in the Coliseum. USC insisted on playing on Saturdays. That was okay with Bill Ackerman; he'd rather play them than worry about who got the Saturday dates. The athletic department was in debt, and Bill had to play USC to bring in some money. So we went on Friday nights, and they went on Saturday afternoons. And we did better than they did. We got all the people that were working on Saturday to come in on a Friday night. It made a big difference for your drawing power to go in first.

The first USC-UCLA games was played in 1929; UCLA lost 76–0. The next year we lost 52–0. Bill Ackerman decided it wasn't healthy for us to play them. They were just too good. The schools decided not to play again until UCLA had a chance to build up the program.

UCLA didn't play USC again until Kenny and I got there. So we never had beaten USC; we just ate their leftovers. And I swear the people at those two schools hated each other. "Goddamn USC, those rich sons of bitches!" I can imagine the betting that went down. It became like a war.

We always met at the Wilshire Country Club before the game:

Willis O. Hunter, the director of athletics at USC, all the officials from UCLA, the president of the student body, the coaches, yell leaders, song girls, dean of students, and anybody else connected with the game.

They'd go over anything that might lead to a problem. See, things would happen. Like we stole Tire Biter once; that was their dog. Or one time somebody from the USC band was walking by and someone from our school poured a whole bucket of blue paint on his uniform. Well, I had to buy that kid a new uniform. So they had this big meeting to try and keep everything on an even keel.

My biggest concern going into that first game against USC was whether or not Kenny could play. At eighteen years of age, in his first year of major college football, Kenny handled the ball 90 percent of the time and then backed me up behind the line on defense. He'd play sixty minutes of a sixty-minute ball game. Kenny got so beat up he'd spend his weekends at the Hollywood Hospital getting glucose dripped into his arm. We were all jealous, "Look at that Kenny Washington lying up there with all those pretty nurses."

Well, before the USC game Kenny told me, "Boy, if we weren't playing USC, I wouldn't be playing. My ribs are really hurt. I haven't told anybody; promise me you won't tell anybody, Woody." And I didn't.

USC hit pretty hard, and if you're hurt internally, it's just going to be that much harder on you. Of course the press didn't know Kenny was injured; they went ahead and promoted the game based on his ability to play. Maxwell Stiles wrote this for the *Los Angeles Examiner:*

> If one man can lick a football team, Kenny Washington looks like the man to do it. But if you are going to stick to the theory that a **TEAM** should beat a **MAN**, then you have to take Howard Jones' Trojans.

We played on a cool, crisp December 4th at 2 p.m. and 80,000 fans showed up. General admission was a dollar sixty-five, children with parents paid forty cents, kids under eighteen could get in for forty cents at the Peristyle end, and they'd always leave a gate open for the crashers. I've never paid to get into the Coliseum in my life.

Even as freshman, Kenny and I used to crash the gate. He'd put on his Lincoln High sweater; I'd put on my Jefferson sweater, and we'd run over the cops and ushers, trying to disappear into the crowd.

This time I was coming in through the players' entrance, ready to play in the biggest game of my life. I don't know how we thought we could beat USC; they'd rotate three tackles on me so I was always trying to block a fresh guy. But we were tough because we played from our hearts. I was so keyed up I must have bounced off three lockers and four doors trying to find the tunnel to the field.

We were down 13–0 in the third quarter when Spaulding pulled Kenny out of the game. He was taking a terrible beating. As soon as Don Ferguson came into replace him, USC scored again. Maxwell Stiles wrote:

> When Don Ferguson missed a tackle on Joe Schell to allow the Trojan substitute right halfback to score Southern California's third touchdown on a 25-yard pass from Lansdell midway in the third period, Spaulding told Washington, "You've simply got to go back in there and do whatever you can."
>
> "I'm ready boss," replied the gallant son of African forefathers.

It was the fourth quarter when the wheels started falling off the Trojans' horse. They were knocking us around like they had been all day when Don McNeil, the Trojans' center, who had probably never made a bad snap in his life, hiked the ball and sailed it wide. It took a crazy hop off Roy Engle's helmet and bounded around like a bar of soap in the tub. We recovered on their 44-yard line. That's when Spaulding put Kenny back in the game.

The ball was snapped to Kenny and he faded back. Our right halfback, Hal Hirshon, took off around my end. I stayed in to block; Kenny needed time. Hal was very fast and he ran a pattern toward the goal posts with Joe Schell hanging out of his pocket. Kenny cut loose with a pass. When everything met at the 10-yard line, Joe leaped to knock the ball down and missed. Hal caught the ball and scored; 19–7 USC.

In those days the team scored upon had the option to kick off or receive. USC figured the pass to Hal Hirshon was just a lucky break for us. They figured they'd kick off, pin us down on our end of the field and run the clock out, after all, they'd been stopping us all day. They figured wrong.

They kicked off, and we took over on our own 28-yard line. We got into our huddle and Hal said, "Kenny, I can beat their safety!"

Kenny said, "Okay, run as fast as you can, as far as you can, and I'll hit you."

The key was keeping that Thundering Herd from stampeding Kenny before he got a chance to throw. With the ball on the 28-yard line, Kenny stood back on the 20 ready to receive the snap. We hiked the ball and Kenny started backpedaling. Hal went deep. A couple of Trojans leaked through but Kenny shucked them off. He ran to his right and set to throw on the 15-yard line.

Hal and Joe raced stride for stride until they crossed mid-field. Then Joe started pulling up. He must have thought, "Screw it. Nobody can throw this far!"

Hal kept running, flat-out towards the goal. Kenny cranked it up and unloaded. Hal caught it in on their 20-yard line and took it for the score; 19–13 USC. Paul Zimmerman of the *Los Angeles Times* wrote:

> Then in the winking of an eye black lightning struck the desolate scene. Black lightning in the mighty right arm of Kenny Washington, spectacular Bruin pass thrower. Two bolts hit the confident Trojans and left them badly shattered.
>
> So sudden was the outburst that in the short space of twenty-six seconds the score changed from 19–0 to 19–13 and the Bruin rooting section seemed on the verge of tearing down the huge concrete stadium. It was just as if some magic wand, waved over the green turf, had swept aside all that went before.

Well, no one ever, even in the pros, had thrown a pass as far as Kenny Washington did that day. That was the longest officially documented pass in the history of American football: 72 yards all together, 53 yards in the air from the line of scrimmage. But Kenny received the snap 10 yards behind the line, and he backpedaled and sidestepped until he was boxed into a corner on the 15. Well, from our own 15 to the other guys' 23, that's 65 yards in the air, not counting the diagonal. Nobody had ever seen throwing like that.

This time, USC decided they would let us kick off. They knew if Kenny got the ball back he might throw it the entire length of the field. They received the kick, but we were so fired up they couldn't move the ball. They punted and we took over around mid-field; there were three minutes left on the clock.

Kenny ran and passed us down to their 14-yard line. On third down we tried to trick them. This time Hal Hirshon got the ball and tried a pass to Kenny in the end zone. But Hal was completely exhausted from running downfield time after time. Hal threw the ball way short and as Kenny turned back for it he slipped and fell flat on his face.

It was fourth down and 13 to go on their 14-yard line. The final seconds were ticking off the clock. A touchdown meant a sure tie with a chance to win on the conversion. Kenny received the snap and faded back. I ran a hook pattern to the 1-yard line; I was wide open. Kenny passed and as I turned, I saw the ball coming at me like a bullet. And like a bullet it went right through me.

We could have won if I held on to that pass. I didn't miss many. But when Kenny threw the ball, he threw it hard. He didn't throw many interceptions; if I couldn't get it nobody could. I've often thought about that pass; I don't know how I missed it. I guess it just wasn't meant to be.

But that was the wildest game this city had ever seen; it set the whole town on its ear. Howard Jones must have smoked up three packs of cigarettes watching his team almost get beat.

Naturally there was a lot of press after the game and the one write-up I'll never forget is this one by Frank Finch in the *Los Angeles Times:*

> Naked as a couple of chocolate cherubs as they sat dejectedly in their dressing room, Strode and Washington consoled each other over the failure to complete that fourth down pass that whizzed through Strode's fingers as he stood in the clear on the one-yard line.

"Sorry Kenny," said Strode, "but that potato was just too hot to handle. It went right through my hands."

"That's okay buddy," Kenny answered. "I knew it was hard but I just had to open up on that one; those Trojans were charging in too fast for me."

CHAPTER EIGHT

The Princess Luana

In our junior year they had a big Labor Day parade downtown on Broadway. They asked Kenny and me to participate in the parade and gave us a car to ride in, a beautiful old Packard with the huge chrome side pipes. It was a two-tone beige and black convertible with great big white sidewall tires and deep burgundy leather seats. We rode in the back, waving to the crowd. That's the kind of celebrities we had become.

We were recognized to the point where we could go anywhere free: the Million Dollar Theater, the Orpheum, the Paramount, the most prestigious places. There was a doorman at the Paramount who dressed up like the guy on the Beefeater's Gin bottle. He was always on the lookout for us. If he spotted us, he'd drag us inside.

Fats Waller used to sing and play his piano at the Paramount. They called him Fats for obvious reasons. He used to get so mad at us if we missed one of his shows. Between sets he brought us backstage with him. Fats liked to sit in his dressing room and drink Ballantine's Scotch. After the show, he'd go out in the alley behind the theater and sing and perform all night for anyone who was around. I still can't believe what we were privileged to see.

We wore the finest clothes: silk shirts and ties, wool garbardine suits, and of course we didn't go anywhere without a hat. We didn't run around in our sneakers either; we always wore hard leather shoes with a good polish.

UCLA made us dress up when we traveled, and we rode the trains everywhere. It was a great way to travel that no one even thinks about doing anymore. The school would lease a whole railroad car for the team and we'd raise hell—water fights, food fights, pillow fights, all that crazy stuff. Some of the guys played cards. Jackie Robinson was quite a card player; he beat the guys out of a lot of money. I never played cards. I was too afraid to gamble in those days. And they must have had a cocktail lounge on the train, but I was never interested in spending time there. I wasn't too sophisticated. Kenny and I would get up to a place like Oregon, get our room in the big hotel, then drop water balloons or spit toothpaste off the balcony.

When we hit the road, all the relatives would follow us. Rocky's brother Julius was killed in 1938 driving up to the Oregon State game. Julius was the fire chief; he was always on his way to a fire and that man loved speed. Here's a guy who made A. J. Foyt look like he couldn't get out of first gear. Coming out of the garage, he'd be going ninety by the time he hit the back gate. He hit a turn up around Visalia and never came back.

Well, if nothing else, old Julius didn't miss much of a game. The Oregon State game was our next-to-last game of 1938. They hadn't beaten us since 1930. Down on Spring Street the bookies had us favored 5–2.

On the opening kickoff, Oregon State returned the ball 84 yards for a touchdown. They didn't score again. In the meantime we gained 338 yards, made twenty-three first downs, and didn't score until the third quarter when Kenny passed for a touchdown.

In the fourth quarter Izzy Cantor had the ball, and the Jewish Jitterbug was running for the end zone. The only person between Iz and the goal line was the referee, Tom Fitzpatrick. Fitzpatrick thought Izzy was going to cut right, so he went right. But Izzy went left, they both went down, the defense caught up, and the play was over.

We still had a chance to win when we got the ball down to their ten-yard line with under a minute to play. It was fourth down and Bill Spaulding decided to send in a kid named Ray Sturdevant to try a drop-kick for the winning field goal.

Ray Sturdevant was the kind of guy who wore a slide rule on his belt and a pocket protector for his pens and pencils. Here was a guy that didn't know the meaning of hand-eye coordination. I don't know how he made the team. Bill Spaulding, being the soft-hearted guy that he was, must have felt sorry for Ray. Actually, Ray could do one thing: He could kick the football like it was shot out of a cannon.

Ray was part of what we called "the live bait crew." For three years he took a regular, daily beating in practice without ever seeing one minute of action in a game. Anyway, Bill Spaulding called Ray's number and he came running onto the field, as pumped up and excited as he had ever been, and reported to the referee that he was substituting for the quarterback.

When we looked up from the huddle and saw Ray running towards us we collectively thought, Oh no!, and waved him off. Ray looked like a popped balloon. He stood there stunned, his head on a swivel going from huddle to sideline, huddle to sideline. Izzy felt so sorry for him he offered to come out of the game and give Ray his chance.

Well, Izzy was a fullback, and Ray had come in to replace the quarterback. In those days, if you didn't come in for the quarterback you weren't allowed to say anything in the huddle for one play. We didn't know Ray had come in to kick. They weren't allowed to coach from the sidelines, so we tried something else and the game ended tied.

The alumnai wanted Bill Spaulding fired after that game. Actually, they wanted him fired after the 1937 season, but Kenny saved him with his big performance against USC. Bill Ackerman decided to let Bill Spaulding finish out the 1938 season and hire a new coach for 1939. So Bill Spaulding's last game, after thirteen years of coaching bad football players at UCLA, was the big game against USC.

The Trojans were tied with Cal for the conference lead. Each school had one tie on their record, but Cal had already played their last game the week before. It came down to which team had scored the most points over the course of the season. USC needed to beat us by four touchdowns to win the conference and get invited back to the Rose Bowl.

That was the big prize; the Rose Bowl was worth a lot of money and prestige to the school that got invited. But if USC didn't go to the Rose Bowl, they were going to Hawaii. Before the season began, USC had been invited to come to Honolulu and play the University of Hawaii in the Pineapple Bowl.

Here's how that came about. We had two Hawaiian kids playing football at UCLA, Francis Wai and his little brother Conkling. They introduced me to poi, the nastiest stuff, it tasted like dead flesh. I thought they were cannibals.

The Wai boys were looked after by John Ford. That's how I first met the old man. Ford spent a lot of time in the islands on his yacht. He'd stow a few cases of whiskey, sail over there, and party for a couple of weeks. That was his idea of recreation. John Ford knew all the locals, and he got to know the Wai boys' father, who was one of the leading bankers in Honolulu. Ford arranged to take care of the kids while they were going to school over there.

All the Hawaiians followed West Coast college football. They didn't have any major college football in Hawaii because transportation was still too primitive. So old man Wai sent his sons to California to get an education and play some football. They ended up at UCLA because they were Hawaiian and they weren't very good football players. They wouldn't have made it at USC, that's for sure.

But the Thundering Herd had the big reputation and the people in Hawaii wanted to see them play in the Pineapple Bowl. The Hawaiians arranged, through our athletic department, to extend the invitation to USC. Johnny Johnson was the guy who actually made the contact; he was part of our athletic administration. He made the offer and USC accepted. But they couldn't go to Hawaii and the Rose Bowl. And if they went to the Rose Bowl, we got to go to Hawaii, because we had the man who did the inviting.

We played USC on a Thursday evening. It was an unusual day because it was very hot and there was a big fire burning out of control down in the Santa Monica Mountains. Only 65,000 people turned out for the game. We scored first; I was standing a foot inside the end zone when Kenny hit me with a pass. Now USC needed five touchdowns to get to the Rose Bowl. Well, they scored six and won the game 42–7.

42–7 was no accident, and we had to carry Bill Spaulding out on his shield. The first time he went up against USC, he lost 72–0; nine years later, his last home game, he lost to USC 42–7. A large part of success is timing; Bill Spaulding's timing stunk.

In those days, they would never fire a guy without making sure he had a place to go. Bill Ackerman made him Director of Athletics. Ackerman told him what to do and Spaulding did it. And Bill won a free trip to Hawaii along with twenty-five of his favorite ballplayers. Kenny and I went, and all the seniors went. I guess the only senior that didn't go was Ray Sturdevant.

We left December 15, 1938 and didn't get back until January 11, 1939. The ship left out of Wilmington Harbor, down near Long Beach. We sailed aboard the S.S. *Masonia* which went to the islands by way of San Francisco. It was a huge luxury liner that was just about as high as it was long, hundreds of feet in every direction, with three smoke stacks that billowed white puffs as she chugged along. It took a little over a week to get there and what a relaxing time that was.

We stayed at the Royal Hawaiian Hotel, which is still there on Waikiki Beach. You can't miss it because it's out of that older era. The architecture has kind of a Spanish feel to it, and it's bright pink on the outside. Back in 1938 the Royal Hawaiian was the only big hotel. Honolulu hadn't been built up yet.

Kenny and I took a trip around the island on the road that travels around Diamond Head, up the Kailua side and by the North Shore. It got a little scary up around the North Shore because the surf was up over twenty feet and the spray made it feel like we were driving through a hurricane. In fact there's a section of the road they call the Forbidden Road because it's so dangerous to travel.

And the Pali Highway was there. That's an elevated highway that cuts the island in half. They told me to flip a coin off the edge of the Pali Highway and when I did, the wind was so strong it blew the coin right back. Down below there was nothing but jungle and tropical flowers of every shape and color. The aroma was like perfume. Once you get that tropical aroma in your nostrils, you never forget it.

When Kenny and I stepped off the boat, we saw people darker than us. Polynesians and Orientals, all manner of mixed breeds. They were walking around with no restrictions. Kenny and I had a lot of freedom in Los Angeles, but there was always a borderline. When I got home the first thing I told my mother was, "I saw the people free." That was my first impression of Hawaii.

I remember looking at Kenny in disbelief. We didn't know how to act. Kenny and I decided we'd better not get involved with any of the Hawaiian girls. We had never been interracial at home when it came to our personal relations, but we felt the Hawaiians might resent us—not the kids but the older generation. And it could have caused quite a stir among our sponsors at UCLA.

We played our game against the University of Hawaii and beat them 32–7. After the game the Wai boys' father had a big party for the team at his house. He lived on the beach and the party was real Hawaiian style. They had laid nets out in the water before the party began and when we got there a couple of locals dressed in pongee skirts pulled the nets in, collected the fish, cleaned them, and put them on the fire. They had a pig roasting in the ground and poi on the table. They set up one long table so everybody could sit together. Tiki torches were burning around the whole area.

Old man Wai had hired some native dancers to put on a show. They danced on the beach. They wore grass skirts that showed more flesh than I had ever seen a woman show in public. And they moved in a way I had never seen a woman move. They glowed in that warm tiki light.

I was wearing my best tweed suit; I had my hair gassed and shining. I held my hat in my hand; I was all delicate looking. When the dance ended, one of the girls came over and introduced herself. I could see in her eyes she liked me.

It turned out she had royal blood. Her name was Princess Luukialuana Kalaeloa, which means: May the rays of sunrise forever shine on you. She was related to Queen Lilly Ukulani, who was the one that gave Americans access to the islands. The princess was a beautiful native girl, with dark skin and eyes that shone. She had long black, black hair that flowed wild. She had a flower in her hair and a body that still makes me blush.

She said, "Woody, I'm having a party for the team. Will you come?"

I said, "Sure, I'll go," but I didn't. I was too afraid of the interracial scene. The day of the party went by and Kenny and I were walking around Waikiki. We walked by a theater downtown and there she was. I tried to hide my head behind Kenny's shoulder as we were walking by, but she spotted me anyway. She grabbed me by the arm and said, "Woody, why didn't you come to my party?"

I stood there floundering for an answer. Kenny was no help; he liked to see me embarrassed. Finally I gave her some weak excuse to get rid of her. I think I promised to meet her somewhere, but I didn't.

When it came time to leave, Kenny and I figured we'd be slick and get there late. We didn't want to go through all that hugging and kissing. We couldn't have all these woman grabbing us in front of everybody from the school. We got there just as they were pulling up the gang plank. The boat started to pull out, and I let out a big sigh. Just then I saw her, the Princess Luana. She was on board, and she was waiting for me. I thought to myself, "This chick is crazy!" And then it started.

She gushed, "Woody Strode, I love you, I love you."

She had her claws in me and she wouldn't leave the boat. She said, "Promise me we will meet again."

I promised, "Yes, we will meet again."

She said, "That's all I wanted to hear." And she dove off the ship, a hundred feet into the water and swam ashore.

I turned to Kenny and said, "Boy, that chick is crazy!"

CHAPTER NINE

The Dead End Kids

During my college years I went with a girl named Lois Evans, a good-looking girl who was studying to be a doctor. We made a good couple because we were both outstanding Negroes. Lois was one of the few black girls at UCLA.

The black guys tried not to get too close to the white girls. If we were attracted to a white girl, we had to pull our reins in. If she didn't come over and snatch you out of the closet, you wouldn't go near her. At the school dances, Kenny and I would stand around the walls, and we were the stars. The wealthiest people's daughters used to come up to us and ask, "May we have this dance?" And we'd dance; that was the protocol.

Even at our own dances, I used to stand back. I was shy with girls. For Kenny it was not a problem, but then he was always more outgoing than I was. I was raised with a more Victorian attitude. But I think by standing back, I became more desirable.

I'd dance; it'd be nice, but I'd get a hard-on and be a little embarrassed about that. We were introduced to sex slowly. My sex life didn't start until I was twenty-one years old in the back seat of that Model T Ford. I'd do everything, but they had to start the motor. Of course we weren't into drugs or alcohol, so we didn't have any false image going. Everything we did had to come right off the top of our heads.

We had morals and integrity back then. I remember Joe E. Brown used to get so mad at Norm Duncan, our freshman coach, because Norm would always swear in front of the players. We didn't swear; we didn't drink or smoke; we didn't lie or cheat. And there weren't any free rides either.

All the years I was at UCLA I had to earn my scholarship. All the guys who were on scholarship did some kind of maintenance work for the school. A lot of the great athletes were janitors; they scrubbed toilets. Kenny and I had good jobs; we used to walk around campus with a stick picking up papers, and we did a little gardening, too. That's how I earned my hundred bucks a month.

In the summer of 1939 Bill Ackerman got Kenny and me jobs working in the service department at the Warner Bros. Studio. Bill had a good relationship with the studio, partly because of Joe E. Brown and partly because Bill took care of them with fooball tickets. Bob Fellows is the guy that got us the jobs out at Warner Bros. He was a movie producer and a big supporter of UCLA athletics.

They dressed us up in brown coats with epaulets and gold-braided ropes hanging from the shoulder. We wore caps like a bellhop in a hotel. We worked as men-in-waiting, porters. We took care of the stars. Bette Davis, Jimmy Cagney, Ann Sheridan, and Olivia de Havilland were some of the big Warner Bros. stars at that time. I remember walking up to Errol Flynn and him saying, "Oh, you and Kenny, I just love watching you guys play!" All the movie stars were football fans.

Every morning the studio would assign us to a sound stage, and we'd stand around and wait for someone to order something. The most important thing was to take care of the director. If he wanted something, snap to. I remember one director who didn't like ice water—it had to be room temperature. It was little stuff like that, and they paid us fifty-seven cents an hour plus tips. I made a hundred dollars in tips one week. Imagine how much money that was back then. I'll never forget the actor John Payne used to give me a dollar every time I did something for him, so I tracked him all day.

One of my most embarrassing moments came when I was told to bring a tray of food to Jane Wyman's dressing room. When I saw her sitting there in that powder-blue silk robe, one leg half out, I was mesmerized by her beauty; she had a face like an angel. She watched me come in the door, and I got so flustered I tripped on the door jamb and fell all the way inside. The food and coffee went all over the carpet. But she smoothed it over for me and helped me clean it up. She said, "You know, I'm a big fan of yours, you and Kenny Washington. How are you boys going to do this year?"

Well, I couldn't think of an answer right then, not under the gun like that. But when Kenny and I got back to school that fall there were a lot of changes on the Bruins' football team. Except for Kenny, we had a whole new backfield. Ned Mathews became our first-string quarterback. Izzy Cantor's little brother, Leo, took over the fullback job. And the school recruited Jackie Robinson to replace Hal Hirshon at right halfback. We had the best backfield talent on the coast and it was up to our new coach, Babe Horrell, to figure out how to make us winners.

Babe Horrell was a tall Aryan type from Pasadena. He came from a big well-to-do family, and all the Horrell kids were star athletes at Pasadena High School. Babe was captain of the tennis and football teams. He played center and guard on the basketball team, and he also made the swimming team and played water polo. He was such a great athlete out there that they named their field Horrell Field.

He went to Cal-Berkley and became an All-American center on the 1924 Andy Smith "Wonder Team," which is regarded as one of the greatest college football teams in history. They were unbeaten the three years Babe centered their line, but they never went to the Rose Bowl. When the Cal Bears got the invitation, they voted to work during Christmas vacation to earn money for presents instead of practicing for the Rose Bowl.

Babe Horrell started coaching for UCLA in 1925. He worked as an unpaid assistant to Bill Spaulding while the school was still over on Vermont Avenue. He and Spaulding were opposite types;

Babe would never leave an old cup, half-full of tobacco juice, lying around the way Spaulding did.

Babe Horrell was high class, cultured and civilized. He always dressed right; he always talked right. But he and Spaulding were alike in that neither one was very good at disciplining the kids. Babe was a nice guy, and he was more like a friend than our coach.

When Babe took over after the 1938 season, his first goal was recruiting Jackie Robinson out of Pasadena Junior College. Jackie was probably the most sought-after athlete on the West Coast. I hadn't met Jackie at that point; I had only read about him. Of course in those days Jackie was famous as a football player.

Jackie Robinson was the first of the Gayle Sayers/O. J. Simpson/Eric Dickerson-type running backs. He had incredible breakaway speed coupled with an elusiveness you had to see to believe. He could change direction quicker than any back I had ever seen. Stop on a dime: boom; full speed in the other direction. They didn't have to do a lot of blocking for him because he was so instinctive. He was shifty and quick and would just outmaneuver everybody.

Pasadena Junior College used to play in the Rose Bowl and Jackie would draw crowds of 20–30,000 people to watch him play. I remember the game Jackie played against Compton Junior College in 1938; that was one of his greatest football games.

He ran back a kick 85 yards for a touchdown. He scored two more touchdowns on runs of 50 and 60 yards and threw for another. The way Jackie ran the sidelines you'd have thought he was playing on a fifty-acre field. Bill Ackerman and Babe Horrell had gone to that game to see if Jackie was good enough to attend UCLA. They took one look at this kid and said, "Yeah, he's good enough," just like their reaction to Kenny Washington. And Jackie Robinson was very pigeontoed, so when he ran alongside Kenny, with his knock-knees, they made quite a pair.

Pasadena Junior College won all eleven of their games in 1938 and the Junior College Championship. Jackie was the unanimous choice as most valuable player. He scored 131 points and gained over 1,000 yards. He and Ray Bartlett, who played end and was Jackie's best friend growing up, were both named to the All-

Southern California Eleven. That was pretty unusual: the two guys who got all the honors were black.

Pasadena Junior College had a pretty unusual team. There were five blacks and six Southerners on the team. Their coach was Tom Mallory from Oklahoma, and he brought the six Southerners with him. At first the Southerners tried to sock hard and hurt and all that stuff, but Jackie and Ray had the same attitude as Kenny and me; if you hit me hard, I'm going to hit you just as hard or harder next time. They had to learn how to respect each other. Then again it helps to have an outstanding team, and the kid that made them great was Jackie Robinson.

Athletically, Jackie benefited from having three older brothers and an older sister who were all outstanding athletes in their own right. They all grew up playing together; each one improved the other.

At that time, Jackie's brother Mack was the really famous athlete in the family. He was a hell of a track and field man. At Pasadena Junior College he set the junior college long-jump record at 25 feet. Then he moved up to the University of Oregon and set a world record in the 220-yard dash. That record stood until Jesse Owens broke it at the 1936 Olympics. Of course, Mack finished second to Jesse Owens in Berlin. Last I heard, Mack was ushering out at Dodger Stadium.

Growing up, Jackie idolized Mack. One of Jackie's first athletic goals was to break Mack's long-jump record at the junior college, which he did. That story became part of the legend of Jackie Robinson, because the National Junior College Track Championships and the Southern California Junior College Baseball Championships were being held on the same day. The track meet was in Pomona, the baseball game was in Glendale, and it took a couple of hours to get from one place to the other. They gave Jackie permission to arrive at the track meet and jump an hour early. On his third jump, Jackie went 25 feet 6½ inches, breaking Mack's record.

They had a car waiting, and as soon as he broke the record, they rushed him out to Glendale. He got there in the middle of the third inning, and his team was down by a few runs. Well, he got a couple of key hits, stole a couple of bases, and basically won the game by himself. He finished the season batting .417, stole twenty-five bases in twenty-four games and was voted the most valuable player in Southern California junior college baseball.

Jackie also lettered in basketball at Pasadena. In 1938 they won the championship and Jackie led the Western Division in scoring. Altogether he lettered in four varsity sports. When it came to athletics, Jackie Robinson could do anything he wanted.

That's why UCLA wanted him. And Oregon wanted him pretty bad, too. They figured they owned Jackie because Mack had gone to school there. Some friends of the school came down and threw the keys to a brand-new Dodge on his porch. And there was an alumnus from Stanford who offered to pay Jackie's way to any school back East just so he wouldn't stay on the West Coast and possibly beat Stanford playing for another school.

Lucky for us we had Babe Horrell, because Babe had considerable prestige, influence, and reputation in Pasadena. He used it all in persuading Jackie to come to UCLA, and Babe made him give the car back. But Jackie wanted to stay close to home anyway. When he announced his decision, he said, "I choose UCLA because I plan to get a job in Los Angeles after I finish school, and I figure I'll have a better chance if I attend a local university."

Jackie came out to UCLA in the summer of 1939. They put him in the extension school so he could make up some units and become eligible to play football in the fall. We also recruited his friend Ray Bartlett, and they became the fourth and fifth black players on our team. The black community liked to point to us as a symbol of achievement. The one guy I haven't mentioned is Johnny Wynn, because I never knew Johnny that well. He was on the freshman team in 1938 and then left school after he made the varsity in 1939. He got some kind of job offer, and I heard he became quite successful.

I never knew Jackie that well either. We were only together that one year. But Jackie was a very intelligent and good-looking young man. He had a very dark complexion with thin, straight features. He had a perfect white smile and steely hard eyes that could flash angry in a heartbeat. To be honest, Jackie Robinson was not well-liked when he was at UCLA. He would never believe there'd be a statue of him sitting out there right now, at the baseball stadium UCLA named after him.

Jackie was not friendly. He had been in a few scuffles in Pasadena with the law, minor trouble. When he came to UCLA he was very withdrawn. Even on the football field he would stand off by himself.

People used to ask me, "Why is Jackie so sullen and always by himself?"

Well, for one thing, Jackie's brother Frank was killed in a motorcycle accident just before Jackie got to UCLA. People hardly ever mention that. But Jackie and Frank were very close. They had a relationship similar to the one Rocky and Kenny shared. Frank encouraged and advised Jackie. I remember Jackie said, "I wanted to win, not only for myself but also because I didn't want to see Frank disappointed."

Jackie's real father, Jerry Robinson, left the family right after Jackie was born. The Robinsons were sharecroppers on a plantation in Cairo, Georgia. Jerry got fed up and took off with a neighbor's wife. They never saw him again. Jackie's mama, Mallie Robinson, packed up the family and moved out to Pasadena, where her brother Burton lived. I believe Burton was a postal clerk.

Burton had a small apartment, too small for the whole family, so Mallie saved what she could and finally got a small house on West Pepper Street, right near the Rose Bowl. The house was a white wood frame California bungalow in a lower-class white neighborhood, and the neighbors were not pleased with the new family on the block. They tried to get rid of Mallie, but she was tough and fought back. And that's where Jackie Robinson grew up.

To someone like Kenny or me, Pasadena seemed like a million miles away based on the crude transportation of that time. It was like Paris, France, as far as I was concerned. Pasadena was where all the rich white people lived. Orange Grove Avenue was millionaires' row. Those people controlled the community, and Pasadena was a segregated and prejudiced town. So it was much harder for someone like Jackie Robinson growing up than it was for someone like Kenny Washington, who grew up with nothing but poor Italians.

See, Jackie Robinson knew where he was from. That's the other reason Jackie had an angry personality. I remember Jackie told this story about growing up in Pasadena:

> I was out in front of the Pepper Street house sweeping up the sidewalk when a little neighborhood girl shouted at me, "nigger, nigger, nigger!" I was old enough to know how to answer that. My older brother Frank told me that, in the South, the most insulting name you can call a white person is "cracker." This is what I called her, and her father stormed out of the house to confront me. I don't remember who threw the first stone but the father and I had a pretty good stone-throwing fight going until the girl's mother came out and made him go back into the house.

Right before Jackie arrived at UCLA, a little story hit the papers that created some tension. Jackie and Ray Bartlett used to play on a softball team sponsored by Pepsi-Cola. They were in what was known as an Owl League, playing overhand softball down at Brookside Playground. They were going home after a game, heading up Mountain Avenue. Jackie had borrowed an old Plymouth from somewhere, and he was giving his teammates a lift home. Ray Bartlett was riding on the running board. When they got to Fair Oaks and Mountain they passed a white guy who started shouting insults at them, called them a bunch of niggers. Eventually they got to a traffic signal and both cars stopped. Ray, without saying anything, reached out and slapped the guy across the face with his baseball glove. The white guy realized the mistake he had made when he saw how many angry kids there were in Jackie's car. When the light changed, he hightailed it.

Well, Jackie was hotheaded, and he wasn't going to leave it alone. He chased the guy and forced him off the road. You can imagine how scared that man was. Ray tried to cool Jackie off, but Jackie wouldn't back down. He was in a rage and ready to kick this guy's ass, but right then the police showed up. Jackie started to defy them, and they ran him in.

Ray, being Jackie's best friend, went down to the police station to see what they were going to do with him. Jackie was yelling, "Ray, get my mother!"

So Ray went and told Mallie what happened. She called Babe Horrell, who, like I said, had considerable influence in Pasadena. Babe got hold of the judge assigned to the case, and I don't know exactly what happened in court, but Jackie was released. They probably put him on some kind of probation. That story followed Jackie out to UCLA and hurt his reputation.

When I went to talk to Bill Ackerman the other day, he told me, "Jackie always seemed to have a chip on his shoulder. I wasn't close to Jackie like I was to you guys. Maybe he was rather ahead of his time in his thinking with regard to the black's situation. I think it hurt him emotionally to see how some of his friends were treated. The result was he kept pretty much within himself; to a certain extent he was a loner.

"Of course, all you kids used to fight for your rights. Ray Bartlett used to be a good fighter for that. I called him Red, you know, because he had that head full of red hair. But Kenny wasn't as vocal as Jackie. Jackie was a nine, and Kenny was a three.

"But Jackie was the best all-around athlete UCLA has ever had, and that includes everybody, even the people playing there now. He was well-coordinated, he had great speed, a lot of strength, and he was very quick."

Jackie became the only man in UCLA history to letter in four varsity sports: track, baseball, basketball and football. He was the national long-jump champion in 1940, and he was the basketball team's highest scorer the two years he played. Baseball was his weakest game, but in football he excelled. In 1939 he led the nation in average yards per carry, a little over 12 yards per run from the line of scrimmage.

With Jackie Robinson on the right side and Kenny Washington on the left, we had the two greatest halfbacks the West Coast had ever seen. And we added to that when Leo Cantor decided to transfer from USC.

Leo was the real football player; Izzy was pretty good, but Leo was great. He was a star quarterback out at Roosevelt High School. In their system the quarterback did most of the ball handling. Leo wasn't really tall, but he was wide, and he was strong. The papers liked to call him Colonel Leo "The Lion" Cantor. Leo gained a lot of yards and scored a lot of points. He didn't think in terms of big gains; he thought in terms of touchdowns, which, of course, is how you win games. Leo was so good that he was the only player Howard Jones ever personally recruited. He went to the Cantors' home and persuaded Leo to attend USC.

Well, we had Izzy Cantor, and Bill Ackerman wasn't about to let Leo go to USC. Bill sent Izzy over to USC, and Izzy worked on his brother. Then Bill sent Mike Frankovich over there, and Mike worked on him. And Joe E. Brown and then Norm Duncan went over there, and they worked on Leo. And Norm was tough; he said, "Look, you aren't going to USC, you're going to our school!"

Finally, Leo decided he'd transfer. Nate and Ned Sugarman were Leo's sponsors, and I'm sure they made it worth his while. And in those days, as long as you hadn't played in any games, you could transfer anywhere you wanted. Leo became a freshman at UCLA in 1938.

Because of Izzy, Leo was immediately accepted as part of the group. And Leo and I became very good friends. We played on the same Air Force football team during the second world war. I remember when we finally got shipped out to go overseas. We were in Honolulu, and it was the time of Passover, the Jewish holiday; that's the best eating time.

Leo said, "Come with me, Woody."

I said, "How am I going to get in?"

"I'm going to tell the Rabbi you're a Jewish Negro."

We did that. I got in and I ate. And all through the years we've never lost track of one another. We used to work for the same plumbing outfit. They used us like human cranes. We delivered bathroom fixtures like those old porcelain and iron tubs that stood on their own feet. You can imagine what a heavy unit that was. Leo would grab it from the bottom, I'd get my back under it and we'd carry that son of a bitch upstairs to somebody's bathroom. We never dropped one, never had an accident. Leo was so strong that we used to bet people he could lift me over his head, like a barbell. He could do that, and we won some money.

Leo was a gambler. Years later, I had 100 dollars I was going to use to check my wife out of the Queen of Angels Hospital. She

90

was having her appendix removed. But Leo got a tip on a horse and he said, "Woody, this is our chance to get even." So we went to the track and the horse, Count Fleet, won at 27–1.

The long shot to make our 1939 backfield was Ned Mathews. Ned was our quarterback. Ned wasn't a big star in high school like the rest of the guys. His first year at Manual Arts he went out for the B team, and they wouldn't give him a uniform. He didn't get a football suit until one of the kids quit and there was an extra one. His junior year he started on the B team. In his senior year he moved up to the varsity, made first-string quarterback, and won the city championship.

Ned ended up at UCLA because his buddy Billy Overlin decided to come over. Billy was the fullback on the Manual Arts team; he was the big gun out there. Ned was more like a little dog who grabs hold of your pants leg and won't let go. Not really dangerous, but damned annoying.

When Ned arrived at UCLA in 1937, he weighed about 150 pounds in full uniform soaking wet. He made the varsity in 1938, but didn't become first-string until 1939. By then he'd put on about twenty pounds of muscle. He was still small, but he learned that blocking is all quickness, technique, and mental toughness. Sometimes he'd be outweighed by fifty to seventy-five pounds; it didn't bother him a bit.

We played a game against Iowa, and they had a big tackle named Luckheed. He went about six-foot-seven, weighed about 300 pounds. Well, we used to have this formation called the Henderson Spread, which brought all the backfield men up to the line of scrimmage except for the deepback, Kenny. This put Ned right across the line from the opposition's tackle. The first time Ned realized he could block this guy Luckheed, he went crazy. Ned, being the quarterback, called the plays, and he kept calling for that play the rest of the game. He said it was just like chopping down a big tree. And after the game, Charlie Kepper, who used to announce football at the Coliseum, said, "That was probably the best exhibition of blocking I have ever seen in the Coliseum." And we beat Iowa.

To show you how valuable Ned was to our team, we had a

testimonial dinner at the Paladium in Hollywood in 1971. Ned was asked to say a few words. As he was walking back to his table, Rocky Washington grabbed him. Rocky turned to Kenny and said, "This guy here you can thank. He made you!"

That took me by surprise because I had never really thought about it, but I have pictures that substantiate it. Pictures of Kenny, Jackie, and Leo breaking loose, with Ned out in front clearing the road.

So those four guys were the nucleus of our 1939 team, and the five of us hung out together quite a bit. Jackie not so much as the other guys, but he'd come with us on Fridays when we'd head out to Boyle Heights for our ritual pre-game meal: pastrami on an onion bagel.

CHAPTER TEN

The Goal Dust Gang

The first football player from UCLA ever to make the pros was Verdie Boyer. He was one of my roommates when I first got to school. He was part of the 1934 team. Verdie was a guard. The next one was Bob MaChessnie, who was an end. He played for the Washington Redskins. But 1936 was the start of the real upswing at UCLA. I guess 1939 was the peak. It was a team that would never quit, never give up. It was sixty-minute football, and the only time substitutions were made was when somebody got hurt.

We were a tough group of dead-end kids, and we came together that year to form UCLA's first great football team. And, to the best of my knowledge, UCLA was the first major university to have four black kids playing key roles. Kenny and Jackie were the first one-two black backfield men, I started every game, and Ray Bartlett saw considerable playing time as a reserve. We were unique in America.

Our success started when we faced Texas Christian University in the first game of the season. TCU was a football powerhouse which hadn't been defeated in their last fourteen games. They finished the 1938 season ranked no worse than third in the nation and a lot of people thought they were the number-one team. Going into our game the bookies had them favored by nine points. We looked at the game as a test to see what our potential really was.

NEGRO STARS LEAD ATTACK
By Bob Hunter (*Examiner*)

Kenny Washington and Jackie Robinson—UCLA's dynamic Goal Dust Twins—went wild in the third quarter last night to spark a inspired Bruin team to a thrilling 6–2 triumph over mighty Texas Christian!

Outside of a decisive 71-yard drive, staged almost single hand-edly by Washington and Robinson, the Horned Frogs held the upper hand.

We didn't lose a game for the rest of the season. Going into our last game with USC, we were undefeated and so were they. If we could beat them, we'd win the conference championship and go to the Rose Bowl for the first time ever. The showdown was December 9, 1939 and it was the biggest, the most colossal, the greatest game ever seen in these parts. Three dollars-thirty cents for reserved, two-twenty for general admission, and a dollar sixty-five at the Peristyle end.

In 1939 USC was the team to beat. They had beaten Duke in the Rose Bowl in January and Duke hadn't been scored upon all season. Not until the last forty seconds of the game when Doyle Nave passed to Antelope Al Krueger for the winning touchdown. It was probably Howard Jones' finest team, and Howard had won five Rose Bowls. The Trojans were really glamorous, as well-known and popular as any football team in the country.

Their biggest stars were Harry Smith, Grenville Lansdell, and Bob Hoffman. Bob was the defensive ace on the team. He was a blue-collar type player. He didn't get much of the spotlight. Lansdell and Smith were two of the glassy-eyed boys. The media loved them.

Harry Smith was a big, moon-faced farm boy from Ontario. He had rugged features, beady eyes, and a crooked smile that made him look like he had just tied someone's shoelaces together. One writer described him as a bull gifted with wings and one of the keenest football minds ever on the line.

Grenville Lansdell was Kenny's counterpart. The papers called him "Froggy Granny, the laughing boy from Pasadena." He was

94

kind of a free spirit who didn't take football too seriously. But he was responsible for getting USC into the Rose Bowl, and he got them through the 1939 season without a defeat.

Just before the game, the All-American selections came out, and Harry Smith and Granny Lansdell were both named to the first team. Kenny Washington only made the second team. I remember the Hearst selections carried a lot of weight because they owned the biggest papers coast-to-coast. Davis J. Walsh, who was the big eye-in-the-sky reporter for the *Examiner,* a Hearst paper, wrote:

> People seem inclined to blame me for the fact that Kenny Washington didn't get on the All-America team. But let's pass that, with the succinct statement that he'd get on mine, if I had one. In fact, I'd start with him and probably pull the rest out of a fedora while blinded at the bottom of a coal hole with the cover on at midnight.

There's no doubt Harry Smith belonged on the team. He was one of the best players in the country, a two-time All-American. But Granny Lansdell was not near the same caliber player as Kenny Washington. In 1939 Kenny led the entire nation in total offense. Tom Harmon of Michigan was second; he was only a junior and he made the first team. Granny Lansdell was three, four hundred yards behind those guys. And Kenny was just as good on defense as he was on offense. After the season was over Kenny had played 580 out of a possible 600 minutes.

But that's the kind of advantage the prestige of USC gave an athlete. USC had the power; they were so dominant in Howard Jones' day. He could have run for Mayor of Los Angeles and won. Granny Lansdell was a good player on a great team, Kenny Washington was a great player on a mediocre team. Dick Hyland of the *Los Angeles Times* wrote:

> Kenny Washington is the best all-around halfback. It was mentioned he is not first-string All-American because he is not a kicker. Maybe no one asked him to kick. Given two weeks, Kenny could kick as good as anyone on Howard Jones' team. I regret Kenny was not given the recognition he deserved on the football field; he is as worthy of All-American as any player in the last ten years.

Kenny didn't make the first team because of prejudiced voting. But to those of us that knew Kenny, it made no difference. We believed in him; we believed he was special and that belief was more powerful than awards or recognition. If it ever bothered Kenny I don't know, he never showed it. The whole thing was a big joke.

Liberty magazine conducted a poll among all the college players to see who the players thought should be an All-American. More than 1,600 athletes were polled and the magazine said that of the eleven players chosen, only one guy of the 664 named received the vote of every player who opposed him. That was Kenny Washington. Tom Harmon was named to the team, but Kenny was the only unanimous choice. As a result, Kenny was awarded the Douglas Fairbanks Trophy as the nation's outstanding player.

NEW ERA FOR BRUINS
By Allan Dale (*Examiner*)

With Saturday's game, an era that has brought the Bruins greater glory than any other will come to an end. The era spans the college days of Kenneth S. Washington, who this year has carried the Bruins undefeated to their last game of the season for the first time in history. Never before has UCLA battled through a season with fewer than two defeats.

Transferring his torch of glory to Jackie Robinson, another star Negro back, Washington will leave behind him a record Bruin backs can look to for inspiration for years to come.

The week before the big game we practiced in secret. Both schools had spies, and we caught two of theirs with binoculars and notebooks. We had guards patrolling the perimeter of the field, and they caught these guys hiding in the bushes. They tied them up and took them out to fraternity row. The kids out there shaved UCLA in their hair, painted them blue and gold and sent 'em home. That's how the war escalated.

There was always a pre-game rally that was held around a huge bonfire, which, if you look it up, means fire of bones. We didn't burn any bodies; we built a structure out of telephone poles set about thirty feet apart. The week prior to the game, all the kids would search the city of Los Angeles looking for wood to fill this structure. They'd steal all the wooden crates from the markets, they'd go up into the hills and collect brush and deadfall. And one year, the USC kids stole all the outhouses from all the construction sites.

The night before the game, they would set off this fire and the flames would shoot hundreds of feet into the sky, thick black smoke would pour out, and sparks would fly at random like fireworks. It may sound dangerous, but we had a lot of vacant lots and land, and it wasn't hard finding a big open area for one of these fires. The kids would stand around and dance while the yell leaders stood on a platform and said whatever they could think of to get the crowd worked up. It was like an Indian war dance, but it was clean fun. There were no drugs; maybe some of the kids drank, but it wasn't a problem.

That year, we sabotaged USC's rally before the big game. A couple of our kids snuck over there early. They soaked the tips of towels in gasoline and lit them. As they ran past USC's woodpile, they flicked the flaming gas off their towels and started their bonfire early. Later I found out from our spies the USC kids had burned Kenny, Jackie, and me in effigy.

"Hey, they burnt you guys up last night, Woody!"

"That's because we're going to kick their asses tomorrow!"

They made figures out of straw, hung us, and burned us. That wasn't racial, that was fear. Just like whenever Pete Rose showed up at Dodger Stadium, the fans would boo the hell out of him. Well, they weren't booing him, they were booing his ability. That's how they show their admiration.

I SPEAK MY MIND
By Davis J. Walsh (*Examiner*)

In the case of USC, the collegiate patrician with just a touch of condescension in its attitude toward the other, and UCLA, the alleged upstart and social climber, it's the kind of thing well calculated to make the feuds of the Hatfields and the McCoys pale and insipid, by contrast. Nothing and nobody are quite normal around here today; everything (and everybody) seem momentarily at the point of violence, real or merely oral.

I said something about the UCLA football team having "sucker-appeal," and meant it. It was certainly meant, anyhow, when I once said the same thing about Dempsey and Ruth and the New York Yankees and the Washington eight oared crew of 1936. It would be, and doubtless will be, said again about Seabiscuit and Hedy Lamarr and sidecars, the Taj Mahal in the moonlight and Mount Blanc, without benefit of anything.

It's zip, 80 yards for a touchdown with UCLA. And it was that way with Ruth when he hit a home run and with Dempsey when he put the bop on somebody's profile. But enough. All of us are suckers for that kind of thing and glad to be.

The Friday before the game, I said good-bye to my parents, cranked up the Model T and drove over to Lincoln Heights to pick up Kenny. He was inside, and he wasn't too happy. His Grandma had him stringing popcorn for the Christmas tree.

He said, "Thank God!," grabbed his bag, and kissed Grandma good-bye. We didn't say good-bye to Rocky; he was upstairs sleeping off the night shift. We'd see him at the game.

Kenny beat me to the car and threw his bag into the backseat. We flipped a coin to see who would crank up the engine. That was a dangerous job because sometimes the crank would fly and smack you a good one. Kenny wouldn't go for two out of three, so I went up front and turned the engine over, and we took off for Westwood.

It was a cool gray, rainy-looking day; Kenny and I raced down Wilshire Boulevard with the top down. All the Christmas decorations were up, and all the retail stores had their best merchandise in the windows. We felt so good, so alive. There was no nervousness, no fear, only exhilaration. We were so excited to be playing in this big game. The City of Los Angeles put the spotlight on us, and that was a very prideful feeling.

We laughed and screamed the whole way; we were a couple of live wires. We got to school, parked the car, and ran over to Kerchoff Hall; that's where we met the rest of the team.

After everybody showed up, Babe Horrell put us on a bus and took us over to the Beverly Hills Hotel to spend the night. They liked to keep us together in those days, to make sure we weren't on the streets and to make sure we went to bed on time.

The Beverly Hills Hotel is probably one of the three fanciest hotels in the city. That's where all the actors and movie producers stay, out there on Sunset Blvd. Being seen by their pool or sipping drinks in their Polo Lounge is as classy as you can get.

I remember sitting in the Polo Lounge with Jackie, Leo, Kenny, and Ned. We were shining in our best clothes. I wore a dark-blue wool suit, double-breasted with big lapels, and a red silk tie. We sat there all quiet and respectful, sipping water and eating apples, listening to Don Nova sing. We talked to some people and answered some questions for the press.

Kenny and I shared a room that night, and it was hard getting to sleep. Kenny decided he'd call Rocky at the police station. That was a mistake; he had to talk football with five or six guys before they would let him through to Rocky. And Rocky just said, "Look, you've already proved yourself. All you guys have proved you deserve to be there. All you have to do is go out tomorrow and give it 100 percent. That's all anyone expects. Now get some sleep. I'll see you at the game."

We got up early Saturday morning and climbed on a bus headed for the Coliseum. It was still overcast and cool, but it hadn't rained; it was good football weather. Game time was two o'clock, but we must have arrived at the players' entrance around ten or eleven. The stadium was empty and quiet. The behind-the-scenes people were there, the hot dog men and peanut men, the ticket takers and beer sellers. They were setting up their stands, packing their trays and racks, getting ready for the mob.

As we got off the bus, I saw Bob Hoffman, the Trojan halfback. He was sitting by himself on the lawn up against a tree reading the funny papers. I always thought that was kind of unusual, that he should be there all by himself. Maybe he wanted to get a good look at us before we laced the gear on. He probably lived nearby and just walked over. But we were all friendly, and we said hello to Bob before we went inside.

The crowd started arriving around noon; we were still in the locker room at that point. I remember sitting with Kenny in the trainer's room waiting to get taped up. As I sat there I could feel the vibration of the crowd. Those thick concrete walls were pulsing, boy, and my heart was keeping time. Kenny turned to me, "You nervous?"

"No way . . . How about you?"

"Nope, I just want to get this thing started."

The butterflies were swirling, and as we dropped our heads to hide the lie, I could see Kenny cross himself.

To this day, it was the biggest crowd in the history of the Coliseum. When I ran out of the tunnel onto the field the sight nearly took my breath away; I nearly hyperventilated. There were 103,500 paid admissions and there must have been another 5,000 when you counted all the press people, the vendors, the officials, and the gate crashers. It was a splashy, colorful ocean of people.

There were thirty American flags flying around the top of the bowl; how many places had room for that? The student sections faced each other across the field and they competed to see who could do the best yells or the best stunts with the color cards. The USC band was on the field, and they were pretty slick. They dressed up like soldiers from Troy with crimson skirts and capes with gold piping. And they had shiny gold helmets with side flaps and red mohawks on the top.

All the Hollywood royalty showed up. Douglas Fairbanks and Joe E. Brown. Jane Wyman and all the stars Kenny and I met at Warner Bros. were there. But nobody paid them any attention. This was a big game; everybody was a fan. And the noise was deafening, like the static from a blank TV station times a hundred thousand. Russell Newland of the *San Francisco Chronicle* wrote:

> The fans made more noise per 100 pounds than any we've heard this season. Even the "hot dogs" were half again as thick as the one-handed "bow-wow" lunches Northern Californians bit into submission.

Our heads were so full of thoughts that nobody spoke before the game. We were like soldiers on their way to the front. By the time we finished all our warm-ups and drills, I was 100 percent concentration towards the job at hand. This time we were ready, and we were in great shape because nobody got to fall off the log. We were ready to go the whole sixty minutes.

We won the coin toss, and Kenny took the opening kickoff on the 10-yard line and ran it out to the 30. On fourth down we punted. USC took over the ball and tried to ram it down our throats. Granny Lansdell and Harry Smith put on a show, with Harry providing the best blocking I ever saw.

He cut Kenny Washington down cold, in the open, twice. The first time, Kenny was on defense, and Harry just laid him out as Granny went on by. That was the first time Kenny had been knocked off his feet by one man all year.

The second time, Kenny was running with the ball and Harry was maneuvering into position to make the tackle. Kenny must have said to himself, "Screw it, let's see how strong this guy really is." Kenny put his head down and drove at Harry as hard as he could. When they hit, all three of them, Kenny, Harry and the ball, hung there, like they were suspended in time. Then Kenny went over backwards, and Harry recovered the ball. I think that's when we realized we were up against the best.

Right after that fumble, USC almost scored. They got the ball down to our 11-yard line. I remember looking over to their sideline and seeing Howard Jones sitting there, his big ears sticking straight out, smoking a cigarette, and acting like nothing in the world was going on.

They snapped the ball to Lansdell and he cut back over center. He was past our secondary before we knew what happened. Then suddenly Jackie Robinson came flying out of the corner. He put 180 pounds of wiry body behind his helmet and planted it right on the ball. This is what Dick Hyland wrote for the *Times:*

> The ball shot off the Trojan's chest like it had been blown from a gun barrel. No man's arm could have withstood that blow from Robinson's body, no bag of wind incased in leather could have done anything but react violently when compressed as that football was between Robinson and Lansdell. There was no individual fault in that play. Concerned, instead, were laws of physics pertaining to reactions.

It seemed like the ball laid there in the end zone for hours. Finally, I got down and scooped it up. Once I had it in my hands, I woke up quick like I had stuck my finger in a socket. I saw a picture of myself in the papers; my eyes looked like a frightened deer's, and I was striding the goddamnedest stride.

Two guys hit me right off. I got to the goal line and somebody else hit me; I kept on going. Suddenly I was in the clear and charging. I was thinking six points when Bob Hoffman brought me down on our own 13. To this day, I don't know where he came from, but he saved a sure touchdown.

The first half ended scoreless. USC outplayed us, and we were lucky to still be in the game. When we got into the locker room, Rocky was waiting for us, and he was mad. He grabbed Kenny by the arm. He said, "You're playing scared, boy. A couple of bad breaks and you start playing scared. Look, you can beat these guys!

"You've got to open up, start throwing the ball downfield. Go with what got you here. You're in a great position to win this game, but you've got to take the fight to them. I believe in you, Kenny. Now go out there and show them what you can do!"

That speech got Kenny fired up. In the second half he came out throwing. He just missed on two touchdown passes to Jackie, and he threw a 44-yard pass the referee ruled I caught out-of-bounds. We started to click and gain momentum. Davis J. Walsh wrote this for the *Examiner:*

> The only trouble was to distinguish one from the other, as the tide of fortune ebbed and flowed. For USC was no defensive, desperately harassed opponent throughout the whole afternoon. Hardly that. It was mostly at the end, when USC having hurled its might and strength and unlimited resource against its opponent, to no purpose, in a scoreless first, suddenly found itself vulnerable to Washington's passes as the minutes began running out on the clock.

There were about five minutes left in the game when we took over on our own 20-yard line. Kenny went to the pass. He threw an 18-yarder to me. Then he hit Jackie Robinson for another first down on the USC 26. He threw another to me for a first down on the 15 and a fourth to Ned Mathews for 5 yards. Then Leo and Kenny, like a couple of bulldozers, picked up our last first down on the USC 3-yard line. Davis J. Walsh continued:

The Bruins had penetrated the lofty reserve of this patrician from University Avenue and had him backed down and seemingly about to be discredited and made to look declasse, with the end of the game in sight. He was all the way back, to be exact, where the shadow of his own goal posts were casting an oblique shadow across his earnest and frantic rear. The goal line was just abaft his anxious pawing cleats and the stands were in a tantrum.

It was first and goal on the USC 3-yard line. The whole series depended on Ned Mathews, just twenty years old, to call the right plays. On first down he called on number thirteen, and Kenny tried to crash through the left side of the Trojan line. That was Harry Smith's territory, and he stopped Kenny for no gain.

Ned decided to try the right side. We opened a hole four feet wide, and Leo Cantor was halfway through it when Bob Hoffman hit him and stood him straight up. After a second, Leo just plopped right where he was.

We called time-out to let Leo recover his senses. We got into our huddle, and Ned decided we'd try to surprise USC and call the same play. That was a mistake, because Leo was still woozy, and he lost 2 yards. It was fourth down on the 4-yard line. The ball was directly in front of the goal post. A little over thirty seconds were left in the game. Going back to Davis J. Walsh:

> It wasn't just one of those things that cry aloud. Crying aloud, as a matter of fact, would have been empty, footless, vapid in the midst of all the bluster and uproar that went on yesterday. The situation didn't even brusquely demand a field goal try. It fairly shrieked for it, bellowed, trumpeted, clamored, screamed and bleated almost obscenely in a shrill, insensate falsetto.

We didn't kick it. Babe Horrell could have called time-out and told us to kick, but he figured Ned had gotten us that far, he might as well take us the rest of the way. In the huddle we took a vote, should we go for six points or three?

Five of us voted touchdown, five of us voted field goal. It was up to Ned to cast the deciding vote. He voted touchdown. All his life Ned wanted to be part of the Thundering Herd; now he had a chance to beat them. He wanted to do it right. He wanted the touchdown.

Ned called a play designed to trick them. Kenny got the ball and faked a run to the left. Jackie, Leo, and I all decoyed to draw the defense away. While Kenny was moving left, he threw the ball back across the field to Don McPherson, who was standing all alone in the end zone. He had his fingertips on the ball when Bob Hoffman stepped in front and knocked the ball to the ground. The game ended scoreless.

Kenny Washington didn't play sixty minutes that day; he only went fifty-nine minutes and forty-five seconds. Babe took him out with fifteen seconds left so the fans would have a chance to give him a hand. It was Kenny's last game as a Bruin, probably his last game ever. And Kenny almost single-handedly built that institution.

When Kenny took that long walk off the field, the fans gave him the greatest ovation ever received by an athlete in the Coliseum. Granny Lansdell, Harry Smith, and Bob Hoffman all came over to shake his hand and give him a hug. It was the most soul-stirring event I have ever seen in sports. Someone told me Jane Wyman was crying in the stands. And as Kenny left the field and headed to the tunnel, the ovation followed him in huge waves. It was like the Pope of Rome had come out.

USC got the invitation to the Rose Bowl that year. Now every time Bill Ackerman sees Ned Mathews or Leo Cantor, he reminds them that they cost the school $100,000. That's how much the Rose Bowl was worth in those days. But we didn't blame Ned; in fact he was named captain of the 1940 team. See, football is so much like life. Every time you get knocked down, you wonder if you want to get up. Sometimes you wonder, "Is this worth it?" But you pick yourself up, dust yourself off, and keep on going.

After that game, Dick Hyland and the *Los Angeles Times* gave me one of the greatest write-ups of my athletic career:

> We may be fairly sure that those of us fortunate enough to see that Trojan-Bruin game witnessed as great a performance of end play as was exhibited anywhere in the United States this fall. When a man does all he is supposed to do on every play, when on top of that he

does things no one can fairly expect him to do, that man is playing great football. Woody Strode was great Saturday; he climaxed a fine football career and from now on he can think, if things ever seem tough, I did my part once. I did my part and a man named Hyland, who loves the hearts and spirits of champions, figuratively doffed his hat to me as another champion.

After the press got through with us, and we had showered and changed, we left the Coliseum. It was dark when we walked out of the players' entrance. It had started to rain, and the streets and walkways glittered in the streetlight. Everyone was gone; only the trash from 100,000 people proved something big had happened that day.

I remember being so mad on the bus ride back to UCLA. Not because we didn't win the game, but because I remembered we hadn't put the top on the Model T. It was a long, squirmy ride home on those wet seats. They smelled awful, like an old dog. It was a quiet ride as Kenny and I drove past the Christmas lights on Wilshire. There was a sadness floating between us. I guess we realized one of the most exciting times of our lives had just come and gone.

I made the turn onto Avenue 19 and dropped Kenny off. Rocky was waiting in the doorway. He put an arm over Kenny's shoulder and they walked in the door together. I turned the Model T around and headed home to spend the rest of the evening with my family.

CHAPTER ELEVEN

What the Hell Is That?

If I had just skated across the goal line and turned in, out: boom, touchdown. We could have done that. But that's all hindsight. Kenny and I thought about that a lot. I guess we felt like we were outfoxing USC. There were a lot of moves we could have made, but I guess God didn't want us to win. Because if we had scored that touchdown, that would have been the biggest game in UCLA history. For us to play sixty minutes and beat the Thundering Herd—can you imagine it? We'd all have statues out there today.

The Trojans beat Tennessee in the Rose Bowl, New Year's Day 1940. That was Howard Jones' last Rose Bowl, and he never lost one. He died of a heart attack in 1940; the cigarettes and the pressure did him in. His 1939 team was ranked number one in the country; we were ranked tenth. Ray Bartlett, Ned Mathews, Leo Cantor, and Jackie Robinson all had another year of football left. In 1940 Babe moved Jackie to left halfback, but without Kenny, the team floundered. They won one game and lost nine.

Kenny and I both had some schooling left before we could graduate. I had about six months to go for my degree, and I planned to stay through the 1940 track season. I wanted to compete in the 1940 Olympics in Helsinki, but the war in Europe cancelled the games.

Well, by 1940 I had been at that institution six-and-a-half years. I'm proud of the fact that I could go there and get all my grades, but I wasn't ever going to be a brain surgeon. I was an athlete, so when they cancelled the Olympics, I decided not to hang around.

My first payday playing football came right after I left UCLA. When I left school, I hoped I could get into coaching or something that would keep me close to athletics; I never thought I would become a professional athlete. But a promoter named Larry Sunbrock asked me to play in two special exhibition football games at $750 per game.

Larry Sunbrock was one of the slickest, slipperiest promoters you ever laid your eyes on. One time he sold 100,000 tickets to the Coliseum for the greatest thrill show on earth. He brought in two old steam locomotives and set them on a track facing each other at opposite ends of the stadium. They sat there building up steam until the boilers were red-hot. The brakes were on full, and when they got to the point where they wouldn't hold any more, the brakeman set the trains loose and they flew at each other full speed ahead. The impact was tremendous. The wheels fell off one of the trains. The other one cracked its boiler, the scalding water gushed out, and the steam filled the bowl. It was spectacular. And Sunbrock used to put on rodeos and pro football events at Gilmore Stadium. That was located over where CBS and the Farmer's Market are today, at Beverly and Fairfax.

Larry Sunbrock got the idea of putting together a college all-star team and playing them against two of the semi-pro teams that were just getting started out here. A guy named Paul Schissler started the semi-pro league. Schissler was a promoter in his own right, a good coach and a smart football man. He coached at Oregon, went to the Chicago Cardinals of the NFL, and then came out here and started the Pacific Coast League.

Originally, there were five teams in the league: San Diego, Fresno, Salinas, Hollywood, and Los Angeles. Then Phoenix added a team. Schissler coached and owned the Hollywood Bears. We played them and the Los Angeles Bulldogs in two exhibition games in Gilmore Stadium.

Sunbrock started by signing Kenny Washington at $1,000 per game. You talk about some money; way back then, that was it. But Kenny was the main attraction; the team was billed The Kenny Washington All-Stars.

Rocky handled the negotiations for Kenny. Sunbrock wanted to pay Kenny with war bonds, but Rocky said, "What good are they? They're in your name; they're no good to Kenny. What the hell is he going to do with them? If you report them lost or stolen, Kenny's out of luck!"

That's when Sunbrock came up with the cash, a thousand dollar bill.

Back then, the guys in the semi-pro league were getting maybe thirty-five dollars a game. Mostly they were guys from USC, UCLA, or Loyola. Not many guys went to the National Football League. There were fewer teams in the NFL, none in the Far West, and there wasn't much money in it yet.

The guys who played football after college played because they loved the game. Everybody had regular jobs, and after work they would practice at Griffith Park. In those days a cop made maybe $200 a month, so thirty-five dollars a week on top of your regular salary wasn't bad for playing the game you loved.

Our first exhibition game was against the Bulldogs and before the game Gloomy Gus Henderson and several of his players went over to pay Rocky a visit. They wanted to know how much money Kenny was getting out of Sunbrock. They were all talking and finally Rocky said, "Look, as far as I'm concerned, the deal is made and Kenny's got his money."

They said, "Well, how much did Kenny get?"

Rocky said, "Hell, it's no secret. He's getting $1,000."

Well, they called Rocky a liar. You don't call Rocky Washington a liar. He went and got the thousand dollar bill. Who had a thousand dollar bill in their house during the Depression? The Bulldogs' eyes were like saucers; they couldn't believe it.

The next day it all came out in the open, and we damn near didn't play the game. The Bulldogs had a gun to Sunbrock's head because all these fans were buying tickets to a game that might not be played. Finally Sunbrock had to promise the Bulldogs a lot more money. We played the game, and it was a sellout, 18,000 people.

Larry Sunbrock tried to weasel out of paying us after the first game. He said, "Why don't you boys wait until after the Hollywood Bears game and then I'll pay you all in full?" That's when Larry Sunbrock got run out of town.

Paul Schissler stepped in and took over the promotion. Of course, Schissler was already interested in Kenny because he wanted Kenny to play for his Bears team in the fall. So Schissler took care of Kenny, we played the second game, and everybody got paid off. I had $1,500 for two games. I went to the bank with a .45 next to me in the car.

Kenny took his two grand and bought a little two-bedroom house down on West 35th Street. He hung around UCLA and finished up his education. In September, he married June Bradley from Long Beach. June was half-German, very pretty, and very light-skinned. They had a little announcement of the wedding in *Liberty*, along with a picture. The caption read, "Kenny Washington marries June Bradley (a girl of color)." They wanted everybody to be sure of what she was. I remember Kenny saying to me, "Sometimes I'm with June and I feel funny because they think I've got a white girl."

After Kenny graduated he became a cop on the Los Angeles Police Department. Can you imagine one of today's outstanding college players becoming a cop?

Rocky got him on the force, and Kenny had a hard time as a cop. I remember one night I was going home and I saw him having a confrontation with a drunk on Central Avenue. I got out of my car and thought I'd have to help him fight this guy. The ignorant blacks had no respect for Kenny. To them, if you achieved success in the white man's society, you were an Uncle Tom.

I probably landed the best job of all the graduates. I went to work for Burron Fitts, the District Attorney, as an investigator. I had all the authority given the cops without having to wear the uniform. I was a hound dog; I delivered subpoenas within the black community. I was like a liaison.

The D.A.'s office was using me, but I was too naive to notice.

As an athlete, I was introduced to everybody. I knew all the pimps, hustlers, bookies, and gangsters. The Mafia was here, and I grew up with those people. But it wasn't like Chicago or New York, organized crime had no big lock on things. If a guy had $500, he didn't have to answer to them, he just opened his own bookie shop.

All the whorehouses were out on D Street in San Bernardino. That's where the red light district was. They closed down shortly before the second world war. We had pimps but they were more like businessmen. Today, I see the pimps on Hollywood Boulevard, and they look like a bunch of pigs. In my day they wore beautiful suits, silk vests, diamond stickpins and spats. They sold the most beautiful women in the world. And those guys moved up to become the hotel and nightclub owners, and their sons and daughters became doctors and lawyers.

Prostitution was illegal on the books, but out here in the Far West it was overlooked. There wasn't anything wrong with going out and getting a piece of ass. And no one got raped. If someone was guilty of rape, they'd torture him, then hang him.

Part of my job with the D.A. was escorting prisoners to the prisons at San Quentin and Folsom. That wrapped me up; I knew right then I'd never make it as a cop. Those prisons looked like dog pounds, the human beings like dogs. I'd take the prisoners up there on the train. They'd be handcuffed, and I'd have my .45 in my waistband. I'd stay over night in San Francisco and come home the next day. I ran into a lobbyist up there once. He had an open checkbook. He was a fan of mine, bought me a $25 dinner.

Working for the D.A., I spent a lot of time at the clubs and after-hours spots up in Hollywood and down on Central Avenue. That's when I saw her again. She came over here looking for me. I was sitting in a Rhumboogey club on Las Palmas and Melrose Avenue. She came walking in with Jackie Coogan and this whole Hollywood crowd, and she was as dark as me. She wore a lace dress that was plunging in the front. She had her hair pulled back and a flower on one side. I was with a group of my friends and they asked, "What the hell is that?"

I was able to answer, "Well, that's a goddamned Hawaiian."

Her group sat down at a table across the room. She had her

back to me, but she kept turning around and looking at me. I started to get embarrassed. I don't care if you're a white man or a black man: if you're in a bar you don't look at another man's woman. But there she was dancing with Jackie and winking at me. I told the guys I was with, "Let's get out of here."

We started to walk out, and as I got near the door she grabbed me. She said, "Woodrow, don't you remember me?"

I just about had a heart attack.

"No!"

"Well, you were in Hawaii two years ago. Remember the little girl that kissed you good-bye and was crying?"

"Oh my God!" It was the Princess Luana.

"Here's my phone number and address. I'm living with Lupe Velez at the Paramount Hotel. Please call me."

"Okay."

We left the club and the kids I'm with said, "You ought to pick that one up!"

I said, "Oh no!" See, we had rules and regulations. That was another man's woman; I couldn't call her. I didn't think it would matter. Here it was two years later, she's full-grown and with this whole high-class Hollywood crowd.

I found out if you're attractive to a Hawaiian girl, she'll come after you. I didn't have to make the moves; she made them all for me. Here was a beautiful, brown, dark-eyed Hawaiian; when she threw her arms around me, my manhood had to stand up; You're either going to be a faggot or you're going to dance. "Would you like to come home with me?" That's the Hawaiian way, totally uninhibited.

A week goes by and I was sitting in the Club Alabam'. She must have had some spies working for her because she found me and cornered me. The pimps took one look at this beautiful Hawaiian girl and they all wanted me to introduce them to her. I said, "No!" I had been treated too good in Hawaii to let that happen. I put my arm around her, to protect her. That was the first move.

She said, "Come on, let's go have a drink!"

"I don't drink."

She said, "Oh, you're a sissy!" That's when I started drinking; she forced me to drink. I was like Gary Cooper, "Yep, Nope," and she pulled me right off the screen and out of my shell.

I said, "I'm going down to Honey Murphy's to get some barbecue. I guess you can come along if you want."

She followed me over there. We were sitting at the bar, and she asked me to go home with her. I was hedging and finally I said, "No, I can't. I'm already going with a girl."

That was Lois Evans. So the Princess got pissed off. She stomped out, got into her car, backed it up and hit the building. Everybody in the place was staring at me, so I went out to see what was going on. I got into the car with her and tried to calm her down. We sat and talked.

She told me she got her chance to come over here when they were looking for someone to double Dorothy Lamour, the actress. That was her introduction to Hollywood. And Luana was a native dancer. She got a job dancing at Ken's Hula Hut. She told me all this and the tears stopped. She said, "I wanted to be with you so!"

She was pulling me to her now, and I didn't realize I was getting caught in her web. I was still living with my parents on 34th and Central. I told her to drop me off at home. When we got there she said, "May I call you?"

I gave her my number. An hour later she called and we talked for five hours. She conned me into taking her out. The next night I picked her up at the Paramount Hotel, right near the studio. She came down in some pongee sarong. Her ass was hanging out, her hair was sort of half-out. She was naked as far as we were concerned out here. I was in shock. She crossed the street and all the cars were screeching their brakes. I said, "Luana, for the love of God, please put on some clothes." And I waited for her while she changed.

I took her back down to the Avenue, and I gave her the grand tour. Finally, she talked me into going to her club in Hollywood. Ken's Hula Hut was a restricted club. We went inside, and sat with a group of Hawaiian musicians. They were about the same color as me, and I didn't feel too uncomfortable. She got up to dance and all of a sudden she was dancing for me. As soon as the music stopped, the band boys shouted out, "Aloha, Woody Strode!"

I was uncovered, and I started flinching because some of the white people walked over to where I was sitting. "Hey Woody, remember when you and Kenny. . . ."

They were all football fans. I had never realized until that night how well the white people liked me. What an education to have this girl pull me into the white world that I never would have invaded without her.

The black community turned on me because I was a star and they thought I should marry a nice black girl like Lois Evans. Lois went to my mother and said, "Mrs. Strode, did you know Woody is going with a Hawaiian girl and she's a dancer in a nightclub?" My mother, with her religious background, thought I was involved in the gangster scene. I got mad at my mother. But my daddy just looked at Luana and said, "Son, why don't you marry her?" He didn't miss a beat.

Well, I didn't marry her right away. I began to shut down because of all the fuss. I moved out of my mother's house and in with this old lady named Mama Kay. That's where Luana and I shacked up before we got married. Every day I would go to the office, get my marching orders, come back and pick up Luana. She'd make the rounds with me as I served subpoenas.

Somebody must have seen us necking in the car because six months later I arrived at the office and the big law book was open on my desk to the page that said, "Common law marriage is illegal in the State of California." They were telling me to go get married. The next day, when I picked her up I said, "Hey Luana, you want to get married?"

"Sure, Daddy!"

And off we went to Las Vegas. The justice of the peace turned out to be a white man who was raised in Samoa. He saw Luana with the flower in her hair and said, "Aloha!" They had this big Hawaiian exchange; finally, the justice said, "So, you kids want to get married? It'll cost you twelve bucks."

Here was the most beautiful Hawaiian girl ever to come into this country and I had her. She was so glamorous. She used to do a moon dance at the Miramar. She'd dance in silhouette with the moon behind her. I'd have to sit in the dressing room and wait for her. When it came time for her to leave, groups of fans would be waiting by the backstage entrance to meet her.

Victor Mature, the actor, wanted to marry her. Right after we were married, we were lying down and he called. Luana picked up the phone and said, "Oh hello, Vic."

He said, "I want you to stop the wedding!"

"Can't, Vic; we just got married." And over the phone he sang "You Can't Be Mine and Somebody Else's, Too."

When I got back to the D.A.'s office, nobody knew I had gotten married. I punched in and then went back out to do my job. By ten o'clock, Walter Winchell's column had called, asking about my marriage. A report had leaked out over the wire service. I got back to the office and they said, "Congratulations and Walter Winchell's column just called."

I called Luana and said, "I don't want any headlines, NEGRO ATHLETE MARRIES HAWAIIAN PRINCESS!" I already had problems with the black community, so you can imagine what a ripple that headline would have caused.

She said, "Don't worry, Daddy, I'll handle it." She was sharp, boy; the Mormons had really taught her. She was able to quiet things down, and we were given a normal little announcement in the newspaper.

But I had to move away from my own people. I was an outstanding Negro and I married out of my race. I found out I was more comfortable living up in Hollywood with the white people and the Hawaiians. The Hawaiian people were like me; they were mixed up with everything under the sun. Some of them have seven different bloods. They were brown, I was brown. There was no color shock. I began to compare. I said, "You know, Luana, they act just like colored people."

She said, "Yeah, and your brother Baylous looks just like my Uncle Joe."

It wasn't planned; it was purely accidental. When it came time to break away from my own race, I just stepped over the fence. The Hawaiian education threw me right into the middle of the most affluent white group, the Hollywood entertainers. The Polynesians were the only minority that had carte blanche, because all the

Hawaiians out here were musicians, dancers, and singers. A lot of the old nightclubs in Hollywood had a tropical atmosphere. People loved that stuff because it was exotic.

The Hawaiians knew Buck Jones, the cowboy star. That's how I met him before he died. I met Gene Autry because he owned one of the clubs where my wife danced. I met Dorothy Lamour through my wife. She played in some of the *Road* pictures with Bob Hope and Bing Crosby. Bing fell in love with the Hawaiian life style. He used to like to dress casually like the Hawaiians. One time they wouldn't let Bing into a hotel in Vancouver because of the way he was dressed. They used to browbeat him over that.

I lived with the Hawaiian boys who played for Bing, in a thirty-five room apartment building on Las Palmas Avenue. That was Dick McIntyre's band. His brother Lonnie was playing at the Lexington Hotel.

My wife was dancing for Harry Owen's band. When she first appeared at Billy Berg's club, which was right around the corner from our apartment, I remember her remarking about the black people all staying upstairs. None of them came down to dance. I told her, "Honey, when you see my people in a club like this, they don't dance because that's like showing off."

Because I was married to Luana, they let me make full use of the clubs. Plus, I was an athlete; I had a lot of fans. The club owners had a meeting at Billy Berg's, and they invited me to come to their clubs anytime. There was a key club on Vine Street, and they gave me the key.

I heard the best music in the world. That's how I learned to play the guitar, just by hanging out, listening and watching. I learned to speak a little Hawaiian, too. This is how I knew I could: I was sitting at a bar and the Hawaiians said in Hawai, "Hey Luana, when Woody goes to bed, let's go out after hours."

I answered in Hawaiian, "Bullshit, I'm going to go, too."

My whole life style changed as I got completely integrated into this Hawaiian community. I learned to eat poi and raw fish. I ate seaweed before anyone had heard of vitamins. I dressed in one-piece skirts; they thought nothing of your ass hanging out. I got so I found I had to correct myself around my own people.

If I had stayed with my own people, I would have probably ended up in the civil service. I don't believe I was cut out for my own culture, based on the primitive side of me. I don't think I could have survived going to church every Sunday with my wife leaning on me. Here I was with a group of happy-go-lucky Polynesians. I saw the last four-and-five-day parties. Drinking, singing, dancing, and passing out. Waking up, drinking, singing, and dancing. You'd believe you had died and gone to heaven.

In November, Burron Fitts came up for re-election and lost. They put a lei around his neck and made a racial issue out of it. They used my marriage to Luana to get him out of office.

I lost the job with the D.A. and finished out the year playing football for the Hollywood Bears. Kenny was already playing, and Paul Schissler asked me if I wanted to come aboard. Of course, Kenny and I were like bookends on the football field, and I said yes.

In those days, Don Hutson, one of the greatest offensive ends ever to play professional football, was getting about $175 a week playing for the Green Bay Packers. Paul Schissler was paying me $100 a game, plus a percentage of the gate. When we filled up Gilmore Stadium, I'd come home with $300. That's all the money I needed.

Kenny was making about $200 a game, plus his percentage. He took home $500 some weeks. We were making more money than the guys in the NFL. Right on the tickets it was printed, "The Hollywood Bears with Kenny Washington vs. . . . . . ." That's the kind of marquee value Kenny had. And Schissler was shrewd; he would pay Kenny so much, and he would pay Rocky so much. That way the players didn't think Kenny was getting that much more than them.

See, Kenny and I were in paradise. When I looked at integration from my side of the wall, I already enjoyed it. If the rest of the country had just moved up to our level, integration would have been much smoother in the United States. But World War II came along and the wound got opened. Everybody started taking sides, everybody got hung up, and we all scattered like quail.

117

CHAPTER TWELVE

The University of March Field

My first off-season with the Bears, I was looking around for something to do. I went to see Cal Eaton, who ran the Olympic Auditorium in Los Angeles, the place in those days for wrestling and boxing. I was thinking about boxing. But Cal said, "Why? You'll get your brain rattled. They'll steal your money and leave you broke. Why not think about wrestling? Let's go down to the Olympic and take a look at some of the wrestlers I've got working there."

He introduced me to Sandor Szabo, Ed Strangler Louis, and Jim Londos. When Cal introduced them he said, "This guy's forty, this guy's fifty . . ."

Sandor Szabo, forty-five years old, looked like a movie star. I had never seen athletes that looked so good at that age. They were the most glamorous wrestlers in the prime of their careers. Strangler Louis could scissor a 100 pound sack of grain and bust it. Jim Londos was "The Golden Greek;" he'd always finish his opponents with an airplane spin and a body slam. Londos was one of the greatest draws in wrestling history.

He was actually more a subdued type. The show in wrestling had just started; they had just left the strangling and the straight wrestling. The show biz started with Jumping Joe Savoldi, an ex-football player from Notre Dame who also played for the Chicago Bears in 1930 before he went into wrestling. Joe introduced the flying tackle. He'd use the ropes like a slingshot to fly across the ring.

They never beat Jumping Joe because he was the box office. The promoters had to protect their investment. It got so some of the greatest wrestlers in the world could not become champions because they were not good showmen. That was the hardest part of wrestling.

On a wrestling show card it says exhibition, and exhibition means you can't go and bet on the best one. But it looks so real, and the fans believe it. They believe it today. Wrestlers put on the greatest show. We had to be in shape to take all the punishment that went down. Jumping out of the ring, hitting the seats. How do you hit the seats? Like a sack of potatoes. If you're tense, you'll hurt yourself.

It's a thin line between the showmanship and the straight wrestling. Straight wrestling is too dull. If I've got a headlock on you and stop your circulation, you'll faint. The fans won't pay to see that. The real artists can hit you without doing any damage. They can throw a punch and land it right on your skin. That's how good you have to be. The guys who miss are not good.

Wrestlers were either a babyface or a heel. The heels usually won and the fans hated them. That's how they developed the gate, because the fans always came back to see the bad guys get beat. That was the key, getting those fans to really hate you.

One time in Pico Rivera, California, the villain was leaving the ring for the dressing room. The stands split to form an entrance way and as this wrestler walked by, a guy in the stands reached down to hit him. The guy missed, slipped, fell over the railing, fell fifteen feet to the concrete floor and broke his own neck.

And in this book I have, called *Whatever Happened to Gorgeous George?*, Joe Jares tells this story about his father:

> Pop was wrestling Spider Galento in Chattanooga one night, and it was sort of a contest between them to see who the crowd hated the most. In such instances the people usually pick a favorite, and he is

forced into being honorable and decent. Galento entered the ring first and by a series of struts and poses had the fans despising him immediately. So Pop came into the ring and showed off his ill-gotten belt. Still, the crowd obviously hated Spider more. So Dad shouted up to the black section, way up in the back, that he was tired of their being deprived and he was going to give them a close look at his belt. He did just that, delaying the start of the match fourteen minutes as he slowly wandered among them. By the time he got back in the ring the whites hated him as much as if he had sung "The Battle Hymn of the Republic" over the loudspeaker.

I started wrestling in 1941 and I wrestled for eight straight months. Actually, I was in training to become a wrestler. Cal Eaton put me together with this old Jewish wrestler, Baron Ginsberg; he was sixty-five years old. He said, "I'm going to teach you how to wrestle. When you can pin me, we'll cut you loose." Sixty-five years old and he kicked my ass for eight months before I could pin him.

In those days the wrestlers were the strongest guys in the world. They had the thickest, most powerful necks. I'll bet you could've taken a wrestler from the old days, tied a rope around his neck, got a bunch of guys on a wheel and pulled him up. Taken him right to the ceiling and hung him and you wouldn't have killed him. You might've cut off his circulation if you let him hang there for fifteen minutes, but you wouldn't have killed anybody. Unless you jerked them, let them take a ten-foot drop. And some might have had enough muscle to take a small fall. Drop ten feet, and at the right moment flex and catch the fall.

I was skinny as far as the wrestlers went; I had all these bones sticking out. Baron Ginsberg used to get me in the flying mare, pick me up on his back, spin me and throw me over his shoulder. I had to learn not to hit the mat on my side for fear of busting a rib. I learned to land on my feet, hit the ropes and come back with a flying tackle. I almost turned it into a ballet.

After eight months with this old man, I had developed the confidence. I went on one tour before the football season started. We went out to San Bernardino and paraded up and down the streets just like the circus had come to town. That would attract the fans because television hadn't hit yet. The wrestlers would arrive in a place like San Bernardino and just take over the town. We didn't look like civilians. Wrestlers don't look like civilians, they look like another breed.

The promoters created the characters, and they would decide if you were good or bad. The handsome wrestlers with smooth faces and lean bodies usually played the hero. The fatter, uglier wrestlers played the heel. And foreign wrestlers were usually bad guys, too.

In my time, I could not play the villain. If I came into the ring and my opponent was a nice, clean white boy and the first thing I do is punch him in the eye, now he's walking around blind. Then I reach in and catch his mouth and rip, run my finger up his nose. A white audience would kill a white wrestler for doing that, but if I did it, we'd have had a race riot. They would've hung me in the ring. That's why the black wrestler was always a babyface. I dressed all in white: white trunks, white shoes. I was the clean colored boy.

Sometimes I'd get the villain down, look out to the audience and yell, "SHOULD I HIT HIM?"

The audience would answer, "HIT THAT SON-OF-A-BITCH, WOODY!" I've wrestled in the most prejudiced states in the country beating the shit out of a white man because I knew the psychology.

The most dangerous job I ever saw anyone take was Mr. Moto after the second world war. He played the sneaky Japanese. He fell out of the ring at the Olympic and 1,000 people came after him. After Pearl Harbor, that was it, that's how dangerous it really was. We'd get into a little town like South Gate and the police would have to escort him from the ring.

In one of my first matches I was wrestling the heel and he was doing all this nasty stuff to me, gouging and punching. My daddy was ringside watching me get beat up, and he couldn't take it. He came right into the ring: "That's my son, get the hell off him!"

I had to get up off the mat and tell him, "It's only a show Daddy." He didn't know.

In September, 1941, football started up, and I left wrestling. We played two pre-season games that Paul Schissler promoted. The first was an all-star game, the local college kids against the local pros. Schissler took the best players from that game and we played the Washington Redskins at Gilmore Stadium. The Redskins had come out in the pre-season to train down in San Diego. They had just lost the NFL championship to the Chicago Bears, 73 to 0. The Chicago Bears kicked everybody's butt.

But the Redskins were really good. They had Slingin' Sammy Baugh, one of the greatest quarterbacks in NFL history, by way of TCU. Bob MaChessnie from UCLA at end. And Wee Willie Wilkens, a 300-pound tackle. There's a story that Slip Madigan, the coach at St. Mary's, was on a recruiting trip and came across Wee Willie plowing a field. He asked Willie which way town was. Willie picked the plow up with one hand and pointed. Wee Willie went to St. Mary's.

The Redskins beat us 30–0. They had forty-eight ball players and we had twenty-eight. Schissler had to pull Kenny out for five minutes and that's when the parade started. They intercepted a pass and scored, and from there it was all downhill.

There was a referee working that game, John Old, who was also a sportswriter. He kept calling penalties the whole game, on both sides. He'd give us a five-yard penalty and then back it up ten more for talking back. In the fourth quarter there was a huge pileup, and John Old got stuck at the bottom. When they finally got to him, he had to be revived and wheeled off the field. That's the kind of football we played.

After the Redskins game, we went into our regular Hollywood Bears' season. On December 7th we were playing at Gilmore Field and at halftime we got the news: the Japanese had bombed Pearl Harbor. They made an announcement about every fifteen minutes until the end of the game. We were walking off the field and Kenny asked me, "What are we going to do now?"

I said, "I don't know about you, but if they put all the names in a hat they won't draw mine. I've never won a prize." That shows how naive I was.

The next week at practice, Paul Schissler showed up dressed like an Air Force Captain. We all rolled on the ground laughing, "What the hell are you doing in the Army?"

He said, "I'm in the reserves."

"What the hell is that?"

Schissler signed up with the Fourth Air Force down at March Field in Riverside. He was in charge of organizing a service football team, the March Field Fliers. The prime purpose of this team was to provide some entertainment and make some money. They played for Army Emergency Relief, a charity for the families of soldiers killed or injured. At practice Schissler said, "If any of you boys get the heat on you, let me know. I'll put you on my team at March Field."

They pulled my name out of the hat and I called Schissler like a little sheep. I was one of his boys. He said, "Meet me on Spring Street in front of the Stock Exchange." Schissler was half-rich, into stocks and all that. He said, "Just pack a minimum amount of clothes, and bring your shoes and your shoulder pads."

The March Field Fliers had the greatest players in the world because everybody got drafted and because Schissler and General Hap Arnold were drinking buddies. Hap Arnold was Commander-in-Chief of the Air Force and a real sports enthusiast; he probably played football himself. He gave Schissler carte blanche to get anyone he wanted. I asked Schissler, "How did you get me on this team?"

"I told Hap Arnold you were the greatest end who ever played. That's how we selected you."

Schissler couldn't get Kenny on the team, because Kenny had to have a knee operation. I'll talk more about that later. But Schissler did go out and steal Leo Cantor from the Santa Ana Air Force team. Leo and Izzy were both playing out there, but Schissler wanted Leo. Leo was the one; he had been signed by the old Chicago Cardinals to play in the NFL before the war came along. Santa Ana recruited him, but Schissler talked to Hap Arnold and Hap had Leo transferred to March Field.

Leo and I weren't assigned to any one group; we were there to play football. We ended up getting the best jobs on the base. Neither one of us could swim to save our lives, so they made life guards out of us. We had to learn to swim up and down that pool. The last test was treading water for ten minutes with our full uniforms on, boots and everything. That's when I almost drank up the pool, and they made me a life guard. I sat on the sidelines with

Woody Strode at UCLA. He was a great
pass catcher while playing left end for
the Bruins.

Woody's mother, Rosa Norris Strode. She gave Woody his Cherokee blood.

Woody and teammate Kenny Washington at the UCLA training table.

Another of Woody's teammates, Jackie Robinson, was a great football player, a terrible baseball player, during his years at UCLA. He went on to become the first black player in Major League baseball.

Freshman year at UCLA. Woody was an all-around track man.

Woody in training for the 1936 Olympics.
Note the gassed hair.

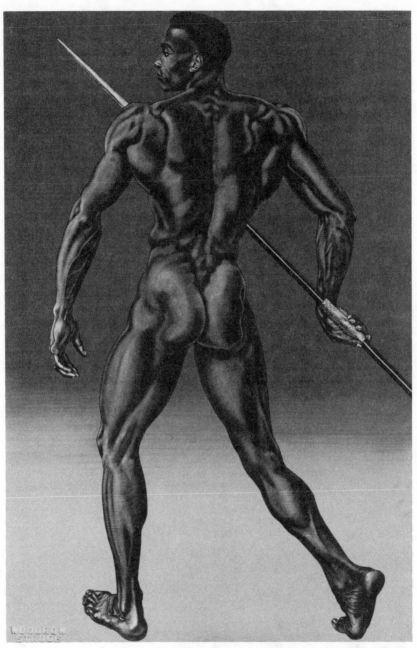

One of two paintings commissioned by
Adolf Hitler for the Olympic Art Festival
prior to the 1936 Berlin Olympics.
(Collection of California Museum of Afro-American
History and Culture, Los Angeles)

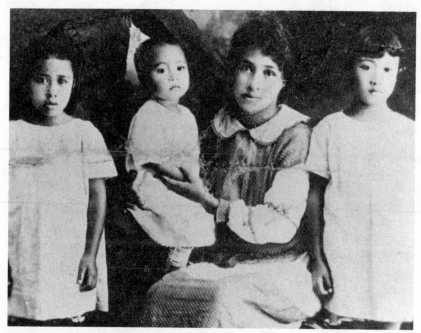

Luana's family: (left to right) Kuulei, Lellani, Esther Kalaeloa, and Luukialuana Kaealohapauole Kaluhiokalani Kalaeloa.

The Princess Luana as a young woman in Hawaii.

Woody at 27, recently married and
playing for the Hollywood Bears.

Having just signed with the Los Angeles Rams, Woody relaxes with Luana,
playing cards.

Two famous passing combinations join forces on the 1946 World Champion Los Angeles Rams: Woody and Kenny on the left, Bob Waterfield (7) and Jim Benton on the right.

Football immortals: Los Angeles Rams Kenny Washington (left), Tom Harmon, and Bob Waterfield, 1946.

Woody was always ready, but the Rams never really gave him a chance to play.
Although Woody was renowned as a great pass catcher while playing for UCLA,
the Hollywood Bears, and the March Field Fliers, the Rams never let him catch
a pass. (Photo by Vic Stein)

Woody, with son Kalai (left) and daughter June, raised chickens and rabbits on their ranch in Montebello.

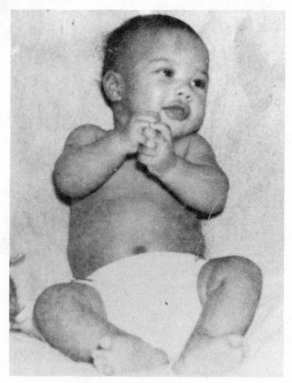

Woody's firstborn, Woodrow Wilson Kalaeloa Strode, was born in 1946. Kalaeloa means "heavenly sky."

June Strode, age 2.

Woody (42) was instrumental in winning the Grey
Cup for the Calgary Stampeders in 1948.

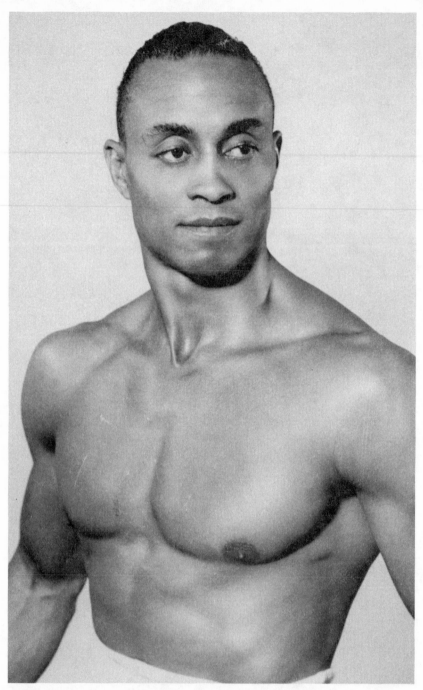

Woody had to play the "clean colored boy" when he starred as a professional wrestler, 1948.

Woody as first mate in *City Beneath the Sea,* 1953. (Photo by Photofest)

They tried to use a dummy for this scene from *Spartacus,* 1960, but it didn't look real, so Woody had to do it. Kirk Douglas is in the foreground.

As *Sergeant Rutledge*, 1960, directed by John Ford. This was one of the first dignified roles for a black actor in Hollywood.

Woody and Clint Eastwood struggle in a scene from the TV series *Rawhide*, 1961.

Luana at an awards ceremony for East
Los Angeles College. She was president
of the night school student body.

Luana and June in
Almeria, Spain. June won
"Miss Tourista."

Kalai in 1969, just graduated from UCLA.

Luana Strode in 1966.

June Strode in her early
twenties.

Woody and Luana
(center) with Mr. and
Mrs. Jumping Joe
Williams. Woody and Joe
swore into the Air Force
together.

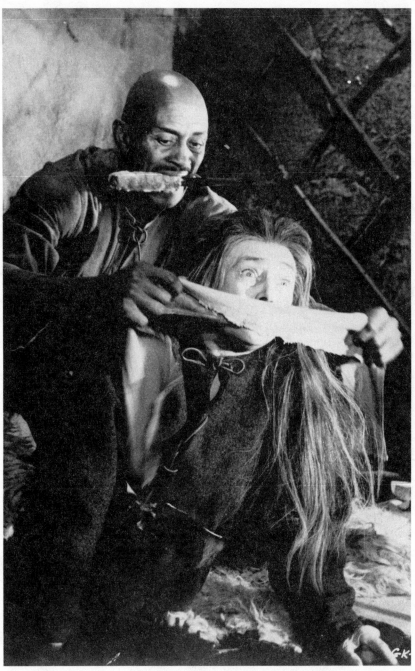

Woody, under orders from Genghis Khan, kidnaps
the lady-in-waiting of Khan's future wife, *Genghis Khan,*
1965.

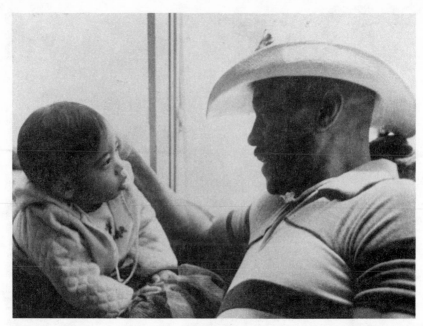

Grandson Joshua Strode helped hold Woody together
after Luana's death in 1980.

In Richard Brooks' *The Professionals,* 1963, Woody's
name appeared on the screen ahead of Burt
Lancaster's. Here, left to right, are Burt, Lee Marvin,
Robert Ryan, and Woody.

Woody in Dino De Laurentiis' *The Deserter,* 1971.
Woody plays a prisoner chosen to join a group of
elite fighting men. (Photo by Photofest)

Christmas in Hawaii: daughter June and granddaughter Luukia.

Woody and Tina were married May 10, 1982, and now live happily on Woody's five-acre ranch in Glendora, California.

Woody Strode today with grandson Joshua and son
Kalai. (Photo by Dick Broun)

my arms folded and never hit the water again. I told them, "If you can't swim, don't cross that goddamn rope," the one that separated the shallow end from the deep end, "because I'm not coming after you!"

When we weren't playing football, that's what Leo and I did. We used to call that place the University of March Field.

We had these long poles, and if someone got in trouble in the water, we'd reach them with the pole. I didn't want to drown trying to save somebody, so we tried to discourage the soldiers from going in the water. Leo worked up a story about how I got my physique based on doing 1,000 push-ups a day. Pretty soon we had all the soldiers doing push-ups instead of swimming. Leo and I started a push-up fad on that campus.

Now, Leo Cantor didn't look Semitic. He was a Russian Jew; he looked like any other white boy. The soldiers didn't know he was Jewish; they'd talk bad about the Jews and Leo would have to sit and listen to it. I remember he told me, "Woody, I can't put up with this shit. It's driving me crazy. I go to bed, but I can't sleep."

I said, "Leo, what's a Jew supposed to look like?"

That's how ignorant I was. I was twenty-seven; Leo was twenty-two. That's when we were introduced to serious prejudice in this country.

When I got into the service, they were lining up the blacks over here and the whites over there. They assigned me to the black outfit that lived in Dusty Acres. They worked in the mess hall, cleaned the latrines and the officers' quarters. They were the service unit. And the base was like a little Southern town. The black soldiers lived in separate quarters, rode segregated buses, and went to a segregated theater and PX.

What a slap in the face that was. For twenty-seven years I thought I was equal. Now we had the goddamnedest war going and I find out how bad things really are. My first reaction to the segregation wasn't madness; it was, "What?" I had never been kicked before. Things I had been doing all my life I could not do now.

They wanted me to go to OCS, Officer Candidate School, because I was an outstanding black based on my years at UCLA and my athletic background. But Schissler was afraid they would steal me away from his team. He said, "Woody, I don't want you to do anything wrong."

I said, "I'm not. I'm here to play football. I'll be a private." And I stayed a private, but as a private I had more prestige than the black officers. That was from athletics. If you're white and rooting for your team and one of the guys on the team is black, well then, he's one of yours and he's all right.

I lived in Dusty Acres for six months before Schissler got me separated from the black unit. He maneuvered the Commanding Officer into allowing the football team to live together. Schissler told the C.O., "You know Woody Strode is one of my best ballplayers. I hate to keep him separated; it's not good for the team. Is there something you can do?"

I ended up living in the gym with the rest of the white ballplayers.

We had the greatest group of athletes from all over the country, from Ohio, Nebraska, Alabama, and Mississippi. It was unique because most of them had never played with a black person before. We got introduced to one another in the gym. We had cases of beer and whiskey; that's how we said hello. Everybody got falling down drunk and they saw that I wasn't any different. I played guitar and sang Hawaiian songs; that was totally new to them. We started to have a good time, and they saw I didn't have any scars on my back.

I remember Jimmy Nelson, one of my teammates said, "I had no idea you guys were like this."

They called Jimmy Nelson, Taterhead; he was an All-American from Alabama. He had kinky blond hair. When we got drunk he said, "Woody, at home they used to call me 'nig'."

"Why's that, Jimmy?"

"Because I got kinky hair."

I said, "Yeah, you may be a half-breed at that."

We had an Indian quarterback from Oklahoma, Jack Jacobs. Indian Jack Jacobs, a great runner and passer. He was the only player I've ever seen that could kick seventy yards in the air. He didn't kick straight ahead, he'd throw his hip into it, kind of from the side. The ball would just hang in the sky, it gave us time to get downfield. And I don't remember any fair catches being allowed; I think we just nailed the receiver.

We went to Seattle to play the University of Washington. The Indian was hurt and so was I. I had a groin pull, and the doctors told me that if I was hit wrong I may never play again. The Indian was wearing an inner tube around his middle because all his ribs were crushed. We got behind a little school like Washington. We were sitting on the bench watching, and in the fourth quarter I looked at the Indian. I said, "Jake, you think you want to get in there so you can throw me the ball and we can get a goddamned touchdown?"

We went out there. I ran downfield, in and out, and crossed the goal line. The Indian was back there sucking it in and boom, we got a touchdown. We did that twice and won the game.

We played all our football out here in the West. The farthest east we would travel was to Colorado. We played an Army base there. We played the other service teams, we played the semi-pro teams, and we played against some of the colleges and universities.

We went to the Coliseum to play USC. I told my teammates, "You know, we never could beat these guys. Let's run the ball right down their goddamned throats!"

We were all grown men; a lot of the team was from the NFL. We had them 35–0 at the half, and Schissler was on his knees. He said, "If you guys keep this up, I'm through forever as a coach." In the second half he substituted for all our first-string players, and we didn't score for the rest of the game.

When we played the El Toro Marines, we built a grandstand for General Hap Arnold. He was like a movie star and the nicest guy in the world. He sat up there signing autographs. By halftime we had fallen behind the Marines 6–0. Well, the generals would bet thousands of dollars on these games. Hap Arnold came into the locker room at the half and said, "We're backing up the boats, if you don't win this goddamned game, I'm shipping you all overseas!"

We came back and won 32–6. That was pressure football; we played for our lives.

It was a tough league, and 1944 was my best year; I caught

nine touchdown passes. After we played the Second Air Force in Spokane, Washington, I got one of the best write-ups of my athletic career from George Davis, who wrote for the *Herald*. It didn't mean a lot; it wasn't a big fat headline, just a little truth spoken out of the side of the mouth.

> While Strode has always been rated highly locally, he's tops nationally according to the Second Air Force Bombers whose star-studded personnel boasts wide experience in the college and pro ranks.
>
> "Strode is head and shoulders the best all-around end I've ever played against," said Vic Spadaccini, great bomber back who used to tear opposing lines to shreds while at Minnesota and with the Cleveland Rams.
>
> "That goes for me too," added Hal Van Evrey, another Minnesota hero who left the Green Bay Packers to join the Army. "Don Hutson can snag passes better than anyone in football history but is weak defensively. But for all-around ability, give me Strode over any end in the National League. Not only has he ideal size, but has plenty of speed and isn't easily fooled."

I played football at March Field for three years. We had a love affair going because we hardly ever lost a game. My last Fliers' game was against the Washington Redskins, and they beat us 7–3. I blocked one of Sammy Baugh's punts. Sammy Baugh was such a quick kicker he only got five punts blocked in his entire career, and I got one of them. Then I got a concussion. I was running downfield on a kick-off and ran right into Wee Willie Wilkins. I hit him in the chest, bounced off and they carried me off the field. They were the only team we couldn't beat.

After that game all the service teams were disbanded and everybody got kicked out of the country. It was time for the big push in the war effort. All the soldiers were mobilized. The government said no more athletes could stay in the country, everybody had to shoulder the gun.

They were going to ship me off with the rest of the black soldiers to Europe, and boy, that was the butcher shop. Schissler stepped in and called Hap Arnold in Washington. He said, "You know General, we've got to send Woody Strode overseas. Well, for the last three years he's been living with all my ballplayers in the gym. They do everything together. I sure would hate to get Woody killed with some other outfit."

The General said, "Ask Woody which way he wants to go."

I was shipped to the Pacific with 140 other athletes. One hundred football players from the South and Southwest and me, plus forty baseball players.

Billy Hitchcock, third baseman for the Detroit Tigers, was the Adjutant. Enos Slaughter of the St. Louis Cardinals was the Commanding Officer. We had everybody but DiMaggio. He got out because he had a bad ankle or something. They issued us winter clothes, and we thought we were going to Siberia. We ended up in Honolulu.

I was on my way to the boat when Colonel Davidson, the C.O., stopped me. I was wearing my fifty-mission hat; that meant you had survived fifty flights. A pilot gave it to me; that was quite an honor. I was wearing some specially made fatigues, all zooted up. I had my slippers on. The Colonel stopped me, and he was ripping me up and down because I was out of order in my dress. As I got ready to salute, I cracked a smile because I was laughing inside. He said, "Because you're laughing, I'm going to take your corporal stripes."

Now I was late for the boat. I pulled up in a jeep. Leo Cantor was hanging over the side yelling at me, "Come on you son-of-a-bitch, they're waiting on you!"

When we got to Honolulu, we were still considered part of the Special Service until the government could figure out what to do with us. In the meantime, they had Leo and me living in the gym with all the other athletes, just like we did at March Field.

We had a fighter living with us named Speedy Dado. He was collecting $1,000 a week under the table boxing. I was listening when the General called. He said, "Who in the hell is this Speedy Dado making $1,000 a week? He's making more than me and I'm the goddamned general. You round up all those athletes and ship them as far into the Pacific as you can!" Now I was going to hell, either Tinian or Saipan.

I got shipped out and Leo Cantor stayed behind. When it came time to get on the boat, Leo played crazy, and he remained in Honolulu. They observed him for one year, and when the war ended, they shipped him home.

Leo and I were lucky. While a lot of guys were dying in Europe or the Pacific, we stayed home and played football. If I shut my eyes, I could believe I did my part for mankind. I didn't realize how lucky I was until I got off the boat in Tinian and watched the soldiers going all the way to Okinawa. That's where the real heat was. The guys in my outfit were complaining. I said, "You see the faces on those guys walking the gangplank? As long as you don't look like that, keep your mouths shut!"

Tinian was the airfield. It was a four-mile spit of land with a few palm trees and military-type structures, basically just one big landing field. There were hundreds of fighter planes and bombers lined up wing to wing. The whole island lit up from the sun reflecting off the planes. That was the group of planes that dropped the atomic bomb on Japan.

After we landed, Billy Hitchcock came up to me and said, "You remember that colonel that busted you for dressing out of order? He runs this place. If I leave you here, he'll ship you to Okinawa. I'm going to ship you to the generals' headquarters on Guam."

That's the kind of protection I had. If I had gone to the Mafia, I couldn't have had better protection.

I ended up guarding B-29s. We had practically secured the island, but there were still Japanese in the outlying areas. They lived on the run in the jungle. They had become primitive, like animals. We had American soldiers who hadn't seen a woman in three years. They were just about as primitive as the Japanese. The first Sunday they came knocking at my door. "Woody, you want to come hunting with us?"

"For what?"

"We got Japanese out here. We find them, kill them, and take the gold out of their mouths."

That's how you become a soldier. That's the kind of killer you have to be.

After I got introduced to the guys, we snuck into the officers' club and filled up a big bottle full of every kind of liquor you can think of, and we stole a case of beer. We sat in a Quonset hut, I played the guitar, and we got drunk. When it came time to turn in, they walked me back to my barracks, 400 yards. I asked them, "Why?"

"We're afraid of Japanese snipers."

That scared me to death. I remember we slept stripped naked except for our boots and socks. The moonlight would shine in through the window. Outside were these clicking noises, like signals. I thought it was the Japanese trying to lure us outside. After a week, I couldn't take it anymore. I asked, "What is that noise out there?"

They all fell out of bed laughing, "We just knew you were scared to death. Those are the goddamned lizards."

I couldn't sleep for a month.

We didn't carry guns. Shoot a gun and they knew where you were. We carried machetes. Somewhere on my left hand I have a scar from where I cut myself on the blade. I was walking and my hand crossed the blade. If it hadn't hit the bone, it would have passed clean through my hand.

After two months I became acclimated. I learned how to climb a coconut tree to get that cool coconut milk. I spent my days hiding out in the Quonset hut listening to Tokyo Rose on the short wave. The Japanese had all the best records, Count Basie, Duke Ellington, Nat King Cole. They had better records than we had. That's how they lured in the listeners; then they'd talk all their propaganda.

One day I was lying back and a male Japanese voice came on the air, "So sorry, please."

For eight months I was in that jungle and I never heard anyone but Tokyo Rose. This voice came on and said what happened; we had dropped the bomb. I went to the Commanding Officer, "Sir. I've been listening to the short wave; I think it's over."

He said, "Well, don't start any rumors."

Then we hit Nagasaki, that was the end of the war. In August of 1945, representatives of Japan surrendered aboard the *USS Missouri*.

Now it was getting-out time. The first stop was Honolulu. They wanted to ship me off to Japan to play occupational football; I still had about a half-year to go before I could get out. That's when I came up with a lame back. They discharged me and sent me home on an aircraft carrier. I hit the Coast at San Francisco. Luana was there waiting for me. She said, "The whole team is on its way up here."

The Hollywood Bears were coming up to play the San Francisco Clippers. I talked to Schissler on the phone. He said, "I've got Kenny with me. I'm bringing your uniform. Are you in shape?"

I suited up and played for forty minutes.

CHAPTER THIRTEEN

The Integration of Pro Sports

During my three years at March Field, Leo and I lived on base during the week and came home to Los Angeles on the weekends. Leo kept his car on base and we'd drive home together. But if I had to make the trip by myself, I would just hitchhike; I never rode the bus once.

Because of the uniform, I never had to worry about getting a ride. Everybody respected the man in uniform; black or white it didn't matter, they'd stop right away and pick you up. There was no fear, no knocking of the heads, because drugs hadn't taken over our society yet. Drugs changed the whole culture of America because the guy who really needs the drug can't afford it. That's when it got into the mad area.

We were into alcohol; that was it. When Leo and I came home on the weekends, we'd meet up with Kenny, when Kenny was in town, at Billy Berg's, drink and listen to the swing. We were all married, so we'd grab the wives and meet at the club. And when we headed back to base we always had four or five cases of whiskey in the trunk.

Whiskey was hard to come by during the war, but Kenny had a connection. He'd get the whiskey for us and Leo and I would fight all the way back to the base. He wanted to charge forty dollars and I said, "Fifty!" I said, "If we get caught, they'll have us in front of the Commanding Officer so we might as well get as much as we can."

The whiskey came from a liquor wholesaler who owned the San Francisco Clippers football team. Kenny played for him during the war years. Normally Kenny would have never left Paul Schissler but when the war came, Schissler went to organize the Fliers and this guy in San Francisco offered Kenny $500 a week to play football; plus he offered Kenny some sort of job working with his company after Kenny retired from football.

Like I mentioned before, Kenny didn't go into the service because of his bad knees. The first really bad injury came at the end of our 1941 season with the Bears. Kenny went to make a cut; he planted his foot and when he went to push off, the knee just gave out. I could hear that thing go clear across the field; it sounded like a guitar string popping.

Kenny had an operation and that got him out of the service. Instead, he went on the USO tour. That's when he gave up being a policeman. When he came back from the tour, he started playing football up in San Francisco. I used to laugh about that; Kenny wasn't physically fit for the armed services, and he ended up making a fortune playing football during the war.

But the government did use Kenny Washington. They sent famous black athletes like Kenny overseas to talk to the segregated black units. He went to Alaska and he went to the Burma Road. That was a 700-mile highway that connected Kunming, China with Lashio, Burma. The allied soldiers used that as a supply route. About the only plane that could make it over there was a DC-3. Kenny told me what a spooky thing that was, and I told him how lucky he was he had bad knees.

The idea behind these USO tours was to keep the black soldiers quiet by promising them things would get better after the war. "Just keep working within the system and things will change."

They had quite a group of athletes, and they'd go over there and entertain the troops, put on a little act, answer a few questions. Joe Louis was a great one for that; he traveled over 70,000 miles during World War II.

Joe Louis was stationed at Fort Riley, Kansas. He was a private with an all-black cavalry unit. That's where Jackie Robinson was stationed. Jackie didn't graduate from UCLA; he left school in 1941 to help his mother support the family. He played a little for the Los Angeles Bulldogs, then got a better offer to play semi-pro football in Honolulu. He was on a ship headed for the mainland when the Japanese attacked Pearl Harbor. When he got home, he was drafted and ended up at Fort Riley.

Jackie played on the football and baseball teams at Fort Riley. Then they transferred him to Camp Swift in Texas, and that leads to this story I found in Chris Mead's book, *Champion: Joe Louis.* Truman Gibson, a Chicago attorney, tells it:

> Jackie went to Camp Swift and was getting on the bus going back to camp when the bus driver, who along with most of the white bus drivers in the South was deputized and carried a pistol and whose firm resolve was to see that Negro soldiers would get to the back of the bus, said, "All right, nigger, get to the back of the bus."
>
> Jackie said, "I'm getting to the back of the bus. Take it easy."
>
> "You can't talk to me like that."
>
> Jackie said, "Well, I can talk to anybody any way I want."
>
> So he [the bus driver] pulled his pistol, and Jackie said, "That's a fatal mistake." He says, "You're going to eat that son of a bitch." So Jackie took it and broke every tooth in the guy's mouth, and they discharged Jackie for the good of the service. That's the Jackie Robinson story.

Boy, that was a tough war, and I have to thank Paul Schissler for saving my life by getting me on that service team. He was a hidden activist, and he sheltered me. Every time I found out what really went down, I was shocked. Years later, I saw a church in Yugoslavia where the Germans mowed down a whole town. That's what Hitler was all about.

After the war I read *The Rise and Fall of the Roman Empire* in four days. My wife was browbeating me, but I was hungry to learn. I began to read books the school never taught me. I never learned anything in school; we just skimmed over everything.

I wanted to know why everybody hated one another. I started reading black papers like the *Pittsburgh Courier* and the *Los Angeles*

135

Sentinel. I had a little education but no real understanding. I'd say, "Well, my family was former slaves and that's why the white men think they are superior to me." I didn't really know anything about it.

World War II was a racial war and what it did was pull the blanket off America's race problems. It was after the war when the equal rights movement got started. The Negro American said, "I fought for liberty; now I want to enjoy some." And slowly the doors started opening economically and socially.

They were getting ready to integrate major league professional sports but nobody knew anything about it. Branch Rickey was the man responsible. He ran the Brooklyn Dodgers and all their farm clubs. He was the smartest of all the baseball men. He was deeply religious, had a keen eye for talent, and most importantly, he knew how to make a buck.

If a man had the ability, regardless of race, Branch Rickey believed he should be given the opportunity to play. They say he was committed to that philosophy years before he signed Jackie Robinson, but he had to wait for the prevailing attitudes to change before he could make his move.

The commissioner of baseball, Judge Kenesaw Mountain Landis from Tennessee, was dead set against the integration of baseball. When Landis died, the power shifted; a more liberal-minded regime took over and Jackie Robinson was brought into the game.

Jackie became a good baseball player during his years in the army. He got out in 1944 and that's when the Negro Leagues came after him. That was Negro professional baseball. Jackie played for the Kansas City Monarchs.

In the meantime, Branch Rickey started his own club in the Negro Leagues; he called them the Brown Dodgers. The club was Rickey's way of scouting the black ballplayers. He realized a lot of players had the talent; how can you ignore a Satchel Paige or a Josh Gibson? It was just a matter of finding the right man. That's when Rickey heard about Jackie Robinson, who was hitting about .350 (just behind Josh Gibson, the Negro Leagues' batting champion of 1945), stealing bases, and rarely making an error in the field.

Rickey liked his talent, but he also liked the fact that Jackie had attended UCLA, that he was well spoken. If a black player was going to make it in the big leagues, he'd have to do it like Joe Louis. Keep the public image clean, be humble and modest, never boast in victory and never mess with the white women.

Jackie had the intelligence and daring that our people could respect. At the same time, he could play the role: not shuffling, just quiet and respectful. This is the role Branch Rickey demanded he play and Jackie agreed. Those of us that knew Jackie Robinson didn't believe he could do it. But Jackie's desire to be the best and the first overcame his anger and bad temper. Kenny and I discussed that many times. They'd have a sign on the locker room saying, "NO NIGGERS ALLOWED!," then he'd go out and play baseball. I don't think Kenny and I could have done that. I don't know.

In October of 1945, Jackie signed for a $3,500 bonus and $600 a month to play for the Montreal Royals, the Brooklyn Dodgers' top farm club. Jackie became the first black man to play in white organized baseball in what they called the modern era.

To the press, Jackie said, "I can't begin to tell you how happy I am that I am the first member of my race in organized ball. I can only say that I'll do my very best to come through in every manner."

All the black Americans cheered.

At first, there was considerable opposition among the big-league baseball players. Rogers Hornsby said, "The Negro Leagues are doing all right and Negro players should be developed and then remain as stars. This thing won't work out."

And Dixie Walker of the Brooklyn Dodgers said, "He's been signed for the Montreal club and as long as he isn't with the Dodgers, I'm not worried."

See, that was a smart move on the part of Branch Rickey, sending Jackie up to Canada. The Canadians weren't prejudiced like the Americans were. Jackie was an outstanding player, and the Canadians were quick to accept him.

The Montreal Royals opened their regular season against the Jersey City Giants in April, 1949. Jackie hit safely four out of five times, with one homer and three singles, stole two bases and scored four runs. Wendell Smith wrote a great article about that game in his column, "The Sports Beat." I'd like to quote some of that here.

. . . There he was—this Pied Piper of the diamond—perspiration rolling off his bronze brow, idolizing kids swirling all around him, autograph hounds tugging at him . . . And big cops riding prancing steeds trying unsuccessfully to disperse the mob that had cornered the hero of the day.

As he left the park and walked out onto the street, the once brilliant sun was fading slowly in the distant western skies. His petite and dainty little wife greeted him warmly and kindly. "You've had quite a day, little man," she said sweetly.

"Yes," he said softly and pleasantly, "God has been good to us today!"

And William G. Nunn of the *Pittsburgh Courier* wrote:

And we felt the thrill of being an American, though black. Because Jackie had come through. He had vindicated the *Courier's* faith in him. He had vindicated the hopes of 14,000,000 Negro Americans and all right-thinking white Americans. We know that millions of these Americans were also pulling for him.

As twilight deepens over the ball park . . . as the American flag waves proudly in the glooming, we bow our heads in silent tribute to a man who opened another saga in the book which is America . . . two men with faith in God and Democracy.

Thank God for a Branch Rickey and thank America for Jackie Robinson.

In Montreal, Jackie was a hero, but the Royals played most of their games in the United States. Jackie was constantly under attack from fans and opposing players. In one city, I think it was Baltimore, a fan brought a black cat to the park; he was swinging it from a noose, and it was dead as a doorknob. He took it down near the Royals' dugout and invited Jackie to "come meet your brother." There were many incidents, and the pressure wore on Jackie until he almost had a nervous breakdown, and his hair turned as gray as an old man's.

But the pressure didn't affect Jackie's performance on the field. He finished the season hitting .349 and won the batting title. He led the league in stolen bases and fielding percentage. Montreal won the pennant and the little World Series against the Louisville Cardinals; Jackie was the most valuable player.

At twenty-six years of age, Jackie Robinson proved he was ready for Major League Baseball. And he proved the black athlete belonged in professional sports. Pro football, the National Football League, was the next group to integrate.

The first Negro to play in organized professional football was Fritz Pollard from Brown University. He was a player-coach for the Akron, Ohio Indians from 1920 through 1925. They won the first championship game in 1920.

It was mostly a white team and the players resented being coached by a black man. That's when Pollard became a master of psychology. He said, "There was one player in particular who didn't like the idea of being coached by a Negro. I solved that problem by letting him carry most of the touchdowns and catch most of the passes in a ball game. After that, he was my greatest admirer!"

Now aside from Fritz Pollard, some of the other early black stars in professional football were Bob Marshall, Ink Williams, Sol Butler, and Duke Slater. Duke Slater was Howard Jones' great tackle from Iowa. He played for the Rock Island Independents and later for the Chicago Cardinals. Smokey Joe Lillard of Oregon also played for the Cardinals. Smokey Joe was the last black player during that era. He quit football in 1933, and from 1933 until 1946 no blacks were accepted in the National Football League.

In 1946, the Cleveland Rams decided to move their franchise to Los Angeles. They were the first big-time professional team we had out here on the West Coast. The Rams were managed by Charles Walsh, better known as Chili. His brother Adam was the head coach. They worked for Dan Reeves, owner of the Rams.

Dan Reeves was a rich man's son. His family owned a chain of grocery stores in New York which he sold for a fortune. He became an investment banker and started his own company. But he loved football and he bought the Rams.

During the 1945 season, the Cleveland Rams won nine games and lost one, then beat the Washington Redskins 15–14 in the championship game. They would have lost, but Slingin' Sammy Baugh threw a pass from his own end zone that hit the goal post and bounced out of the end zone for a safety.

So the Rams were the NFL champions of 1945. The next year, Paul Brown started the All-American Football Conference. What Branch Rickey was to baseball, Paul Brown was to football. He became coach and general manager of the Cleveland Browns.

Like Schissler, Brown coached service football and that brought him in contact with the best athletes, white and black. He had a history of giving black players a chance. And he knew that in order to provide top-notch football, he needed to sign the best black players. It was only a matter of time before he signed one of his black players to the new league. Plus, they needed the black player as a drawing card at the ticket window.

Now, I believe if Paul Schissler had gotten the pro football franchise in Los Angeles he would have used the entire March Field Fliers team. All of them were all-pros anyway. Kenny and I would have been about the only two who had not played in the NFL. There probably wouldn't have been a racial incident. It would have been much easier, but when Dan Reeves brought the team out here they already had an unwritten rule: no blacks in the National Football League. But the NFL wasn't blind to what was happening in the All-American Conference, and I think because they were afraid of the competition, they realized they were going to have to sign some black players.

When the Rams moved out in 1946, they had a run-in with the people of Los Angeles about playing in the Coliseum, based on giving Kenny Washington a tryout. See, the Supervisors of Los Angeles and the Coliseum Commission weren't convinced they wanted pro football in the Coliseum in the first place. In 1926, the Chicago Bears, with Red Grange, came out to play an exhibition game. They drew so many people to the Coliseum that USC got scared that pro football would hurt their box office, so they locked the pros out.

But the Coliseum was the only place the Rams could play, based on its size and location. And because the Coliseum was publicly owned, the Rams had to get approval from the Supervisors of Los Angeles as well as the Coliseum Commission before they could play there. Like I said before, the initial concern was over what effect the pro-game would have on the colleges, USC and

UCLA. Well, they worked out an agreement that gave the Rams a certain number of available Sundays on which to play their games.

When it became obvious the Rams were going to make the move, a group of black sportswriters, led by Hally Harding of the *Los Angeles Sentinel*, asked Chili Walsh why there were no Negroes playing in the NFL. Harding had the support of Leonard J. Roach, who was the chairman of the Coliseum Commission, and together they asked, "Can Kenny Washington have a tryout?"

"I'm sorry, but in the National Football League we have no coloreds."

The commissioner answered, "Well, then you can't have the Coliseum."

That's how they blackmailed the Rams into signing Kenny Washington.

Of course, Kenny had been a football star from high school through college and with the Hollywood Bears, even though semi-pro ball was like sandlot compared to the NFL. But to show you how popular Kenny Washington was, they gave him this special sportsmanship award at the Coliseum and more than 80,000 people showed up to give him a standing ovation. The people out here loved Kenny, and they wanted him to play for the Rams.

Chili Walsh invited Kenny to try out for the team. Two months later Chili contacted Paul Schissler about buying out Kenny's contract with the Hollywood Bears. I don't know how much Schissler got, but he sold them the contract. Paul got out of coaching and became an executive for the *Los Angeles Times*. The Pacific Coast Football League folded.

On March 21, 1946, the Los Angeles Rams signed Kenny Washington to play football in the NFL. Rocky handled the negotiations for Kenny. They talked to Kenny, and he told them to take a copy of the contract down to the Newton Street Police Station so that his uncle could take a look at it. So Rocky looked over the contract, and I don't know how much they wanted to pay Kenny, but I don't think that was an issue. Rocky wanted to make sure that they weren't signing Kenny to use as window dressing. Rocky had them add a no-cut clause that insured Kenny on getting paid for one year even if the Rams did use him for publicity purposes.

Chili Walsh assured Rocky that they were genuinely interested in Kenny not only as a drawing card but also because of Kenny's ability. They agreed to Rocky's no-cut clause and Kenny signed. The Rams were smart in signing Kenny, because with Kenny on the roster they were assured of drawing X number of people. The Rams almost folded when they first started playing out here, and without Kenny they probably would have.

Of course, the signing made big headlines in all the newspapers. Here's what Bob Oates of the *Examiner* wrote:

RAMS SIGN KENNY WASHINGTON, HUGE OFFER ACCEPTED BY STAR

Washington and Robinson, the Bruins' prewar "Touchdown Twins," have hence become the first two members of their race to lead the way into modern day, big-time athletics.

The Rams declined to announce terms of the contract. But one said, "Kenny asked for plenty and got it."

Washington, now 27, generally is described as the greatest halfback ever produced in the far west. He is the mightiest drawing card in coast football. When the Coliseum sold out all its 104,000 seats on the occasion of UCLA's scoreless tie with USC in 1939, Kenny was the main magnet.

The Rams hadn't even talked to me yet. But when Kenny signed, they had to get him a roommate. He could have gotten along with the white boys on the team, Bob Waterfield and Jim Hardy and all of those boys from UCLA and USC. But the thinking then was that he had to have a running mate, another black person to live with on the road. They asked him to select somebody. Kenny told them he wanted me. They spoke of my marriage to a Hawaiian. They tried to use my marriage to keep me off the team. But Kenny had power at that point and he said, "I want my buddy." That's how I came to play for the Los Angeles Rams.

So the three of us, Jackie Robinson, Kenny Washington and I were the three responsible for integrating pro sports in America. And what most people don't realize is that Kenny Washington was the first black athlete signed to play pro sports on a major league professional team. In 1946, Jackie Robinson was still playing for the Montreal Royals; he didn't move up to the Brooklyn Dodgers' club until 1947.

A lot of credit has to go to UCLA and Bill Ackerman for making that happen. To back that up, I found this article by Vincent X. Flaherty in the *Examiner*.

BRUINS AID PRECEDENT SHATTERING STEP

Undoubtedly, UCLA wielded some influence in making the situation possible, for all three boys made the upward step the same year, shattering precedent.

With Robinson, Washington, and Strode blazing the trail into professional sports, other teams have followed the example. For one, the Cleveland Browns of the All-American Pro Football Conference have signed a Negro player and now the Washington Redskins are scouring the country in search of outstanding Negro football stars.

Although there were many good Negro fighters before him, Joe Louis, the heavyweight boxing champion, did much toward elevating the Negro athlete's station in life. Joe's fistic career has been an exemplary one, and it is significant that Kenny Washington, Woody Strode, and Jackie Robinson are the same high type athletes both from a point of skill and character.

CHAPTER FOURTEEN

Just a Roommate

After World War II, I played in an all-star football game with all the great players from the Pacific Coast, plus all the great players who were hanging out after the war. The press asked me to compare the great athletes.

In my generation, nobody was better than Jim Thorpe. He won the decathlon and pentathlon at the 1912 Olympics but had his gold medals taken away because he had played some semi-pro baseball. He was also one of the most feared players in early American football.

Thorpe was a combination Sac-Fox Indian and played his college football for the Carlisle Indian Institute. He played professionally for the Canton Bulldogs, and when the American Professional Football Association was started in 1920, Jim Thorpe was named its first president.

Thorpe was a friend of Bill Spaulding's, and one time he came to UCLA to visit. Bill Spaulding said, "Woody, I want you to meet Jim Thorpe, the greatest Indian football player that ever lived."

And I shook his hand, "Mr. Thorpe." I know Spaulding must have told him I also had Indian blood.

Then there was Red Grange, the man who really popularized professional football. George Halas of the Chicago Bears stole him away from the University of Illinois, and they both made a fortune barnstorming the country. Grange was making $100,000 a year back in the twenties. He was the "Galloping Ghost."

And how do you figure a guy like Ernie Nevers, a fullback from Stanford who went on to play for the Chicago Cardinals? He still holds the record for the most touchdowns scored in a single game, six. I saw him play a game with two broken ankles. That's almost unbelievable.

I think Bronco Nagurski was possibly the finest athlete ever to carry the ball. Bronco was a Canadian who went to the University of Minnesota. He made All-American at tackle, then moved to the backfield and made All-Amerian at fullback. I had never seen a lineman become a running back. He ended up playing every position for them except center, quarterback, and halfback. Bronco went on to become a big star with the Chicago Bears.

Bronco Nagurski was just a big strong bruiser for his day. He weighed about 235 pounds and boy, was he tough. Once Bronco was in a second-story hotel room. He and some buddies were getting drunk, fooling around, and Bronco fell out of the window. He hit the pavement, and a crowd gathered around him. A policeman broke through the crowd and asked Bronco, "What happened?"

Bronco said, "I don't know. I just got here myself!"

Now, there were very few passers as good as Sammy Baugh. I was put on the spot because I was standing with Indian Jack Jacobs and they asked me, "Woody, who's the best passer in football: Jack Jacobs, Sammy Baugh, or Kenny Washington?"

I said, "Sammy and the Indian inside 35 yards, Kenny 50 yards on out. But if you give me Kenny Washington and Bronco Nagurski, you can have everyone else."

And I can't leave out Sid Luckman, who was possibly the smartest quarterback, even up to this day. He's another one who played for George Halas and the Chicago Bears. Sid was the first of the modern T-formation quarterbacks in professional football. In the 1943 championship game he was down three touchdowns to Sammy Baugh and threw five touchdowns to win. And he's the one who led the 73–0 massacre of the Washington Redskins in the

1940 title game. That's when the T-formation took over football, and the passing game really opened up.

The Rams had a great T-formation quarterback named Bob Waterfield. He followed Kenny and me out at UCLA. They had to redshirt Bob until they brought in the T-formation. Bob went to UCLA on a gymnastics scholarship; that's how good an athlete he was. He took UCLA to their first Rose Bowl in 1942. Then as a rookie with the Cleveland Rams he won the Most Valuable Player award. He was the only rookie to be unanimously voted MVP and he didn't even make All-American at UCLA. That was in 1945, when the Rams beat the Redskins for the NFL championship.

I played against Bob when I was with the March Field Fliers. Before the game my old line coach, Ray Richards, came up to me and said, "You know Woody, this is our young ball club. Tell your boys not to hurt them."

I said, "We'll carry you," and we only beat them by six points.

Bob Waterfield was a local boy; he played for Van Nuys High School out in the San Fernando Valley. That's where he met his sweetheart and future wife, Jane Russell. She was the actress Howard Hughes made famous by virtue of her full-figured talent. Kenny Junior used to sit in her lap at the practices; he was only five years old and he thought he had already died and gone to heaven.

Bob Waterfield grew up watching Kenny play football. Bob was a fan, and he ended up breaking a lot of Kenny's offensive records at UCLA. You might think there was a little friction between Kenny and Bob over who was going to quarterback the Rams, but Bob loved Kenny. And Kenny was quite fond of Bob. I remember Bob told the press, "Kenny was the best football player I ever saw in my life and that includes everybody I ever knew. And he was also a great gentleman." Bob Waterfield was a tremendous gentleman as well.

In addition to Bob Waterfield, the Rams had Indian Jack Jacobs and Jim Hardy at quarterback. Hardy was from USC; he was a hero out there because he threw five touchdown passes in two Rose Bowl games. They also had Tom Harmon from Michigan, Fred Gerhke, a scatback from Utah, and Bob Hoffman from USC. The

Rams had no shortage of good backfield men. So naturally the question was, "How is Kenny going to fit in?"

Adam Walsh said, "We'll use him where we can get the most good out of his many outstanding abilities. There is always one thing that any player can do better than anything else and we will use Kenny where his assets as a passer and runner will give us the strongest possible four-man combination on the field at one time." In other words, Adam Walsh didn't know how he was going to use Kenny.

Well, just before the season started, Kenny underwent another knee operation which took some of the heat off Adam Walsh. Kenny had re-injured the knee in 1945 playing with the Hollywood Bears. We were playing a game against the San Diego Bombers and Kenny dropped back to pass. Just as he let go, he was clobbered. When the pile cleared up, Kenny got up limping. Kenny said it was just a pulled muscle, but he didn't do any running for the rest of that season.

They ended up operating on both knees, and Kenny spent the spring and summer rehabilitating, trying to get ready for the Rams' first exhibition game in August. He worked out his knees playing handball at the Police Academy. Bob Waterfield really worked with Kenny so Kenny could make the most of his shot in the NFL.

Kenny was able to get his knees in good enough shape to play, but at twenty-eight years of age he would never be the same. Had he gone straight to the NFL after he got out of UCLA, there's no telling the records he could have set. Dick Hyland wrote this article for the *Los Angeles Times* about Kenny that really lumped me up.

> Try this test: stand Ernie Nevers, Red Grange, Tommy Harmon, and Washington on a sideline prior to a game. You can pick but one of them to play 60 minutes for you. And great as the others are, you must pick the ex-Uclan. His all-around ability was greater than any of the others with the possible exception of Nevers. He gets the nod over the greatest of Stanford players because in college Nevers was continually being benched for injuries while Kenny was rarely off the field in tough games. He was a durable duck indeed.
>
> Your flinger was quite a Washington fan when Kenny was an undergraduate. In fact, he became most unpopular with the Trojans

by laughing in print at the pretenses of Trojans to all-narrow, provincial, prejudiced pickers. Had Kenny Washington been signed by a National League team in 1940, he would undoubtedly have been, with one year's experience, one of the greatest of professional backs and a drawing card from one end of the league to the other.

But that was six years ago. In the meantime Washington has become a beaten-up ball player who is neither so strong nor so quick in his reactions as he was before the war. He has a trick leg which kept him out of games on many occasions last season and he has lost just enough of his speed to enable tacklers who would have missed him or run into his murderous straight arm when he was at his best to handle him with punishing tackles which in turn help cut down his speed, strength, and effectiveness.

Coming into the National League with a reputation, Kenny Washington is going to find himself on a hot seat every time a ball is snapped into play. No one can ever doubt his courage who saw the whappings he took as a collegian. But doubting his physical ability, as demonstrated last football season, to take the beating he will get is something else again. I suspect that long before the coming season is over Kenny Washington will be used mainly as a "spot" player, entering games to heave long passes when Coach Adam Walsh thinks they might succeed.

Kenny Washington will work his head off to prove this prediction wrong, and I hope he does.

A couple of years ago, a writer from *Sports Illustrated* called me to talk about the integration of professional football. I told him, "No, this is the worst incident that ever happened in my life, and I don't want to talk about it."

Then he insulted me. He said, "I heard you were just a roommate."

I had the ability to play in the NFL but the Rams weren't concerned with that. They spoke badly of my marriage to a Hawaiian, and I think if they had their choice they would have selected somebody else. They weren't really glad to have me, so I spent considerable time sitting on the bench, collecting my $350 a week.

My signing with the Rams wasn't a package deal per se, but they realized that Kenny would be a loner on the road. They didn't want Kenny to face it by himself; that's why they hired me. Sometimes the team would stay at the Hilton and Kenny and I would have to go find somewhere else to stay. If we were lucky, we'd stay with a friend or relative.

Traveling with the Rams made a big impact; we discovered how popular we were across the country. The black kids outside California used to tell Kenny and me how much they enjoyed listening to our games on the radio while we were still playing at UCLA. Until that time, we didn't realize what a unique thing we had done. We discovered that very few blacks received the opportunity Kenny and I received. I never became bitter over it, maybe at a few individuals, but never at the total picture.

I mean, this was the way it was. We had it better in Los Angeles than any other area of the country, but we still suffered from prejudice. You accepted it as a way of life. We knew it was wrong, but you could only talk about these things if you were on a plateau where your voice had some impact. That's the level Jackie Robinson reached and that's why he is better remembered than Kenny or me. But Jackie had to suffer through worse abuse than we did in order to reach that level. I saw that affect Jackie, and I think it was all the pressure that forced Jackie into an early grave.

When Jackie Robinson was brought up to the Brooklyn Dodgers in 1947, a number of the players signed a petition to keep Jackie off the team. They went to Branch Rickey, who was signing the paychecks, and said, "I don't want to play with him!"

"Well, okay, there's the door." Which is basically what Branch Rickey did. "If you don't want to play with Jackie, then you're going to play for somebody else. Or not at all."

I don't think people gave too much thought to Kenny and me playing for the Rams. Hell, Negroes had helped found the National Football League only twenty-six years before we signed. And black players had been part of the league up until 1933, which was only thirteen years before we signed. So the precedent had already been established. Now, if you look far enough back into baseball's history you'll find that Jackie Robinson wasn't really the first black either.

Baseball is an older game than football. They played baseball during the Civil War years. There were a lot of black players in that era. And when the game went professional, in the period after the Civil War, blacks were still playing; they were just labeled Indians or Cubans. One black pitcher was sent to Cuba for a while to lose his identity, so that his team could bring him back as a Cuban. It's when the game grew into the national pastime that we began to be left out. Basically, that's what happened in football; it just happened over a shorter period of time.

So in baseball that wasn't a smooth transition. Jackie's signing was earth-shattering because Branch Rickey had to fight the whole league. And he had enough guts and push and whatever else it took to do the job.

I don't think even Rickey could have realized what the overall impact would be. Kenny and I didn't have those problems with the Rams, not with the players at least. It seems like the only thing the Rams players were concerned with was who's making the most money. And that's the way it should be. It's just a business.

There were thirty-three players on the Rams' roster the year I signed, and ten of us were from the West Coast. Out of those ten, five of us were from USC and three of us were from UCLA. On the USC side there was Bob Delauer, who played center and kicked field goals, Jim Hardy, Pat West, a fullback, and Jack Banta and Bob Hoffman, who were both on the 1939 team. And on the UCLA side there was Kenny, me, and Bob Waterfield. Hell, we had all grown up with each other, so there were no problems there.

Bob Waterfield was the guy who tried to get us into the white hotel back in Chicago. That's where we played our first game as Rams. We arrived at the airport in Chicago, stepped off the plane, and Kenny walked up to me pouting. They didn't talk to me because I wasn't considered. I said, "What's wrong?"

He said, "You know, we can't stay at that stinking hotel!" They wouldn't let us stay at the Stevens Hotel with the rest of the team.

I said, "What? I stayed there during the track season." That shows how Bill Ackerman protected us. I said, "What do they want us to do?"

"They're going to give us $100 apiece to go find some place else to stay."

I said, "Well, what the hell, let's be segregated!"

We headed across town and got a room at the Persian Hotel, which is a slum now. Back then it was the most plush Negro hotel in the city. They booked the greatest jazz bands into that place. Count Basie was playing in the club downstairs, and all the white people had come to hear him play.

Kenny and I got a seat at the bar and ordered a couple of Tom Collins's. Around midnight Bob Waterfield showed up. He was checking in on us. Bob said, "You crazy sons of bitches, what are you doing here this late at night?"

"Just sittin' here enjoying this club!"

He said, "Look, we've made arrangements for you two to come up town with us and stay in the hotel."

I told Bob, "Forget that, boy. I'm going to be segregated, spend this hundred dollars, stay right here, and listen to the Count play his music."

Bob said, "What the hell," and ordered himself a drink.

Here I was thirty-one years old, Kenny was twenty-eight, and we were getting this kind of education. I remember the first time we saw Harlem. We had gone there to play the Giants at the Polo Grounds. We saw the whole separation scene back there: the Polish people, the Italians, the Jewish people all had their own areas.

We had never seen so many black people in one place as we did in Harlem. We stood on the street gawking. I used to joke about it. I said, "You know, we were acting just like white people would!"

There weren't many racial incidents that I can remember on the football field. You're out there trying to beat each other up; how do you know when a guy's trying to hurt you because you're black? There were times when certain players would try to take a cheap shot. In one of the early games, Kenny had made a block and the play was going away from him. He was flat on his back when their left end came across and took a run like he was going to kick off. Kenny happened to see him coming and raised his head. This guy just missed or he would have kicked Kenny's head clear up to the press box.

Jim Hardy saw the play and after the game we were all sitting together and Hardy asked about it. Kenny told him, "It's hell being a Negro, Jim." Kenny didn't mean any self-pity by that; it was just a social comment.

When I got to the Rams, they stuck me on defense. They figured that would be the butcher shop. I was always primed but they never let me catch a pass. Those were the first years of the specialty player, of platooning the offense and defense. I weighed only 210 pounds, and I had to go up against National Football League linemen that weighed 250 pounds and more. I think the Rams' brass was hoping I'd get killed out there. It didn't matter; I knew how to play football and I survived.

At first, the Rams weren't inclined to give Kenny or me any playing time. We played an exhibition game against the Redskins and Kenny got in for only one play in the first half, plus a few minutes before the final gun. I didn't play at all. People began to question why. Gordon Macker of the *Daily News* wrote:

> The scam of advertising names to hustle the chumps and then letting the names be only numbers in the program (25 cents please) seems to be an accepted practice with the pro promoters. Well this town won't go for it.

At first I didn't feel bad; I just felt embarrassed. I resigned myself to the situation. I was making more money than I had with Schissler and I wasn't getting banged up. I was in the NFL and that was like a prize.

But I did have one great game in the NFL. It was against the Chicago Bears. The first half went by, and I didn't get into the game. At halftime I was walking to the dressing room and I ran into Fred Davis. Fred had played on the March Field Fliers and then was signed by the Bears. He said, "Woody, what the hell are you doing on the bench?" I didn't know how to answer, and that's the first time I really felt bad about not playing. I just hung my head and walked off the field.

In the third quarter Adam Walsh was looking for somebody to come off the bench and crash the Bears' line. The Chicago Bears had the biggest, baddest linemen in football. They had a play where they would spread their linemen a yard apart and when the ball was snapped everybody would pull out around the end. The end had to hold his ground and wait for this huge thundering herd to run him over. It was like looking down Times Square at all the skyscrapers. Nobody on our team had the guts to stay in there and fight.

Adam Walsh knew I was crazy enough to do it, and he put me in the game. We lined up, and I got on my marks like it was a track meet. When the line pulled out I knifed between them; when they stood up to block, I hit them before they got off the snap.

I was getting through their line and each time I broke through I punished their left halfback, Dante Magnani from St. Mary's. Five times I dropped my shoulder and laid him out. The sixth time, he couldn't take it anymore and he flinched. I went right around him and caught Sid Luckman looking out the window. I sacked him for a ten-yard loss, undressed him right there in front of 70,000 people.

I proved I could play, but for whatever reason the Rams weren't interested in using me. When somebody broke down, or they couldn't find anybody with guts enough to go out there and do the job, they'd stick me in and I would shine. But in my generation, players never defended their right to play. We just tried to prove ourselves in practice, which I did.

If a kid had my record today, he'd be in a court of law defending his right to play. The press would be right on top of them, "What are you doing sitting Woody Strode on the bench?" Well, I had to sit and suffer those lashes because I opened the door. Kenny and I opened the door. Soon, every black with the ability was running up and down the field.

The second year, we played an exhibition game against the Redskins and they only put me in the game once. I sat on the bench as they prepared to cut me from the team. The next day, I was released. George Trafton, the line coach, broke the news to me. He said, "Woody, it's not because of your ability that you're getting fired. They're trying to say you're too old and that they're trying to rebuild. I tried to tell them Negroes don't age like white people."

I was only thirty-two, and I was in better shape than anybody on the team. I could still outrun everyone but Tom Harmon. So Trafton told me the news and a tear came to his eye because he didn't know how to say so long.

Then I found out what really went down. I went to see Kenny, who had been picked up for another year. I said, "Kenny, why did they release me?"

He said, "It's not your ability; it's your life style. Dan Reeves does not approve of your marriage to Luana and your Hawaiian life style." The old school was still in force upstairs and I got affected by it.

The Sunday after I got cut, Kenny sent some of his friends from the old neighborhood over to my house. They knocked on the door, "Woody, we'd like to talk to you."

"Excuse me for a moment," and I went and put some clothes on. They came inside. They said, "Kenny sent us over. We were having dinner last night and we heard Dan Reeves and Bob Snyder talk about cutting you from the team. They were falling down drunk and they were talking so bad about you and Luana that we sent our wives home. We don't like what they're doing. Do you want to fight them?"

The mob was asking me this. I looked at them and said, "You know, I've lived here thirty-two years and I've never had a racial incident. I don't want to start one now." And anyway, how do you fight someone with 100 million dollars? I'm talking about Dan Reeves.

Well, in 1971, Dan Reeves died of cancer and a girlfriend of Luana's called. She told Luana, "Don't let Woody show up at the funeral." I don't know what that was all about, but pure hate was somewhere in their line. I never forgot that. But I'm not happy about anyone dying. They must have assumed my attitude was, "Thank God the old bastard is dead."

So when the guy from *Sports Illustrated* called, I told him, "If I have to integrate heaven, I don't want to go." That's how bad it was. I always compare my situation to the way a white person would have reacted. They don't want to be where they aren't wanted either. If I'm not welcome in your cocktail lounge, you're liable to poison me. You might spit in my food. You might cook a rat and say, "We'll just give that son-of-a-bitch anything." Any white man would have reacted the same way. "Don't go into that restaurant boy; you're liable to eat some mice."

"Why?"

"They don't like white people."

"Well, where else can we eat?"

That's exactly what a white boy would say. I'm the same way. We're not that far apart, but they try to tell us we're different. I don't know how to beat the drums or chant or do voodoo. I'm no different because we're all exposed to the same culture, the same dreams.

CHAPTER FIFTEEN

A Hero In Dogtown

In December, 1946, my baby boy was born. I couldn't sleep for the three weeks prior because of worrying and fretting. He kicked and thrashed so much I thought he was going to smother. Finally, when the day came, I drove Luana to the Queen of Angels Hospital in Hollywood and out he came without a hitch.

We named him Woody. He was a beautiful baby, and right from the beginning you could see a lot more of the Hawaiian in him than me. His skin was a smooth cocoa brown, and he had big, luminous eyes like his mother.

We were still living in the apartment up in Hollywood, and when we brought little Woody home the Hawaiians put on a big luau for Luana and the baby in one of the vacant lots across the street. Everybody who came gave us a dollar; that's a Hawaiian custom for the firstborn. And they gave him his Hawaiian name, Kalaeloa; that means heavenly sky. Kalai is the name he goes by now. Officially, his name is Woodrow Wilson Kalaeloa Strode.

Well, after I got cut from the Rams, I completely shut down. I kept myself busy cleaning and cooking, washing diapers and taking care of the baby. He and Luana were my only joy at that time. The New York Yankees of the All-American Football Conference contacted me and asked me to come back for a tryout. At first I said,

"No, they don't want me to play football," and I was through integrating anything. But finally, not knowing what else to do, I decided I'd give it a try.

When I walked into Dan Topping's office—he was the general manager—he said, "Son, from the way they talk about you, we thought you were fifty years old!" Regardless, I didn't make their team. Once the Rams said my career was over, as far as the rest of football was concerned, that was it. "At his age, at this point in Woody Strode's career, he does not have the ability." And that ended my football career in the United States.

I took the train home from New York. On the way, I stopped in Chicago; I had some cousins living there. I got drunk for one week and licked my wounds. I was a warrior, I didn't know anything but football; now they weren't allowing me to play. I didn't know how I was going to support my wife and baby.

When I got home, Luana said, "Les Lear's been calling you from Canada. They want you to play football up there."

Les Lear played guard beside me on the Rams. A lot of that team had been cut one way or another, and some of them moved up to Canada to play. The Calgary Stampeders hired Les as their player-coach. He was allowed four Americans on the team; he reached for the best ones he could find.

I called, and Les said, "Woody, I got a job for you. Bring your shoes and your shoulder pads"—because he couldn't get the equipment up there—"I'll get you all the money I can." He sent me a contract offering $5,000 for the season, eighteen games, 100 dollars a week expense money, my hotel and transportation all paid for.

When I stepped off the plane in Calgary, it was like stepping back into the Old West. It was cowboy country; they were into cattle, oil, and grain. Their land was wide open. The plains between Calgary in the Alberta province and Regina in the Saskatchewan were just an extension of our great plains here in the United States.

At that time, you could get on the highway and hit a curve that would last a mile. As far as the eye could see there was nothing but acres and acres of flat land. They had Black Angus cattle up there, and I thought the Canadians were crazy, because when the temperature dropped below zero, they'd just back the cattle up against a mountain and drop hay. The cattle would all stand there bunched together. That's how they kept from freezing to death. And that was the healthiest meat in the world, because all the unhealthy weak livestock died.

The Canadian Indians used to bring wild game to my hotel room. I'm part Indian, but you never walk up to them and announce it. They'll see it in you. They came to all the football games, and it took them a month to ask me what kind of Indian blood I had. I told them, "American Blackfoot." The guy who asked me had an interpreter talking for him; he replied, "We are Canadian Blackfeet." Well, that made us like brothers. And the Canadian Blackfeet were the richest Indians I ever saw; they owned oil fields and herds of Black Angus.

Now, when you try to visualize an American Indian, you usually see them naked except for a breechclout. The Canadian Indians wore suits they handmade out of deerskin. They wore fur-lined moccasins and feathered headdress. That was the difference between the American Indian and the Canadian; the Canadian Indian didn't get urbanized, reservationized. They were still living off the land. They would hunt and fish for six months and store enough meat to last through the winter.

When the Canadian Indians harvested their grain, they'd leave a stubble one or two feet high. Across the road the white people would shave their fields clean. Well, on the Indian land you could throw a rock into the stubble and out would fly geese and ducks. The Indians were much closer to the land than the white men.

The Sarsi Indians were the land barons. They owned all the land from Calgary to Banff, 60 miles to the west. Banff was the most spectacular place. In the springtime the lakes and streams would swell from the melting snow that covered the great Rocky Mountains. The water was sky-blue and the lakes reflected those purple, snow-covered Rockies like a mirror. The streams ran quickly and as the current flowed over the rocks, the water would back up into little white ice cream-colored puffs.

In the 1800s they built the largest, most grand resort in the world in Banff. Part of the attraction was a set of natural hot springs which were part of the national park there. After a game we'd drive up in weather thirty degrees below zero and soak out all the soreness in those hot sulfur baths.

In 1947, Canadian football players were still playing both ways, offense and defense. We practiced on a frozen hockey field. They laid the chalk marks right on top of the ice. I had to wear the old canvas pants that I hadn't worn since high school. I was playing pro football with eighteen-year-old Canadian kids, plus three other Americans: Pete Thodos, Rod Pantages, and Keith Spaith, our quarterback. Keith had tried out for the Rams but didn't make it. Les Lear brought him up to Canada, and he became a legend in their league. He married the daughter of the head of the Grain Exchange and became set for life.

We went undefeated my first year because we used the Rams' playbook. In those years, the Rams had the most innovative offense. The hardest thing about playing for the Rams was learning their system. I had never seen so many plays and had so many patterns to memorize. My Calgary teammates were just kids and ignorant about the game, so Les gave us only seven plays. Around end, off tackle, over guard, center; he simplified it.

When we made it to the championship game, the whole town of Calgary packed up and made the trip east to Toronto. It was like traveling from Spokane, Washington to New York City. Two thousand cowboys and Indians climbed on the train with us, and everybody else followed in cars and wagons. But then, the people of Calgary wouldn't have turned out to see the Queen of England like they did to see the Stampeders play football.

See, the western territories, Regina, Winnipeg, Edmonton, and Calgary, that was dog territory. All the sophisticated, urban people lived in Montreal or Toronto; so when the town of Calgary traveled east to Montreal, that was like the American pioneer turning around and heading back to Boston. I've got this article written by Douglas MacFarlane for the *Toronto Daily News* that describes the scene.

> The Stampeders, with their ponies, their chuck-wagon, their Indian chief cheerleader, their flap-jacks and their western brand of enthusiasm, had taken over the town long before game time. All morning

Saturday, the Calgarys paraded at the drop of a tuba note. They finally wound up at the city hall, fried some flaps for some jacks, gave a guy by the name of Hiram [the mayor] a ride on one of their ponies, and headed for the stadium. It was quite a piece of mobile vaudeville by the time it hit Bloor St. One prairie schooner even had a little prairie schooner tagging along behind. There were wagons and trucks and cars and doggies and on them all were people peculiarly dressed in great big hats and great big boots and all of them shouting great big boasts.

We played Ottawa in the title game. Here's what happened: Ottawa had an extension play that started as an end run. While the play developed, they would lateral the ball back as they approached the sideline. On the fourth lateral, they dropped the ball. I was at that spot, and I reached down and grabbed the ball. I could see the whites of the referee's eyes; he didn't blow his whistle, so I ran the ball 45 yards for the winning touchdown.

I was the hero. I left the field on my teammates' shoulders, a bottle of rye whiskey in my hand. No black athlete in the world had ever done that. I was their prized bull.

That night we partied in the Royal York Hotel, the best hotel in the city. I met an Indian friend out front, and he let me borrow his horse, a pure white multi-breed. I saddled up and walked that horse right up to the front entrance. The doorman watched me coming, frozen in his boots. My Indian friend held the door for me as I moved inside.

The lobby floor was marble cut into big squares with a black matrix. There were round marble columns that stretched fifty feet to a vaulted, cathedral-type ceiling. The night crowd was milling in tuxedos, dinner jackets and long, flowing gowns. The high-class conversation stopped when they saw me, like someone took a hammer to the alarm clock.

I walked that horse right through the crowd. I was wearing a white linen cowboy-type suit, reddish lizard-skin boots, and a navy blue silk scarf around my neck. I held the reins and my rye whiskey in my left hand, my white ten-gallon hat in my right. I walked to the center of the lobby and pulled back on the reins. I kicked that horse hard and he reared up and spun around. I leaned way back in the saddle, looked up towards the ceiling and let out a war cry. The place erupted in applause and shouting. And when the police showed up, I sliced through them like cutting a cake as I charged out of there.

The next day I was in all the newspapers. Anybody else they would have locked up. But because I was a black American and we had just won the national championship, something Calgary had never come close to doing, I got away with it. And Tom Brooks, who owned the Stampeders and Imperial Oil—a multi-million-aire—would have paid any fine. Now I'm one of the immortal guys up there.

After I became a star in the Canadian Football League, I took a beating out on the field. I could measure how good I was playing by how bad they tried to get me out of the game. I remember Les telling me in one of the early games, "Woody, when you leave the field, don't take your helmet off or somebody might hit you in the head with a bottle!" That's how dangerous it was.

After I broke my ankle at the beginning of the 1948 season, Les Lear decided we needed another pass-catching end to help take the heat off me. I told Les, "We need to get Sugarfoot Anderson."

Sugarfoot's real name was Ezerett. He was sweet; he liked to wear a lot of lavender perfume. He had a long, oval face and a big, toothy smile. He was an immaculate dresser and quite the ladies' man.

Sugarfoot was about six-feet-five; he had my body, only bigger. His arms were longer; his fingers were an inch longer than mine. His hands were so big, he caught passes one-handed. And he was very theatrical; he'd try and make a catch look harder than it was. He'd make a tackle and be the last one to get up, that kind of thing. But he was another one of our good ball players who never got a chance to play in the NFL.

Sugarfoot and I played together on the Hollywood Bears. He was out of the University of Kentucky. He and I caught most of Kenny's long passes. In 1945 we were playing the Bulldogs and Kenny threw me a 65-yarder for a touchdown. Kenny used to call that the exhibition plan: run as fast as you can, as far as you can, and I'll hit you. When we got the ball back after my 65-yard touchdown, I looked at Sugar in the huddle. I said, "Sugar, you'd better tighten your laces." The next play, Kenny faded back and hit him for a touchdown, 75 yards in the air.

After I brought Sugarfoot up to Canada, we roomed together at the hotel in downtown Calgary. We had a suite with a juke box and all our favorite records. We didn't need an icebox; we'd just sit a case of beer outside the window and five minutes later we'd have ice-cold bear. Once, after a few drinks, Sugarfoot thanked me for bringing him up to Canada.

"You know, Woody, I pray to you and God."

"Why, Sugar?"

"Because you brought me to Canada." He said, "When I was a little boy, my mother picked cotton, and she used to drag me through the field on a sack." I had never heard a story like that.

I told him, "I'm jealous of you. You're getting more out of this than I am." For the first time he was around white people who loved him. He hadn't had that kind of licking-off before.

Sugarfoot still lives up there. His wife became something like a supervisor for the city of Calgary. His kids were born here but raised in Canada. They're Canadians. Fifteen years after I quit playing, they all came down here to check me out. We were just getting over the race riots in Watts. I asked them, "What are you doing here? Go back to Canada; there's too much hate down here." They had a whole different existence up there. They learned to play hockey and ski and all that stuff.

I always felt good about bringing Sugarfoot Anderson to Canada. That was one of the good marks on my life. And with Sugarfoot on the team, the Stampeders went undefeated for the second straight year. We got to the Western Division championship game, and in the first half I separated my shoulder. They froze it at halftime. I went back out to play the second half, fell and tore all the rest of the muscles. After the game, which we won, I was walking out of the hotel in Regina. It was ten below zero and I had a chill. I turned to Sugar and said, "Sugar, something's wrong with me." And then the pain and the throbbing started.

The doctor came to see me. He said, "Woody, do you want me to give you a shot for the pain?"

"No!" I said, "Give me some whiskey." And the Canadian boys brought me some of their finest rye whiskey, emptied half the bottle, and filled it up with beer. I drank that, and they picked me up and carried me to the train. I sat on the bunk while they fed me this mixture until I passed out. That's how the pain left.

When I woke up the next day, I was in Calgary. I couldn't pick up my arm, but there was no pain. I had made it through the shock. Now I had to get prepared for the national championship two weeks away. Les Lear said, "I want you to run and keep your legs in shape." I had my arm in a sling, and I ran around the track holding my arm.

After two weeks, I could get the arm up to shoulder level but I couldn't get it over my head. I couldn't do any pass catching in the workouts. Right before the game, the Canadian kids grabbed my wrist and dug their fingernails into the skin. The doctor shot me with novocaine five times. It was one of those old-fashioned metal syringes with a six-inch needle. The doctor put that right into my joint. I played the first half. At halftime I went into the dressing room and the shoulder started hurting real bad, but I could still maneuver. The doctor said, "Woody, do you want me to shoot you up again?"

Well, I didn't have the guts to take that needle five more times. I said, "No! I think I can make it like I am."

I went as far as humanly possible, but I had to take myself out of the game with five minutes left. I stood on the sideline and watched my team lose. The pain flared and tears came to my eyes. There was nothing wrong with the rest of me; I just couldn't move that arm at all. And I couldn't take another needle in my shoulder. You can imagine that needle going right into the joint. If I had had some fat, it might have been okay, but right into the bone, I couldn't handle it.

Before I left Canada to come home to Los Angeles, a Doctor Townsend contacted me. He said, "Woody, I know your shoulder is in bad shape. Let me check it over before you leave." He x-rayed me standing up and he couldn't see the separation. Then he put a weight in my hand and the shoulder just fell apart. Because of the poor healing, calcification had started. He said, "I've got to perform an operation."

They gave me sodium pentothal. That's when they first started using it, in 1948. They said, "We want you to start counting."

I said, "One." I woke up on the edge of the bed with the nurse feeding me. They had my arm all bandaged up like a chicken wing against my chest. They had it so tight the blood couldn't turn the corner. The aching in the joint was terrible. I said, "Nurse, could you please bring this down a little?" She loosened my bandages, and when Doctor Townsend found out, he went through the roof. He said, "For that, I'm going to put you in plaster." He put me in a cast, and I stayed in that Canadian hospital waiting to heal up.

After three weeks, they took the cast off, put me in a sling, and I flew home. That's when I saw my baby girl June for the first time. We named her June after Kenny's wife. She was the most beautiful baby, and she grew into the most beautiful woman. Well, with two kids at home, I learned that $5,000 a year was not enough. I had to find a way to make some more money.

I went to see Cal Eaton and asked him if I could become part of his stable of wrestlers. He said, "Fine; as soon as your shoulder's healed up we'll put you back in the ring." Then Tom Brooks sent me an extra $1,500 to help me get by until the shoulder was fully healed.

I went to the Olympic Auditorium just about every day to exercise and watch the wrestlers work out, stay in touch and visualize the new moves. At first my arm was no bigger than my wrist. I started exercising the arm by just flexing the muscle. Then I got a little five-pound weight and worked out with that. I returned to the ring as soon as I got my physical look back, even though I was still healing inside. The wrestlers said, "We'll take your bumps, Woody, you just wrestle. Don't worry; we ain't going to slam you." They let me heal in the ring.

When some money started coming in, Luana and I began thinking about getting another place to live. With two kids, that one-bedroom apartment in Hollywood was getting pretty small. Luana had a Samoan friend, Chief Santini, who performed a knife dance at the Seven Seas Club in Hollywood. They'd light the tiki torches on stage and the Chief would stand there in his pongee skirt, twirling knives while the natives beat their drums. It was quite exciting. Anyway, the Chief owned a little ranch in Montebello that he was looking to sell. So Luana and I went out to take a look.

It happened that Gorgeous George, a friend of mine and one of the most famous of the old-time wrestlers, had a turkey ranch out there. He raised 12,000 lavender turkeys. He painted them lavender; the whole ranch was painted lavender. I asked George how much it cost to raise turkeys. He said it was very expensive. I told him, "Well, maybe I could raise some chickens." And I bought the ranch.

I raised 4,000 chickens and 1,000 rabbits on this ranch. My kids loved it; it was like a playground. One of the smartest moves I ever made was moving those kids to the country. Right across the street there was a dairy, and as Kalai got older he liked to sneak over there and ride the cows. They could go hiking and fishing out there, too.

The ranch house was quite big. I had enough room for my mother and my brother Baylous. Baylous took care of the place when I wasn't in town. He plucked the chickens and skinned the rabbits. We'd sell the meat, the skins, and the feathers to an old man that used to come by in an old flat-head Chevy pick-up truck. The eggs I'd sell myself at the after-hour spots and night clubs.

Physically I was 100 percent when I went back to Canadian football in 1949. That's when my football career ended. At the start of that season I got hit in mid-air as I was going for a pass. I must have been three feet off the ground when this guy went right through me and busted two ribs over my heart. They couldn't tape them; they couldn't inject novocaine right over the heart. I tried to play, but I was running downfield worrying about who was coming to hit me.

I walked off the field and told Les, "That's it. I'm through!"

He said, "What the hell, Woody, you're in better shape than anybody on the field."

I said, "What do you think I was doing out there. I was listening for the footsteps."

He said, "You're right; that's it."

Many people ask me how you quit playing football and I tell them, "You just run out of guts."

But Tom Brooks gave me my five grand anyway.

CHAPTER SIXTEEN

"Hit That Son of a Bitch, Willie!"

While I was playing football in Canada, Kenny Washington remained with the Rams. He retired after the 1948 season. He sent me a telegram up in Canada asking me to attend his retirement ceremony at the Coliseum. I was recuperating in the hospital; I wired back:

> JUST HAD A SHOULDER OPERATION STOP
> SEE YOU WHEN I GET HOME STOP
>
> WOODY

I got home in time for Kenny's big farewell from the City of Los Angeles. Eighty thousand people showed up, and the Supervisors of Los Angeles presented him with a special plaque honoring Kenny as an outstanding citizen and sportsman. Afterwards, there was a party at Kenny's house. I met Richard Nixon there. I'll never forget him saying to me, "Mr. Strode, if you ever get to Washington, D.C., I want to show you the city."

Kenny played three years for the Rams. He was thirty years old when he retired. He told me, "Hell, even a half-step slower is fatal." When you sidestep a guy, you need that extra step to avoid being hit. "Not only that, I notice I get up a lot slower." Kenny had sense enough to know that sooner or later he would get seriously hurt.

After Kenny retired from football, he tried to get into major league baseball. He had a couple of tryouts as a third baseman for the New York Giants, but it came along too late. He developed some kind of growth on his wrist which hampered his swing. He ended up playing a few games in the semi-pro Pacific Coast League. But here again he had been away too long. At age 31, Kenny's days as a big-time athlete were over.

But Kenny did play some great football for the Rams. In 1947, when he set the record for the longest run from scrimmage, I think he was pretty much considered first string. Whether Kenny was hurt over not getting his chance sooner in the NFL, I don't know. We never discussed it. I think he was deeply hurt over the fact that he never had become a national figure in professional sports. Many of us who were great athletes years ago grow old with that hurt. It's a shame that people have forgotten about Kenny Washington.

When Kenny quit athletics, he fell right into the business world. That wouldn't have happened if he hadn't reached a certain level of fame as an athlete. He went to work for the Buckingham Corporation; they handled the distribution of Cutty Sark Whisky. J. D. Elliot had the prime contract for the United States, and he hired Kenny as his public relations man. Kenny made quite a good living, and he traveled quite a bit, too.

The older Kenny and I got, the less we'd see of each other. After the Rams, we were always separated because of our livelihood. When we got together, we'd make a run at all the bars. He'd get me drunk, and I'd never pay for a drink because everyone gave them to Kenny for free. After six or seven drinks, I'd have to leave him downtown. The trip back to Montebello was too far for me to spend the whole evening with him.

I loved football, and I probably played longer than I should have. When you start getting injured like I did towards the end, that's a sign to hang 'em up. After I retired, I had something to fall back on, wrestling. For five years I stopped watching football; that's how you get it out of your system. One day Kenny and I were sitting in a bar on the West Side. We were watching the Rams and the Redskins play on TV. They had face masks on their helmets. I had never seen that before. I said to Kenny, "What in the hell are they doing now?" I couldn't get over how the game had changed. I couldn't understand how somebody could catch a pass with a couple of bars right across their face.

When I quit football, I came back to Los Angeles and started wrestling full-time. We wrestled all over the City of Los Angeles and the Southland. Cal Eaton put the matches together, and he told me where to be. On Monday nights, I was in San Diego, Tuesdays was Southgate, Wednesdays the Olympic Auditorium, Thursdays was the Valley. On Friday nights, I'd go to Santa Monica and Saturdays was San Bernardino. We'd crisscross Southern California. Then I got stuck on the desert circuit: Fresno, Bakersfield and Indio. Indio's near the border, and the Mexicans used to pack the arenas. They were great fans.

I wrestled Gorgeous George out in Indio. His real name was George Raymond Wagner, but in 1950 he had it legally changed to Gorgeous George. Of course, George wasn't really pretty. He was a big, tough bruiser; he had a body like a block of granite. He had a fat, round face that always looked flushed, like he had just blown up a dozen balloons. His nose was kind of a split-level job; I'm sure he'd broken it several times. George did have good teeth, but he was gorgeous more from his manner than his looks. He used to say, "I do not think I'm gorgeous, but what's my opinion against millions of others?"

George brought in the golden era, when all the main-event wrestlers made fortunes. In those early days of television, the late 40s and early 50s, you could catch wrestling on the tube just about any time. It was the number-one rated show for years, but the TV exposure didn't matter; the fans still packed the arenas. And Southern California was the biggest market. In 1949 George appeared at the Olympic Auditorium thirty-two times and sold it out twenty-seven. He was more popular than just about any movie star. He couldn't ride the train because people would mob him.

They even wrote songs about him. I remember one went:

> *He has an armful of muscle and a head full of curls,*
> *He wrestles with the fellows and thrills all the girls;*
> *a two-ton truck with a velvet sheen,*

171

Gorgeous George is the man I mean.
He has a chest like a mountain and a face like a dream,
He starts women swoonin' and makes men scream.

For years, George was just another wrestler. The Gorgeous bit started one night in Oregon. George stepped in the ring with a beautiful royal-blue, sequined robe his wife made for him. Before the match started, George was very careful taking off the robe. He made sure it didn't touch the canvas and folded it up nice and neat. He laid a towel down on a stool outside the apron and set the robe on that. The fans couldn't stand this ugly wrestler being so prissy about his robe, and they let him have it.

George's wife, Betty Wagner, was sitting up in the stands. Betty had a temper, and she couldn't tolerate the fans heckling and booing George over the robe she had made for him. She stood up and slapped one of the hecklers. When George saw his wife fighting in the stands, he went up to defend her and all hell broke loose.

The next night the arena was sold out; they all came to see the too-neat wrestler. Well, George was no fool; this time he was even more careful taking off his robe and folding it neatly. From that point on, George became a master at antagonizing the crowd. That was the key to success in the wrestling business. And that's how the greatest villain in wrestling history was born.

As the act developed, George hired a valet to help him prepare for his matches. Over the years, George had a number of valets, but they all looked the same. They dressed up in morning clothes; dark jacket with tails, gray, striped pants, vest, bow tie, derby hat and white gloves.

When George entered an arena, "Pomp and Circumstance" would play over the loudspeaker. The spotlight would search for, find, and follow George and his valet as they made their entrance. His valet would always climb into the ring first. He carried a spray bottle of Chanel No. 5 on a silver serving tray. Actually, George called it Chanel No. 10: "Why be half-safe?" The valet would set the tray down, take the perfume and spray the ring, the opponent, the referee, everything in sight. Only then would it be acceptable for George to enter the ring.

Gorgeous George always had his hair done in the latest ladies' fashion. Usually, he had long, flowing, golden curls. He held his 'do in place with a gold hair net and gold bobby pins. He called them Georgie pins, and he would pull them out and throw them to the audience as souvenirs.

Before a match began, George's valet would remove the hair net, and George would walk around the ring slowly, showing off his golden locks. Then the valet would remove his robe and carefully put it away. In his prime, George must have had 1,000 robes. He had every imaginable style and fabric: fur-lined, embroidered, sequined, you name it. Finally, when everything was ready and the ref called the wrestlers to the center of the ring to check them for hidden weapons, George had his valet spray the ref's hands with Chanel No. 10 before he would let the ref touch him.

When I wrestled George, it was one of my easiest matches. He won. Of course, I knew in advance who was going to win, the box office. Everyone made money when they wrestled Gorgeous George. The fans came to see him, not Woody Strode. It was like dancing, and he was leading. You had to allow him to perform.

The only thing wrong with George was his voice. He had that old, rough New York accent with "dems" and "dose." If he had had a high, female voice it would have been perfect, but George never did a lot of talking in the ring. And he'd never get himself soiled, even though he was a dirty fighter. He'd either stick you in the eye and blind you, put his fingers in your mouth and rip or punch you when the referee had his back turned. If he pinned you, he'd have his foot on the rope, which is a disqualification; the referee would never see it. It had to be a good match, but George would always win.

The promoters had to protect their investment. Gorgeous George made over $2 million in the ring way back then. And he died tragically. He died broke and drunk with walking pneumonia in a hotel on Skid Row in downtown Los Angeles. I went to see him during that period. I walked into the room and he was lying down on a dirty mattress on an old steel-frame bed that looked more like a hammock. His forehead was wet with perspiration, and he could barely get the words out between coughs.

He called for his son, and a beautiful, brown-headed kid walked into the room. "Woody, this is my son." He said, "My wife divorced me. She said that I'm always on the road and that I'm not compatible. She used to sew my robes; that's how I made my fortune." He went through the whole trauma with me. It was the first time I had ever seen anyone truly brokenhearted, and he became an alcoholic behind that.

The last thing George ever did was a show in Las Vegas at the Silver Slipper. He would stand up on stage and parade in his outfit and throw Georgie pins to the crowd. Finally, he got too weak and messed-up to make that scene. He was only forty-eight years old when he died and it was over his marriage. He couldn't figure out how the woman he married and went through the whole struggle with could leave him penniless twenty years later.

Now, when they wouldn't allow me to play football in this country and I had to go to Canada, I cried on the phone because I missed Luana so much. I'd been married eight years and now I had to leave. Luana bought and packed all these delicate-looking undershorts for me. I said, "Mama, why are you packing those?"

"Daddy, I don't know where you're going to pull your clothes off." She told me without actually coming out and saying, "I know you're going to go to bed with someone else and that's okay." That's why I appreciate the Hawaiian people. They have a whole different outlook on sex. Before I got shipped overseas at the end of World War II she said, "Daddy, if you're going to sleep with someone, please let it be a prostitute."

I always denied it, "Oh no, Mama, I wouldn't." But she knew; she was shrewd, and as long as I didn't get emotionally involved on the road, she could accept it. That's why we were together forty years.

When I got into wrestling full-time, Luana and the kids never traveled with me. I grew up on the road; that's where I became a man. I took care of everybody at home, my wife, my kids, my brother and my mother. I sent the money home every week. I just kept my expense money.

For my first three years in wrestling, Cal Eaton would not let me leave Southern California. When I wrestled in Burbank, which was quite prejudiced at that time, they used to put Tiny Roebuck, a 300-pound Indian wrestler, in the ring with me as a referee. They put him there to bodyguard me; I didn't know that at the time.

Three years later, when I had really learned the psychology of the profession, they let me travel outside the state. I was like a prize fighter who was brought along slowly. Three years of fighting preliminaries and I was making $300, $400 a week, which was a pretty good living. I couldn't have made that kind of money doing anything else.

I couldn't become a headliner until I learned to let them throw me out of the ring. When they got me near that top rope, I used to hold on for dear life. Finally, I overcame the fear. All you have to do when they toss you out is grab the top rope; that slows you down. When you hit the seat, flop like a sack of potatoes. The first time I made it, it registered: I'm not going to get hurt. We used to shoot our television promotions outside the arenas, and it got so they could body slam me on the concrete. All you have to do is make sure your feet hit first. Then I learned how to pick up a 250-pound guy in an airplane spin. It was all leverage. Jim Londos, the Golden Greek, showed me how to do it by grabbing a guy between the legs and lowering a shoulder into him to lift.

After I became a headliner, I would walk into the ring like I was going on stage to perform Hamlet. The better you looked, the more the women went after you. The women were great wrestling fans. There was a wrestler named Barone Leone, an Italian with long black hair and a thin black moustache who used to eat raw meat on television and yell, "KILL!" Every woman wanted to go to bed with him. Women were more attracted to the wrestlers than the movie stars. They liked the bodies and all that, and they used to love the villains. The women were sadistic.

For nine years, I watched these wrestlers control the town. I watched the cops come in black unmarked wagons to carry the villains away from the arenas. The villains couldn't park their cars at the arenas; the fans would rip them up. And the wrestlers always had big cars, Lincolns and Cadillacs, because they spent so much time on the road. Being on the road was the most dangerous part of wrestling. A wrestler could get killed out there.

One of the first places I hit when they put me on the road was Texas and that was a little strange. I got into the ring down there and the referee had a pistol and blackjack in his pocket. They were running through the introductions and I whispered to the referee, "What's going on?"

"Oh well, we had a race riot here a week ago." There I was stripped naked except for my white shorts and shoes, standing out there like a neon sign. When the match started, I snatched my opponent down on the mat. I said, "Listen you son of a bitch, we're going to wrestle from the floor." I wasn't going to stand up and give those fans a clear shot at me.

I remember Buddy Young would not enter the arena in Dallas because it was segregated seating. Buddy was one of our greatest running backs, from the University of Illinois. In 1954 he was integrating football in the state of Texas. He was playing for the Dallas Texans of the old American Football League. Buddy and I were friends; we all knew one another. He told me, "How can I integrate football and then come and watch you wrestle in a segregated arena?"

I asked the promoters, "If I want to go out in the audience, where would I sit?" Well, because I was a wrestler, they'd let me sit ringside. But my people had to sit way up in the back. I did see the wealthiest black people I ever saw in Dallas, Texas. They became wealthy because of segregation.

The Texas blacks had their own stores, doctors and lawyers; whatever they needed, their own people provided it. In the South, the white man wouldn't compete with you. He allowed you your own piece: "Here, this little piece of shit is yours. Just stay there and nobody will bother you."

When I left the arena in Dallas, I waited out front for Buddy Young to pick me up. A wealthy Texas cowboy approached me and said, "Son, I really enjoyed your match. We don't have a nigger in Texas like you. Welcome to Texas!" That was a compliment.

When Buddy Young arrived, I got in the car and we drove over to his house. We sat around his dining room table drinking beer, eating and talking. I asked, "Buddy, how do you play football under these conditions?"

He said, "You know, when these Texans decided to integrate football, that was it. There isn't anybody stupid enough to cross them and mess with me!" That shows you how the Southerner thought, "This is our nigger, and he's going to play!"

Only one time, in Missouri, did I have to integrate the ring. I got away with it because Gust Karras, the promoter, took me and stuck me in Kansas City, Kansas, right across the state line. They had integrated wrestling there, and Gust stuck me in the ring with a bunch of white villains who beat the crap out of me all night. When I moved across the border to Kansas City, Missouri, I had developed sympathy among the fans. I stepped into their ring on a Saturday night. When the match started, I didn't defend myself for fifteen minutes while that villain pounded me. The crowd started hollering, "WILLIE,"—to the Missouri fans every nigger was named Willie—"HIT THAT SON OF A BITCH!" That's how Americans are; even the most prejudiced want to see a fair fight.

When I stepped out of the ring after that match, the white kids started coming up for autographs. I began signing and they asked, "Who have you wrestled?"

"Barone Leone, Gorgeous George." They looked at me in shock. They had never seen a white man and a black man in the ring before; that was all brand new to them.

When I got to Montana, they were promoting tag-team matches. They gave me an Indian partner because my look is so close to theirs. Kid Fox, my Indian partner, knew I had mixed blood, but we didn't discuss it. Nobody made a big issue out of it, but I'd have felt funny if they had made me stick a feather on my head.

When I went back to Canada to wrestle, Mr. Bell, who owned all the race tracks in Calgary, asked me, "Why don't you advertise your Indian blood?"

I said, "Mr. Bell, all of us in America, all the Negroes are mixed breeds one way or another. If I advertise I'm an Indian, the black people will figure I'm putting them down. The Indians already know. Let's just leave it at that." I didn't want to put a headline out there; that would have been a bad psychological move. That's what being a breed does to you.

When I wrestled in Canada, the whole Blackfoot Nation would show up at the arena. They walked in wearing their deerskins and moccasins. The squaws would have papooses strapped on their backs. They'd bring their dogs with them. They would stand in a tight group, smoking pipes and watching. The promoters would approach me and say, "Woody, all the goddamned Indians are here again!"

"Well, goddamit, don't insult anyone. Send the Chief back here to see me." One night the Blackfoot Chief sent a squaw to my dressing room before a match. She measured my feet, my inseam, my waist, my shoulders, even my hands. She made me a complete deerskin outfit. Then they made me an honorary member of their tribe.

They didn't like the way the villains were treating me, so they taught me how to fight a bear. They brought me to their village and drew a ring in the dirt. They had this old brown bear, and they tied his mouth shut with a leather strap; they had his claws cut off. I stood in the middle of the ring with this bear while the Indians shouted instructions I couldn't understand. That's how primitive it was in Canada.

I wrestled only four nights a week up there because we spent a lot of time on the road. Sometimes, we'd have to drive in weather thirty degrees below zero. It didn't bother the Canadians; they'd drive ninety miles an hour listening to the weather report on the radio, trying to outrun a storm. They'd try to hit the wild game with the car. If they hit something, we'd throw it in the trunk and it was so cold it would last all the way from Winnipeg to Regina and all the way back to Calgary. Then we'd pull it out and have it for dinner.

The Canadians would get on some desolate, iced-over highway and never hit the brake. They'd just gear down if they had to. One time, between Edmonton and Calgary, we slid off the road in a four-door Lincoln Continental. I was with some French-Canadian wrestlers who averaged about six-feet-four, 250 pounds; I was the littlest guy in the car. The car hit a snow drift and ended up in a ditch. Get caught in a situation like that and you'd freeze to death.

Six wrestlers got out of the car, picked it up, and put it back on the highway.

Well, before I was done wrestling, I had wrestled all over Canada, the Midwest, the South, and Hawaii. I was on television quite a bit; I think KTLA, one of the local TV stations in Los Angeles, still has some footage of me wrestling. That's how a Hollywood theatrical agent discovered me. He saw me wrestling on the tube, and he came after me to do some half-assed acting jobs. He signed me up, and I slowly fell into the acting business. After a certain point, I realized I could make a living at it, and I never looked back.

CHAPTER SEVENTEEN

An Introduction to Hollywood

In 1951, I went over to Honolulu to wrestle for five months. Hawaii was a paradise for wrestlers. The Hawaiians loved the show and paid good money for the top draws. Jim Londos hung out there quite a bit; that's how he kept his golden color. I didn't need to work on my tan, but I could make more money in one day over there than I could in a whole week over here. One night I earned 600 dollars for a fifteen-minute bout.

After the Honolulu tour, the promoters wanted me to go to Tokyo and stay another five months. Tokyo was another financial paradise for wrestlers. I could've made a lot of money over there, but my kids were starting to grow up. Kalai was five, June was three, and they barely knew who their father was. Luana was browbeating me to spend more time at home. So I took a break from wrestling.

I got a job working at Chrysler. I was thirty-six years old and had never worked a regular job. They put me on the brake assembly line. That was a good job because the brake line you could control; you could stop it down if you had to. The other lines were running all the time; there was no way for those guys to shut down and catch up or rest. But if I got behind, I'd just stop, put in that little cotter pin and send it on its way.

While I was working at Chrysler, I ran into some friends I didn't know I had. They were fans from the football years. They owned a big Esso gas station on East 2nd Street. They asked me what I was up to.

"I'm working for Chrysler."

"Oh well, why don't you come work at our gas station? We'll give you a hundred dollars a week, clear."

I said, "Okay, but I've never worn a money changer."

They dressed me up in a brown monkey suit. It had a short, waist-length jacket, and the pants had a black strip down the side. I wore a little oval patch above my left breast pocket that said, "Woody." And they made me wear one of those service station hats that make you look like you're wearing half a football on top of your head. On Saturday nights I was out there making change on eighteen pumps. When we closed, I'd mop up around all eighteen. That kept me in shape. I've never had any ego about how I earn a buck. If I could make a buck, I'd go down, get a truck full of carrots and sell them.

I was working at the gas station when Sid Gold called me. Sid was a theatrical agent. He saw me wrestling on the tube, and he said, "Woody Strode, I'm a big fan. You have a look I think I could sell. Would you be interested in making some money?" He said the magic words, and he lined me up with a tryout for the *Ramar of the Jungle* television series.

They built the Ramar set at the old Nasseur Studios, which is Fox Television today, over on Sunset and Van Ness. *Ramar* was shot on stage four, and in those days they would create an entire jungle scene inside the sound stage. They started with a huge painted backdrop maybe 120 feet long and fifty feet high. They would paint a few large trees and bushes in the foreground and then everything else would fall off in perspective towards the horizon. Then they'd build out from the backdrop. They'd lay down a carpet of grass, throw a little dirt on it, wheel in trees and bushes on platforms, throw a few vines around and finish it off with some grass huts. It didn't always look real, but it got the job done.

Ramar of the Jungle starred Jon Hall as Ramar. Of course, he was very handsome; Hollywood wasn't into ugly actors. And he

182

had a beautiful body; he was half-Tahitian. He's the one who dove off the high mast in John Ford's *Hurricane,* a classic picture.

Anyway, they had a casting call at the studio; I drove over there. On the way I was thinking about the jungle shows I had seen and how the actors would always speak gibberish, pretending it was some African dialect. When I got there, all the other actors were milling around talking about subtleties of performance and methods of acting. I thought to myself, "No, that doesn't work." Then I met a man on the set from South Africa. We got to talking and I asked him, "Do you know any African words?"

He said, "I know a little Swahili," and he taught me a few words. So when I got up and tried out, it actually sounded like I was saying something.

That's not why they chose me. What they needed were some African warriors, and because of my physical presence, I fit the role better than the actors. With me, all they had to do was give me a loin cloth and put a spear in my hand. I wasn't quite dark enough to play a real African, but in those days it didn't matter. Plus, I could take the spear and hit a tree with it; they didn't need to run a wire for me. I ended up doing nine of those *Ramar* shows in a row.

My first big payday came a couple of years later fighting Johnny Weissmuller. Johnny got too old to make the Tarzan pictures, so they developed the *Jungle Jim* TV series especially for him. He played a white hunter-adventurer on the loose in the African wilds. He called me on the phone and said, "Come on, Woody, come and fight me on the show!"

Johnny Weissmuller knew me through Luana. Because of his swimming background, he was knowledgeable about the Hawaiians. I never knew him as a great swimmer; I knew him strictly from the Tarzan pictures. As Tarzan he was like an alligator in the water. He was the only guy who could hit the water and keep his body up; he kept his head entirely out of the water. When he was really moving, his arms looked like a cartoon character's legs running. His arms would spin around like a windmill in a typhoon, and the water would make a V around him, like the bow of a boat.

They offered me $300 to fight Johnny on his TV show. The

camera was on me for one shot. We were fighting, and I threw Johnny down. He was on his back; I dove at him, and he threw me over with his feet. Bam, he won the fight. We shot that out at Universal, and when I got my $300, they made me promise not to tell the other actors how much I made. That was a whole week's pay and the fight scene only took two hours.

That was the twilight of Johnny Weissmuller's career. He got into the swimming pool business after *Jungle Jim*, then he got sick and went downhill from there. But I did get a chance to tell him he was my idol. I remember he asked me, "How do you stay in shape, Woody?"

"I used to watch you, Johnny, and I worked out every day because I wanted to be just like you." I wanted to swing through the trees with a chimpanzee as my best friend and fight lions to the death with my bare hands.

In those beginning years I couldn't make a living as an actor, so I went back to wrestling in between acting jobs. I was wrestling up at the Hollywood Legion Stadium on El Centro Avenue when I got my first big contract from the studios. RKO was making a $2 million picture called *Androcles and the Lion*, based on the play by George Bernard Shaw. Alan Young was the star; he later played Wilbur on the *Mr. Ed* TV show. They were looking for someone who was in good shape to play the lion in a costume. The producer was a Pakistani named Gabriel Pascal, a very wealthy man. I interviewed with him, and he gave me the job, $500 a week for eight weeks.

To prepare me for the role, they sent me out to the World Jungle Compound, about 40 miles outside of Los Angeles. I worked with a guy named Mel Koontz; he was the lion trainer. For three weeks, I went out to that lion farm, and I brought the kids with me every day. That was Luana's idea, and I was so mad at her after the first day. When June, who was barely talking, saw those strange-looking animals she just welled up and started crying to the point where I thought she'd never shut up. She still remembers it.

We went out there for three weeks and watched the lions. I'd study their walk, how they roared, how they ate, all their mannerisms. Then I'd get down on all fours and try to imitate them. Kalai would get down there with me letting out his little roar. It was like a vacation; I thought I was stealing the money.

Three weeks later, they called me into the studio and measured me for the lion suit. The suit was made out of real lion skin that was cut and sewn into a pair of overalls. The paws were made out of foam rubber that had fur and claws glued on. My upper arms were all tied up in a lion skin vest that was more like a corset. They let me sit in that suit for one week getting used to it. I had to learn to move and breathe all tied up like that.

A week later, they brought the lion head. That was the gimmick, it weighed forty pounds. It had a football headgear inside that strapped to my head. My eyes looked out through the lion's neck. With my arms all tied up, I could just barely touch the lion's mouth.

The first day of shooting, the music was playing and Alan Young was dancing. I was sitting in the background on my haunches like a big cat would. All I had to do was follow Alan Young's movement with the lion's head. Special effects got behind me and pulled wires and tweaked levers. They kept my mouth moving and my eyes blinking. That first shot went on for two hours and because I was on my knees the entire time, my circulation had quit. They laid me down and pulled the lion head off. I look at the director and said, "You know, you guys got all that money back in two hours." I lost seven pounds of water a day making that movie.

So that was the beginning for me, and that's when I began to meet the stuntmen. They told me they all turned the job down. I said, "Yeah, but I got $500 a week!"

They said, "Yeah, well it was worth about $2,500 a week! That's why no one else would take the job." I'm just glad I was in good enough shape to survive it.

I developed a good relationship with Gabriel Pascal and I thought that would keep me working. But he died shortly after we finished the picture, and I went back to wrestling. Finally, *The Ten Commandments* came along. That one starred Charlton Heston and was directed by Cecil B. DeMille.

DeMille was quite a man. He was a small, round, bookish-looking man with a balding head, but he had a dynamic personality.

He wore a silver whistle around his neck and always had a mega-phone in his hand. Wherever he went, he had a lackey who trailed him with a stool. If DeMille went to sit, the stool was there waiting for him. He didn't turn and snap or motion. He sat and the stool was there.

DeMille probably did more than any other man to make Hollywood the center of the film world. His influence is legendary, and he had a passion for Biblical stories, which he would turn into giant spectacles with casts of thousands. DeMille loved physical actors. That's why Victor Mature played Samson. That's why he picked Charlton Heston to play Moses. When he saw my photo-graph, I had the look, so I got a job playing a slave. I was Moses' mother's litter carrier.

Chico Day, who was DeMille's first assistant, contacted me and offered me $500 a week for five weeks' work. I accepted. Well, in the meantime, they couldn't find the right black actor to play the King of Ethiopia. Chico called me and said, "Woody, Mr. DeMille would like you to meet him at the studio."

"What's it all about?"

He said, "You might play the King of Ethiopia."

"How long is the job?"

"One week."

I said, "Chico, I don't want to be a king. I don't want to be a star. I had five weeks guaranteed as a slave!"

He said, "Well, you've got to see the old man."

So I walked into his oak-lined office. He was sitting with his feet up on the desk, looking through one of his Bibles. He had a collection of rare Bibles. He looked up, and I looked at him, looked him dead in the eye. He said, "Son, you mind dropping your pants? I'd like to see your legs."

I had my jeans on; I unbuttoned them and lowered 'em down until they were baggin' around my ankles. He looked; he rubbed his chin; he said, "Fine. You're the King of Ethiopia." Chico and I left the office, and I was cussing at him all the way across the lot. I said, "Goddamit Chico, I just lost a five-week job. You're making a movie star out of me and now I've only got one week's work."

He said, "Shut up, Woody. We'll work something out."

Four days later, I was finished as the King of Ethiopia. I went to wardrobe and returned the king costume, $2,000 worth of feathers, lion skins, boas and jewelry. Chico called down and told them to put me into a slave's outfit. I put on the skirt, the sandals, and the little skull cap with the brass knobs around the forehead. Chico came down and dragged me to the set. I had to stand around in that costume for two hours waiting for Mr. DeMille to finish directing Chuck Heston in a scene.

When he was done, Chico got the old man's attention and brought him over to look at me. He didn't recognize me. Chico said, "Do you know who this is, Mr. DeMille?"

"No I don't. Who is it?"

"That's Woodrow!"

Mr. DeMille would never call me Woody; that was too crude. For my screen billing, if you ever see *The Ten Commandments,* it says Woodrow Strode. He said, "Oh well, Woodrow would be fine for the slave scene." Then the old man leaned into me and said, "Son, don't you ever tell anyone you got two roles in my picture." And not only did I get my five weeks as a slave, I ended up working fifteen weeks.

Just before Mr. DeMille finished shooting the picture, Luana presented him with a very rare King James Bible. She found it in a little bookstore downtown. He was directing a scene that was costing $10,000 a minute. In between takes, Luana walked over to him about as shyly as I'd ever seen her. She presented him with the Bible. He stopped and talked for fifteen minutes. He said to everybody, "I want to thank Luana Strode for this magnificent Bible. I've searched everywhere for this particular edition. You know, I collect these things."

When I left the picture he said, "Son, I know you wrestle. But I don't care where you are in the world, if I'm going to make a picture, you get on a plane and come home because you've got a job." Well, as fate would have it, *The Ten Commandments* was the last picture DeMille directed.

With no other opportunities as an actor, I went back on the wrestling circuit. In those beginning years I had no identity. I had to rely on Sid Gold to find me acting jobs that paid good enough and lasted long enough, to make it worth my while not to wrestle. I was strictly a mechanic. They told me what to do; I did it, and took the money and got out of there.

In 1958, I landed a part in *Tarzan's Fight for Life* and that started me on the road to recognition as an actor. Sol Lesser was the producer of the original Tarzan pictures; then Sy Weintraub bought the movie rights. Sy told me I had the part but that I'd have to shave my hair off. I said, "You've got to be crazy!" They offered me $500 a week.

I said, "Okay!"

I went to the make-up artist, and he said, "Woody, let's cut a Mohawk in there before we take it all off." He made the cut.

"Woody, the Mohawk looks great."

"Yeah, well how in the hell do I have a Mohawk in the middle of the African jungle?"

He said, "Let's see what Sy Weintraub thinks."

We went to see Sy. He started arguing with Sol Lesser about what kind of Indian I looked like. Somebody said, "A Mohawk Indian," and Weintraub said, "No, Cheyenne." That went back and forth for a while. After they got through with the discussion, Sy Weintraub said, "Yeah, he looks perfect for the African part. Just put the African scars on him." They took all kinds of license— whatever looked good.

We made the picture at the MGM studios. They wanted me to fight a lion and they only wanted to pay me $350 to do it. Well, I knew what that job was worth from *Androcles and the Lion*. I told them for a thousand bucks I'd do it. We got into a little sashay about that, and that's the only scene where they had a stuntman stand in for me. But I did the whole film with a Mohawk, and after we got done, I didn't know what to do about my haircut. The only thing I could do was shave it all off and let it grow back.

I was ashamed of my bald head because I was still wrestling. When I stepped into the ring, I wanted to be Gorgeous George. Beautiful hair and locks and looking as good as I could. That was part of the show. Now I had a bald head. I wore a hat to hide my embarrassment. I looked like a robot, all my bone structure was sticking out. My cheek bones were jumping off my face. But everybody said, "Magnificent!" And when I went to interview for my next picture, *Pork Chop Hill* with director Lewis Milestone, he said, "The bald head's perfect."

People started comparing me to Yul Brynner, whom I got to know working on *The Ten Commandments.* When Yul had hair he was just another actor. It was his role in *The King and I,* with the shaved head, that made his career. And when he got darkened down, he looked just like my brother. He had the same type body as me, just on a smaller scale. When you see him on the screen, you'll notice we have similar qualities. And people remember me now because of my shaved head. If I had worn a suit of clothes, what could I have done?

After I finished working for eight weeks on the Tarzan film with Gordon Scott, my agent said, "Boy, I think you can make a living as an actor. You've got a little bank account; why don't you stick around?" Sid was always pulling on me to stay in town. And that's when I gave up the wrestling career for good.

After *Tarzan* I picked up the role in *Pork Chop Hill* with Gregory Peck. From there I went to *Spartacus* with Kirk Douglas and from *Spartacus* to *The Last Voyage* with Robert Stack and Dorothy Malone. Then I starred in John Ford's *Sergeant Rutledge.* All this happened in 1958 and 1959. In 1960 I had four pictures in release with the biggest actors in the world. By then I had a whole career going. But I was never under contract to the studios; they weren't signing black actors. Only our comedians, the song-and-dance men, had contracts. Bill Bojangles Robinson, Hattie McDaniel, and Stepin' Fetchit were some of our early stars. They had the "Yassuh" approach. That's the only way they could make it. Well, I wasn't funny, and I couldn't dance, but I always seemed to have something going. So I wasn't the first, but I was one of the first to play dignified roles.

I remember when I was in Las Vegas making *The Professionals* for Columbia Pictures about the time Floyd Patterson was fighting Muhammad Ali. The black actors were criticizing Stepin' Fetchit. He was one of our greatest comedians and the first black actor to get star billing. I took a stand for him. I said, "If it hadn't been for Stepin' Fetchit, I wouldn't be here. Somebody had to start it."

They're going to do his story some day and all this history will come out. John Ford loved the guy; so did Will Rogers. In fact, John Ford directed a couple of pictures in which Will and Step shared star billing. As a child, the only black movie star I had ever heard of was Stepin' Fetchit. He made two million dollars during the 1930s. He owned sixteen cars. I saw him when I was a kid; he was driving a pink convertible Rolls Royce.

CHAPTER EIGHTEEN

Buffalo Soldier

In Hollywood today, Harry Belafonte is by default, the top Negro star, actor, producer, having completed a historic bolt from oblivion to world wide fame. Sidney Poitier is the highest paid motion picture performer. Who can demand as much as $150,000 plus percentage for a movie. An outstanding teacher as well as one of filmland's finest actors, Juano Hernandez is the dean, or the "elder statesman" of the clan. But the busiest, most promising of them all, the fastest rusher toward the wonderful state of stardom is Woody Strode, the marvelously built, studious and hard working former football, track and wrestling hero.

That ran in *Ebony* magazine in 1959, right after I finished working on *Pork Chop Hill*. Here's how I got that job. A black actor named Jimmy Edwards also worked out of Sid Gold's office. Jimmy was famous for a Stanley Kramer film called *Home of the Brave*. You've got to see that one, it's a classic.

Home of the Brave came out in 1949. It's about segregation in the Army during the second world war. Jimmy played the lead, a black soldier who gets more abuse from his own men than he gets from the enemy, but by the end of the picture we learn he's an equal. Well, that was probably the finest job that had been done by a black actor in the motion pictures.

Home of the Brave was the highlight of Jimmy Edwards' movie career. There wasn't much for him after that, and it broke his heart. He drank heavily, couldn't control it, and died of a massive heart attack. He got lulled to sleep by Hollywood because he thought he was an equal. He was a nice-looking black, dark, handsome and a great actor. He was a stage actor, although I don't know much about that part of his career. He found out color was the whole thing. I had a personal relationship with Jimmy, and he warned me about becoming involved socially in Hollywood. He told me, "Woody, you'll never be white. Don't try to become part of their society."

I was lucky. I had good advice all the way through my career. I watched Paul Robeson, the great singer and actor whom I knew, get destroyed. He was one of the finest blacks we ever had. I saw what happened to these guys, and I learned from them. I remember when Sid Gold first picked me up, I had the spear in my hand. He said, "Woody, why don't you go to acting class?"

I said, "Look at the black actors. They're starving to death. I'm not going to school to study, become an artist, and then fall apart." I never tried to take acting too seriously.

Anyway, I was in Sid Gold's office one day and Jimmy Edwards said, "Woody, I just got a part in Lewis Milestone's new picture, and there's a part in it that's perfect for you. Take this script, go home, learn the lines, and then we'll go over it." That was *Pork Chop Hill*. Milestone was the one who made *All Quiet on the Western Front,* which set the standard for all war pictures.

Pork Chop Hill is based on a true story. It's about a group of American soldiers who were ordered to hold a hillside in Korea for twenty-four hours until peace could be declared. I played the part of Private Franklin, a reluctant soldier. He saw no reason why he should get himself killed fighting the Koreans, fighting for a cause he didn't understand. Several times during the film, Franklin shirks his duties. Gregory Peck, the commanding officer, is constantly on top of Franklin, trying to get him to shape up.

There's a bunker scene near the end of the picture. The Koreans have taken over our trenches. Gregory Peck is looking for Franklin. He knows Franklin is ducking out of the fighting. He walks to a bunker, sticks his head in, and says, "Is anybody in there?"

There's a long silence; I'm hiding in the shadows. I say, "Don't you move, I'm aiming straight at your belly. What's the counter-sign?"

"Oh Franklin, you know there isn't any countersign."

"The hell there ain't. They gave it to us last night. Now you just say those words or I'll shoot."

"Franklin, everybody's fighting and dying. . . ."

"Well, you ought to see how I live back home. Hell, I ain't so sure I would die for that. I'll be damned if I'll die for Korea."

It was a nice scene, and what James Edwards did was teach me to underplay. Before I auditioned for the part, I went home and learned the lines and then met him up at his house. It was like an emergency course. He would play the scene for me, then I would step in and copy him. He said, "Woody, you're so big. Don't shout the lines, underplay, just let the words come out." And before I went on the interview with Sy Bartlett, the producer, and Mile-stone, Jimmy said, "When you get to the office, if you hear the other actors reading, get out of the room. Don't get on their level." He was afraid if I heard their performance, I'd do it the same way.

I went to the audition and waited. I heard the other actors through the door. They were shouting, "DON'T YOU MOVE, I'M AIMING STRAIGHT AT YOUR BELLY."

I told the secretary, "I'm going into the bathroom. Would you knock when they're ready for me?"

They called my name, and I slid into the office. I had the script rolled up in the back pocket of my blue jeans. I didn't know how to act properly. I said, "I've got a scene for you," and I played the bunker scene. I reached way down to the bottom of my stomach and pulled the lines out in a whisper. "Don't you move, I'm aiming straight at your belly." Menacing. If I was a midget, I would have had to shout, but I had stature so I underplayed. Well, every black actor in Hollywood showed up for that job, and I got it.

When it actually came time to film the bunker scene, I got sick to my stomach. I asked Jimmy, "Why?"

He said, "When you get mad, you're used to letting it out, hitting somebody. You can't do that here. You've got to hold it inside. That's what's making you sick. You've got to let that emotion work for you."

193

I was in over my head, but Jimmy walked me through it. And that turned out to be one of the best scenes in the picture.

There's another scene in *Pork Chop Hill* where Gregory Peck and I are walking up a hill. We have a confrontation. Five minutes before they rolled the camera, Jimmy was coaching me from the sideline. I made the march up the hill. I played the perfect scene. Milestone yelled, "CUT. PERFECT! PRINT IT!" I didn't look at Lewis; I didn't look at Gregory Peck; I looked at James Edwards to see how I'd done. Jimmy grabbed me by the arm, shook me hard, and said, "Woody, you son of a bitch. That's your director; that's your star; they hired you. Why the hell are you looking at me?"

"Because you're the one who taught me how to do this stuff!"

Pork Chop Hill was my first good dramatic role. The reviews weren't great, but I got one good review in the *Los Angeles Examiner* from Max Stiles, a writer who had known me as an athlete.

BIG STRIDE FOR WOODY STRODE

Woody, who the late famed artist Stowitts claimed has the finest physique of any athlete he ever saw, plays in this picture of the Korean war a role that should put him well along the way already followed so successfully by Chuck Connors, the old first baseman of the Angels.

FIRST TIME HE EVER WORE CLOTHES IN A FILM

The voice out of the dark came first. After a minute or so, not realizing it was Woody all the while, I wondered when Strode was going to come on the scene. And then, suddenly, there in the darkness, I was able to recognize him. He looked like a brown man's Yul Brynner with a deadly rifle in his hands and hate in his eyes.

This was the first time Strode ever wore clothes in a picture, and his transformation from a body into a fine, competent actor left me actually amazed.

I went straight from *Pork Chop Hill* to *Spartacus*, the biggest picture in the world at that time. *Spartacus* is about a Roman slave, trained to be a gladiator, who escapes and leads a slave army against the Roman Empire. Dalton Trumbo wrote the screenplay based on the novel by Howard Fast. Stanley Kubrick directed and Laurence

Olivier, Charles Laughton, Peter Ustinov, Tony Curtis, Jean Simmons, and Kirk Douglas starred. Kirk Douglas played Spartacus.

All the primary shooting was done on the back lot at Universal. My whole fight sequence was done out there. They went somewhere in Ventura to shoot the slaves revolting. And they went to Spain and hired the Spanish Army to stage the big battle scene.

They paid the Spanish Army one dollar per man. If they had used American extras, it would have cost ninety dollars per man. They got 10,000 soldiers for $10,000. The film cost $12 million and when you see the sets, the scenery, the costumes, they couldn't duplicate that film today for $100 million. It took Stanley Kubrick two years to make that picture. He was thirty-one years of age; he had made *Paths of Glory* at twenty-seven. A genuine camera nut, he really knew how to construct a shot.

Kubrick couldn't find anyone physical enough for my part in *Spartacus*. They needed a black actor who could scale a twelve-foot wall up to a balcony where Sir Laurence Olivier was sitting, watching the fighting in an arena down below. The first hop up the wall was ten feet. I had a triton in my right hand; it was twenty-five pounds of wood and iron with three sharp points like arrowheads. After the first hop I had to reach, grab a wire with my left hand and pull myself all the way up to the ledge of the balcony. I was going to kill Sir Laurence with the triton. Well, even at forty-five years of age, I was about the only actor in the world who could do that stunt.

Here's how Dick Williams of the *Los Angeles Times* described the scene.

> . . . and when enraged slave Woody Strode charges Olivier and friends, the Roman sharply stabs him in the neck, although the slave has already been skewered by a guard's spear, and blood spurts up over Olivier's face. This is gore unlimited when displayed in technicolor on a giant screen.
>
> Some of the film's most absorbing moments are the well-shot sequences of the gladiators being trained: the petrifying clash between Douglas, armed with short Thracian sword, and Strode with forked triton and net . . .

Kirk Douglas and I played slaves sent to this gladiator school run by Peter Ustinov. Ustinov explained his role this way: "I play a sort of headmaster whose specialty is teaching men to carve each other up for the sport of patricians." Well, the patricians decide they want to see Kirk and me fight to the death.

I had to learn to fight Kirk from a crouch like an animal. Kirk is only five-feet-seven or eight, I'm six-four, so I had to crouch down to make it look like a fair fight. Even though I fight him from a squat, when you see the picture, you know I'm bigger, but Kirk was in great shape, so it was believable.

Some actors, like Alan Ladd, are self-conscious about their height. They used to dig a hole for whomever was acting with him. The other actor would stand in that hole and that would bring them eye-to-eye. When Alan Ladd did a picture with Sophia Loren, she had to lie down on the beach so people wouldn't see how much bigger she was. I noticed that right away. But then I'd look at an actor like Jimmy Cagney. He wasn't mixed up emotionally about his height. I remember he fought Mike Mazurki in a film; Mazurki was also a wrestler turned actor. Mike went about six-feet-five, Cagney couldn't have been over five-feet-seven, and Cagney kicked the shit out of him using karate. That's how good an actor Cagney was; he had the attitude that made it believable.

Kirk Douglas had that same tough-guy attitude. He and I rehearsed our fight scene for three weeks before Kubrick rolled any film. For eight hours a day we'd stand in one foot of sand, sweat pouring out of our bodies. Kirk and I each wore a piece of cloth around our waists that looked like a diaper, sandals and a leather and chain-mesh protector over our left arms and shoulders. Kubrick, with his pants rolled up and a golf-type hat on his head, would circle us, looking through a lens he wore around his neck.

I had the triton and a net that was like a small fishing net. Kirk had a short, broad sword and a shield. I'd throw the net and try to tie up his sword or tangle his feet; he'd counter by swiping at me with the sword. I'd try to poke him with the triton, and he'd block it with the shield. It was offense and defense, circling, looking for an opening. After three weeks it became like a ballet. And the weapons were real; they didn't need to add any sound effects.

196

The most dangerous shot is when I just graze Kirk with the points of my triton. It was like throwing a phony punch; I had to just miss, and the camera angle had to be just right. Except it was more dangerous because the spear was heavy, long, and hard to control. Special effects put red paint on the points of my spear. Kirk was standing an arm's length, a spear's length, and six inches away from me. Kubrick set the camera at an angle behind him. Kirk said to me, "Woody, if we get this shot, and you don't open me up, we're going to get good and drunk tonight."

It was the last shot in the sequence and Kubrick said we'd only do one take because it was so dangerous. When we hit our marks, Kubrick yelled, "Now!" I swiped. I had to be perfect, and we got the shot. Afterwards, I met Kirk in the dressing room. He pulled out a bottle of whiskey, and we downed a few stiff ones.

That fight scene is probably my most famous moment on the screen, and it lasts only seven minutes. When Stanley Kubrick finished the film, it was six hours long; the studio made him cut it in half. And they wouldn't let him make the final cut. My fight scene would have lasted fifteen minutes. I just wish I had what they threw away; Stanley Kubrick was a genius.

After four months, I left *Spartacus* to work on two other films, *The Last Voyage* and *Sergeant Rutledge,* and then came back to *Spartacus* to work the last day of the picture. It was a Saturday and that meant golden time, double overtime. All I had to do was my opening scene where I come on the set and wash my face. Kirk Douglas turns to me and says, "What's your name?"

Slowly, I turn to face him. "You don't want to know my name, and I don't want to know yours. Maybe one day I might have to kill you!"

The Last Voyage was an Andrew Stone film. It's a good action picture, and you can still catch it on the tube once in a while. It's about a luxury liner that starts to go down because of fire and explosions aboard the ship. I play a crew man who helps Robert Stack save Dorothy Malone. She gets caught under a big pile of debris; we save her just before the ship goes down.

Andrew Stone wrecked a real luxury liner, the *Ile de France,* in Osaka Harbor. The Japanese navy surrounded the liner, and they started to flood the dining room with sea water. The dikes broke, the walls shifted, and 5,000 tons of water rushed in. The ship took on a twenty-seven degree list; it almost turned over in the harbor. You see it all happen in *The Last Voyage,* it's unbelievable.

We stayed at the Osaka Grand Hotel, one of the fanciest hotels in the world at that time. It was all steel and reflective glass; that was a brand-new look in 1959. And that's when I first saw a transistor radio. I bought one at the store in the hotel. I walked outside, pulled up the antennae and got the BBC. That was magic.

When I got home, John Ford was waiting for me. His chauffeur, Bill—we became dear friends—came to the Selznick Studios and told me the old man wanted to see me. When I arrived at his office, the first thing Mr. Ford said was, "How's Luana?"

He said, "Did you know your wife went to school with my children?" Like I said before, John Ford would vacation on his yacht in Hawaii. He sent his son and daughter over there to go to high school; that's where they met Luana. He knew my wife's mother and all the Kanakas; he knew the whole family.

He said, "I adopted the Wai boys." Well, I knew that because I played football with the Wai boys at UCLA. One of them played second-string end behind me, and John Ford's daughter used to pout all the time because I was the first-stringer. Anyway, we talked and finally he said, "I hear you're trying to be an actor."

I said, "Well, you know, say the line, get the money." I was underplaying him.

He said, "I got a little thing going called *Sergeant Rutledge.* I want you to play the title role." I didn't get too excited because I thought he was joking.

John Ford was interested in telling a story using the Ninth and Tenth Cavalry as the backbone. After slavery came the last of the great Indian wars. Around 1866 the United States government built a cavalry out of former slaves, young, tall, strong Negroes who could ride horses. They were trained to think and act like Indians. They learned to fight hand-to-hand and with a knife. They learned to use a rifle. They put pebbles under their tongues; that's how you get moisture in the desert. They learned to track and read smoke signals, and they ran, ran, ran to get into condition.

They were led by white officers; the highest rank a black soldier could reach was first sergeant. And after they were trained, the government set them loose on the Indians like you would a bloodhound on a fox. When the Indians first saw them, it was the dead of winter. The soldiers hid in the snow under buffalo skins, so they became known to the Indians as the buffalo soldiers.

The buffalo soldiers would track down the Indians; then the infantry would come in and wipe them out. The last of the great Indian leaders, like Geronimo, the Apache chief, were chased down by the Ninth and Tenth Cavalry. I learned that history from my mother; she grew up while that was still going on.

Sergeant Rutledge is about a top sergeant in the Ninth Cavalry. He's accused of murdering his Post Commander and raping his daughter. They catch Sergeant Rutledge at the scene of the crime; the major and his daughter are lying dead on the floor. The sergeant would have been a cinch to die in that generation.

It turns out the father of a young boy, who was a friend of the dead girl, did the killing and the raping. They found a little gold cross the girl wore in his coat. There's a big trial and Sergeant Rutledge is exonerated.

John Ford had a big fight with Warner Bros. because they wanted an established actor like Sidney Poitier or Harry Belafonte to play the title role. Ford said, "They aren't tough enough!" He didn't care that I didn't have a lot of acting experience. He wanted somebody who could portray the image of a fighting man. He didn't want an actor who needed a double. John Ford had power; he won his fight with the studio, and I got the part.

He told me, "Woody, I've had a terrible time. I had to fight to get you. The studio figures you aren't an actor, and I told them it had to be you. Can you ride a horse?"

"Yes, sir!" In truth, I hadn't been on a horse for ten years.

He said, "You're going to lead a cavalry charge and there's no way I can use a double. You'll have all the Indians chasing you, the chief and all his braves."

"Yes, sir!" And I started shaking.

To prepare me for the role, they flew me to Ace Hudkin's ranch in Arizona, and I trained for four days. They gave me a bay-colored, combination quarter horse and thoroughbred with four white stockings and a white blaze on his forehead. It was a beautiful animal and one of the finest running horses around. The first thing John Ford wanted to see was how I got on the horse. He said, "You're a cavalry first sergeant and you've got to mount this horse properly."

Well, this horse was fiery and smart. A horse knows when you don't know what you're doing. I stepped up, made a slow approach. I grabbed the reins in my left hand, put my boot in the stirrup, and grabbed the horn with my right hand. I was holding the reins too loose, trying to coordinate all this movement and trying to make it look good for the old man. I was looking at my boot in the stirrup when this horse swung his head around to hit me. I just did get out of the way or he would have knocked me cold. Cliff Lyons, the cowboy in charge, said, "Woody, I'd better give you a tamer horse."

I was disgraced. John Ford was off to the side shaking his head. I said, "No, this is the one that can carry me." Four days later I looked like I had been born in a saddle. I was confident. Riding a horse is like riding a bicycle; once you learn, you never forget.

The whole production company assembled at the Navajo reservation, which was also in Arizona, and we started shooting the film. In my opening scene, I'm riding to escape, because I know the Army is going to hang me for murder and rape. I have to run my horse along a ridge, pull up, and survey the scene below. Two hundred yards down the canyon, I see the Indians waiting to ambush my unit. I have to make a choice: should I help my men from being massacred or should I escape? Well, you know I've got to help my men. I pull my horse around and start my run 200 yards down the mountainside. I cross the Pecos River and save my unit on the other side.

As I started down the mountain, I had this crazy idea. I pulled my rifle and carried it, John Wayne-style, over my head. I didn't realize that nine-pound Winchester was going to weigh about 150 pounds by the time I got out in the middle of the river. About half way across I could feel myself starting to roll out of the saddle. I just barely made it up the embankment on the other side. I skidded to a stop. I yelled, "THE INDIANS!"

Ford screamed, "CUT!," and I fell out of the saddle.

When we really got into shooting the picture, John Ford played every scene for me. He would stand in front of the camera and play my part; then I would step out there and try to do it exactly like he showed me. Sometimes I would be listening to him, but I wouldn't be looking at him. Boy, that would really make him angry. He'd scream at me, "WHY AREN'T YOU WATCHING ME?" He'd stomp on my feet, slug me, throw rocks at me. One time he said, "BEND OVER, YOU SON OF A BITCH!," and swatted me with the butt end of my rifle.

I thought the old bastard hated me. Goddamit, I was a gentleman, but I looked at him and thought, "I'm going to hurt that old man!"

In one scene he really upset me. I was supposed to be spying on the Indians. I was sneaking through the bushes, he hollered, "WOODY, YOU SON OF A BITCH, QUIT NIGGERING UP MY GOD-DAMNED SCENE!"

I had been tiptoeing, like I was scared. He wanted me to move with intelligence and cunning. Sergeant Rutledge wasn't a tiptoer; he was proud and dignified. And John Ford knew how to pull that out of me and put it up on the screen.

Like the scene where I save Constance Towers from being attacked by the Indians. Constance Towers was a classic Hollywood beauty; blonde hair, small, straight nose, perfect white teeth, the whole package. I kill off some Apaches and drag her into a train station to hide. The Indians manage to wound me, and as we walk into the station, I'm on the verge of passing out. In the original script, she is supposed to help me out of my shirt and treat my wound.

John Ford edited that scene for the white people in the country who couldn't have accepted this beautiful white woman touching my skin and treating my wounds. He said, "Constance! Don't touch Woody!" Ford would always direct like that while the camera was rolling. "Woody, unbutton the shirt. Now ease out of it."

Ford's directing, I'm suffering, and I pull the shirt off. "No! Miss, please, don't touch me!"

I lie down on a pallet and turn so the audience can see I'm

201

wounded. I pass out. Constance walks over to where I'm lying and grabs my Winchester. She crosses the room and turns an old rocking chair to face me. She settles in, lays the rifle across her lap, and waits, protecting Sergeant Rutledge. What a high-class scene that was.

The second time I saw the completed picture was in Texas. I was down there working on Ford's *Two Rode Together*. One night he said, "Woody, your picture is playing in town. Let's go check it out." The picture ended and a group of cowboys came over to where we were standing. They said, "Boy, we didn't resent one minute of that. It was beautiful, beautiful!"

Now, in the big courtroom scene, when the question is asked, "Why did Sergeant Rutledge commit these crimes?" I had the most emotional moment in my acting career. John Ford was really smart. He knew how to get the fire going, how to get all the emotions out of me. When he wanted to turn me on, boom, he'd just hit the switch.

The day before the big scene, Mr. Ford invited me to come over to his son Pat's house. The old man met me there and offered me a drink in the biggest old-fashioned glass I'd ever seen; it was more like a beer mug. And as much as the old man liked to drink, he'd kick my ass if he knew I was drinking. So when I got to Pat's house and he said, "Let's have a drink," my eyes narrowed. It was three o'clock in the afternoon; a sign was flashing in my head, "BEWARE!" Normally, I would never drink on a job, but he told me to drink so I did. By the time night fell I was falling down drunk. Somehow I ended up on Sunset Boulevard whooping and hollering up and down the street. Pat Ford found me and shoved me into his car.

The next morning I woke up in Mr. Ford's green room. That was like his sitting room, adjacent to his bedroom. As a matter of fact, I fell asleep on his bedspread. And if you ever see the movie, in my courtroom scene close-up, you'll see the imprint of his bedspread on my face.

I woke up wondering, "Where the hell am I?" Then I realized, "Oh God! What the hell am I doing in this house?" I was terribly hung over, still a little drunk. I struggled up and snuck by his room.

He was sitting, propped up in bed with his eye patch on, reviewing the script. I went downstairs to the kitchen. Pat Ford was sipping a cup of coffee. He said, "Come on, let's go to the studio before the old man gets up."

Pat drove me to the studio. When Mr. Ford showed up, he didn't bother with hellos or talking to any of the production people, he came right over to where I was sitting. He leaned down, stuck his nose right in my face and sniffed. "Oh, you've been drinking, have you?" He said it real loud like he didn't know.

"Yes, sir. I'm sorry; I've never done this before."

I was playing right into his hands. We sat down, and I ran through a few lines. He interrupted, "Oh, you know your god-damned lines, do you?" I had never known a director to get mad over an actor knowing their lines. He sat there, fists clenched, tight as a coiled rattlesnake ready to strike. He studied me, his good eye piercing through that wrinkled, craggy face, as I ran through my dialogue. When I finished, he growled at me, "Do you think you can do the courtroom scene now?" He wasn't really asking me; he was telling me, "You'd better say 'em right or you're through!" He had me in the pressure cooker.

I said, "Yes sir, I'm ready!"

I took the stand. I felt like an exposed nerve and the old man was twisting the knife. He had me all pissed off, emotional, teetering right on the edge. I sat real stoic while the prosecuting attorney started to parade in front of me. With a huge radio voice he said, "This Negro raped this little girl and killed her father. If he's innocent of the crimes, WHY DID THIS NIGGER TRY TO ESCAPE?" Then he turned to face me, "WHY'D YOU COME BACK, NIGGER?"

By then, the goose pimples were all over me and the floodgates opened. "Because the Ninth Cavalry is my home and my self-respect. If I deserted them, I wouldn't be nothin' but a swamp runnin' nigger. And I ain't that, I'm a man."

That broke me up. And I stood up and broke the chair. We had to shut down so I could pull myself together. Mr. Ford said, "Now Woody, stop those tears. It's a sign of weakness." And that was the truest moment I ever had on the screen. Every time I see that picture I get the goose pimples all over again.

That's how lucky I was to hook up with John Ford. He knew how to pluck me like a harp. That old man not only directed me, he split my personality. I almost had a nervous breakdown doing *Sergeant Rutledge,* but it helped me become an actor.

When we finished the picture, they had a special screening at Warner Bros. Mr. Ford invited me to go with him. Ward Bond, Spencer Tracy, John Wayne, Lewis Milestone, all his drinking buddies were there. Mr. Ford said to me, "Come on down front, Woody. I'm going to hold your hand."

Well, I hate to admit it, but I had started smoking in those years. I must have smoked up three packs of cigarettes watching myself star. When the picture ended, the old man looked at me and said, "I know you're in shock, but what do you think?"

I said, "Hell, you did everything but ride the goddamned horses for me!" And that was true.

Then came the reviews; *Variety* on April 8, 1960 said:

> While star billing goes to Jeffrey Hunter, Constance Towers and Billie Burke, it's actually Woody Strode who dominates. As the giant-sized Negro first sergeant who is eventually proven to be a victim of circumstantial evidence, Strode gives an unusually versatile performance. Ford uses his camera to accent the actor's natural physical strength, to build an image of a man of action and heroic proportions, while Strode fills out the design with many shadings of character.

I stole the review, and of all the pictures I've made I think I'm closest to *Sergeant Rutledge,* because of John Ford. He put me in the saddle. I remember after the picture he invited Luana and me up to his house in Bel Air. I jumped back like the rattlesnake had struck. I never thought he liked me. I went home and told Luana.

She said, "Oh, I haven't seen Papa Ford in years." So we took the kids up to his house and that started a relationship that I didn't realize was going to carry on until his death in 1973. We became the closest friends because I was honest, strong, and crude. I reminded him of an earlier time in history, a time he was in love with. I became one of the few men that could call John Ford Papa.

CHAPTER NINETEEN

Papa Ford

John Ford was born Sean Aloysius O'Feeney on February 1, 1895. His parents were Irish immigrants, and he was the youngest of thirteen children. One time he asked me about my mother and father. I told him about my mother and the slave scene. I told him about the free side and the relationship that side had with the Indians. I said, "My daddy was a brick mason."

He said, "Well, goddamit, my father was a saloon keeper." He got right down in the gutter with me, made me an equal, and told me his whole life's history.

He followed his brother Francis out to Hollywood in 1914 and worked as an actor, stuntman, propman, grip, what have you until he got a chance to direct in 1917. For the next fifty years there was no more prolific or consistently good director in the world.

By the time I got to him, he was in his mid-sixties and a hard-nosed, crotchety old Irishman. He was a big man, probably as big as me in his prime. He had a full, jowly face with a nose like a lump of putty. He wore glasses, and he had some sort of ailment in his left eye. You'd never see him without an eye patch or dark glasses. And he was always burning a big cigar.

John Ford was a romantic and a dreamer. He was an artist,

although he would never admit it. He had a great visual sense. He'd use a doorway or a group of trees to construct a shot like putting a frame on a Rembrandt. And he didn't have to spend a day scratching his head trying to figure out how to shoot something; he relied on an instinct that told him when a shot was right. If someone were to ask him, "Mr. Ford, the green tie next to the tea kettle, what were you trying to say?"

He'd probably answer, "Well, what did it mean to you?"

He was a noisy, humorous man who was probably most happy when he was on location kidding around with the crew. He liked to think of himself as one of the troops rather than the chief. And when he made a friendship, it was lasting; he was fiercely loyal. That's why you see the same actors over and over again in his movies. Harry Carey Sr. was his first big star. Then there was Ward Bond, Henry Fonda, Jimmy Stewart and, of course, John Wayne.

He loved to get inside people's heads and find out what made them tick. He loved to needle and make fun. He liked to put me on, and I never knew whether to believe him or not. I think it was Walter O'Malley who said, "Half of an Irishman's lies are true." That description fits John Ford to a T.

Like most Irishmen, he hated the British, and quite often he would put a British character in one of his films so he could make him look like an idiot. If his movies had a flaw, it was usually because he would overdo the comedy angle. He didn't know when he was going too far. And because his parents were immigrants, he developed quite an interest in a person's ethnic background. I remember sitting at his kitchen table one day sharing a pot of coffee and he asked me, "Woody, why don't you ever talk about your Indian blood?"

I said, "Papa, in this country you can say you're Irish, French and German, and no one would think twice. But if you say Irish, French, and Negro, what a big fat laugh. In America, if you have one drop of black blood you're colored."

He said, "What're you going to do?"

"Sit here and drink this coffee."

He said, "No. That's not what I meant. I'm going over to the studio." He walked over to me and grabbed me by the jawbone.

He leaned into me until I could smell the coffee and Cuban tobacco on his breath. He looked me in the eye and said, "Woody, I want you to come to the studio with me. I want to screen test you. I think maybe you'll play Stone Calf in *Two Rode Together*.

We went to the make-up department and they put a Sitting Bull-type wig on me. But with my smooth skin and that long-haired wig, I looked just like a squaw. I complained about looking like an old lady. Ford said, "Wait a minute, let's try a Mohawk." Well, there I was again.

We shot the screen test and Ford got into a whole new argument with Warner's over using a black actor as the Indian chief. But, in costume, I looked so much like an Indian that the studio bosses couldn't argue. I have so much Indian in my look that back when we were making *Sergeant Rutledge,* Ford made me take my hat off in that hot Arizona sun so that I could get as dark as possible. He made me grow my hair about a half inch so there would be a distinction between the Indians and me. He wanted me to show as much Negro as possible. I never did get black enough, but I did get a nice dark, dark, dark.

So I got the part of Stone Calf in *Two Rode Together* which starred Jimmy Stewart and Richard Widmark. We traveled to Bankersville, Texas and set up the production in an old fort that had been converted into a museum. We went through pre-production, learning lines and rehearsing, while we waited for the Navajo Indians to show up. John Ford was a blood brother to the Navajos and liked to use them in his pictures. He knew how to speak their language, and he taught me enough to get me through my dialogue.

Ford had to build my respect with the Indians because as Stone Calf, I was representing Many Mules, who was Chief of the Navajo Nation. I had to learn to ride bareback and after being in the saddle, what an insecure feeling that was. But after one week of practicing I got so I could tie the reins, drop them, pull my bow, and shoot at a full gallop. And that bareback riding really made my legs strong because of the strength and touch required in controlling the animal.

When the Navajos arrived at the fort, John Ford told me,

"Woody, the Indians are here and I don't want you drinking with them. They're wild enough as it is." He gave me a big lecture.

I was living in a room that used to be the armory. It was swept clean except for a little twin bed, a table with a wash bowl and pitcher, a wooden ladder-back chair and a single, bare incandescent bulb hanging from a wire from the ceiling. I was propped up in bed, memorizing my lines when a knock came at the door around eleven o'clock at night.

I opened the door and there were two sullen-looking Indians standing in the half-light. They both wore black cowboy hats with eagle feathers sticking out of the hat bands, plaid cowboy shirts, jeans, and moccasins. Their coal-black eyes just about disappeared in the darkness.

"The Chief wants to see you." That's all they said. I threw my script onto the bed and followed them into the night.

They escorted me to the Chief's quarters. Many Mules was laying in bed with a quart of whiskey in his hand. He was eighty years old, and his long gray hair flowed over the pillows. His skin was like old leather, but his eyes sparkled. He wouldn't speak English, so he had his translator tell me, "Have a drink, Woody!"

Well, I knew John Ford would kick my ass for drinking with Many Mules, but here was the Chief of the Navajo Nation, like the President of the United States, saying, "Have a drink!" So I drank. Pretty soon I was wound-up and my curiosity got the better of me. I said, "You know, I've never seen a war dance. Could you show me how that's done?"

"Where?"

"How about right out there on the parade grounds?"

Out in the middle of this old fort was a well with a four-foot adobe wall circling the hole. That's where we assembled. Next to the well there was an old half-rotten buckboard wagon the museum people used as a prop for the tourists. We pushed it out a few feet and torched it. I took my boots off, rolled my pants up and joined the rest of the Indians in a circle around the fire. The fire crackled and sparked. Many Mules stood by the well, his arms folded across his chest, while the light flickered across his body. He looked toward the drummer and nodded.

The Indians, already full of alcohol, started slowly. They took a few steps, boom, raised their arms, boom, released and yelled. I followed, imitating. Then the booze and the spirit of the ancestors took over. It was like a hundred years of history had washed away in a heartbeat. I didn't think; I just reacted.

The spell was broken when John Ford came running out in his pajamas. "WHAT THE HELL IS GOING ON!" The prop guys showed up with extinguishers and put the fire out. The Indians fell out of their trance. Many Mules gave the order, and the party broke up. John Ford was so mad he just stared at me, didn't say a word. Just stared for about 30 seconds and then left me standing there.

The next day the old man had my ass pinned down. He was ripping me up one side and down the other. I was in disgrace. When he got through tearing me apart, I went to breakfast. I filled my tray and got ready to sit at the table with him, Jimmy Stewart, and Richard Widmark. Ford refused to let me eat at the table with them. He said, "Woody, you can't eat with us. You're a nigger. You have to sit by yourself."

I said, "Papa, what could I do? When the Chief tells you to drink, you drink."

I think Ford secretly enjoyed the dance. And I think it was that part of me that appealed to John Ford. But he couldn't have me upstage him in front of the entire crew. As much as he liked to be one of the guys, he ruled his set with an iron fist. Maybe that's why he won six Academy Awards and the New York Film Critics Award four times. An interviewer asked Orson Welles which American directors appealed to him most. Welles answered, "The old masters . . . By which I mean John Ford, John Ford, and John Ford."

And he didn't achieve that level of success by letting other people call the shots. You never told John Ford how to play a scene. The young directors today are working with actors who make five million dollars a film plus a percentage. The actor says, "I won't do it that way. I'm going to do it my way," and the directors have to listen. John Ford would have strangled an actor like that.

But Ford had a very human, understanding side, too. While I was working on *Two Rode Together*, I got a telegram from home. My mama had died. I said, "Papa, my mama just died. I've got to bury her and I haven't got the money. I need $1,500."

He said, "Go down to the office and tell my son Pat to write you out a check."

After I buried her, went through the funeral and the whole sad scene, the old man walked up to me. He raised his eye patch and said, "Have you paid me my money back yet?"

I said, "You old son of a bitch, you just took the final payment out of my last check!"

He kept an eye on his money; that's an Irish quality. But he was the first director to pay me $1,000 a week, and what was more important, he kept me working. I made three pictures in a row for John Ford without working for anybody else in-between, By the time I got to *The Man Who Shot Liberty Valance,* I was up to $1,500 a week.

In *The Man Who Shot Liberty Valance,* John Wayne plays a rancher; I play his right-hand man, Pompey. Jimmy Stewart plays a young attorney, and Lee Marvin plays the outlaw, Liberty Valance, a man so cruel he carries a silver-handled whip with nine knotted tails he uses on anyone that dares cross him.

The movie starts with Jimmy making the trip west to set up his law practice in the new frontier. His stagecoach gets held up by Lee Marvin and his gang. Jimmy tries to defend a woman passenger and Lee nearly beats him to death with his whip. The stage gets to town and John Wayne and I pick up Jimmy and carry him in a buckboard wagon over to Miss Hallie's, played by Vera Miles. She runs the town's restaurant; she and John have a romance going. We start patching Jimmy up and John says, "You're in pretty bad shape, pilgrim."

Jimmy says, "I got to do something. I don't want to kill him; I want to put him in jail."

John says, "I know the law books mean a lot to you, but not out here. Out here a man settles his own problems, pilgrim." That's how John Wayne and "pilgrim" became connected.

The picture came out in 1962, and it's still one of John Ford's most popular films. I didn't have much dialogue, but since I was John Wayne's right-hand man I was in almost every scene with him.

That's the only time I ever worked with John. We were never very close. He was a great guy and I needed John, but as far as John Ford was concerned, I didn't need anyone but him. Papa was very jealous of his relationship, so he put a wedge between us. See, John Wayne and John Ford had a father-son relationship that went all the way back to 1928 when Wayne acted in his first Ford feature, *Hangman's House*. They were very close and, of course, John Ford made John Wayne.

Once I was sitting with John Ford when John Wayne called him from Texas. John Wayne was producing, directing, and starring in *The Alamo*. He was calling the old man to see if he would come down and help direct the battle scenes, which the old man did without taking a credit.

But Ford used to needle John Wayne mercilessly. For instance, John Wayne was a football player at USC before they pulled him into the movies. At that time he was still known as Marion Michael Morrison. He was never a great football player, but somehow he got into their hall of fame. One time Ford yelled, "Duke," and he pointed at me, "there's the real football player." Or Ford would tease John over the fact that I had served in World War II and he hadn't, which really pissed John Wayne off. Like most big stars, John Wayne had an ego.

Towards the end of filming *The Man Who Shot Liberty Valance*, John Wayne and I almost came to blows. We were getting ready to do the scene after Wayne realizes he's lost his woman to Jimmy Stewart. John gets rip-roaring drunk; I gather him up and help him to the buckboard wagon. He takes the reins; I climb in the back. We make a full-speed run back to his ranch, which we had just remodeled for Miss Hallie. He staggers inside and burns the place down.

As we filmed the scene, the horses started running away and John couldn't control them. I was kneeling in the back of the wagon as we made our approach to the ranch. John was working the reins, but he couldn't get the horses to stop. I reached up to grab the reins to help him, and John swung and knocked me away.

When the horses finally stopped he fell out of the wagon. I jumped down, and was ready to kick his ass. Ford raced over,

"Woody, don't hit him! We need him!" Then he turned to the crew, "All right, we're going to shut down for a little while." The old man had me sit for two hours and cool off. That's how mad I was; I was shocked, and it was John Ford's fault for pitting me against John Wayne.

When things calmed down and we got back to shooting, we were getting ready to shoot the scene where John Wayne sets fire to the ranch house. I had to go in and drag him out of the burning room. John Wayne wanted to use his double for the scene; I didn't have a double. Ford said, "Duke, Woody is an old man"—I was forty-seven—"and he's got to carry you and he doesn't need a double!" John Wayne played the scene.

That's how John Ford controlled and manipulated. Sometimes he would holler, "Duke!," and whatever John Wayne was doing, I don't care if his pants were down around his ankles, he'd stop and come running.

I told the other actors, "You see Duke running? He's a millionaire. He doesn't have to do that. But that old man made him a millionaire. That's respect."

I don't care how big a star you are: if the director cracks the whip, you dance. That's what you're getting paid for. And John Ford was the greatest director I ever worked for. I always give John Ford credit for making me an actor.

CHAPTER TWENTY

The Mongrel

Toward the end of 1962, Sid Gold lined me up for a part in Sy Weintraub's *Tarzan's Three Challenges*. Just before I left for location in Thailand, I got a call from a wrestling promoter in New York. He offered me $500 a night to come back and wrestle. Five hundred dollars times five nights is $2,500. That was almost twice what I was making in the movies, so I had to accept. And I figured the wrestling would help get me in shape for the movie.

The first match was in Buffalo, New York. They put me in the headline event against a black wrestler named Bobo Brazil. He was the champ of that territory. He went about six-feet-seven, 300 pounds, and beautiful, like a piece of black onyx. Bobo was famous for the "Coco Butt;" he'd grab you by the ears and slam his forehead into yours—*bam*, lights out. Then he'd jump on top for an easy pin.

That first night, Bobo got me up in the air, ready to body slam me and I remember thinking, "Oh God, I hope I can remember my name after this." At forty-eight years of age I thought I could come back, but I couldn't. My skin had gotten soft; my body couldn't take the punishment. I hit the mat and my teeth shattered. My sacroiliac gave out on me.

After the match, the promoter sent me to see an old lady in

upstate New York. She took her shoes off and walked up and down my back, trying to pop my spine back in place. That's when I really gave up wrestling for good, in 1962, the same year Tarzan and Elvis Presley's *Blue Hawaii* were the salvation of the MGM studios. If the studio had needed someone to play Julius Caesar, Elvis Presley would have played Caesar. That's where the box office was.

I spent five months in the jungles of Thailand working for Sy Weintraub. Jock Mahoney played Tarzan; he was the thirteenth Tarzan. He and I battle for control of the jungle.

The final fight takes place on a rope net, like the square rigging of a ship laid flat, twelve feet off the ground. It took us five days to learn to balance and fight on that net. Of course Tarzan beats me, and I had to go limp and fall backwards into a huge black kettle full of boiling oil. To fall backwards without looking, what an awkward thing that was. The kettle was full of silver paint and dry ice to make it look like boiling oil. I had to grab the sides of the pot and hold myself underwater as long as my breath held out. That way they could get a few feet of film so the audience would know I had really died.

If you've ever seen that fight scene you might notice that Jock Mahoney looks real skinny and sick, like the Before picture in a Charles Atlas ad. Well, going into that picture, he *was* Charles Atlas, one of the strongest men in the world, a stuntman turned actor. But he jumped into the Klong River, the dirtiest river in the world, ten times worse than the worst open sewer, and caught tertiary malaria and amoebic dysentery.

He was deathly sick; he couldn't eat. His lungs filled up with fluid and he developed pneumonia. After every fight scene we had to put him in an oxygen tent. Anybody else would have died but Jock Mahoney. I begged him not to go into that river, but he didn't believe he'd get sick; he believed he was Tarzan. That's what made him great.

After the final scene, we rushed Jock from the jungle location in the back of a Land Rover. His body was burning up. A little Japanese girl working on the picture had a thermometer; his temperature read 104 degrees. When we got to the hotel I picked him up and carried him inside. We put him in a tub and packed it with ice. I had some antibiotics and I fed those to him. It took the doctor an hour to show up. He asked me, "What have you done for him?"

I said, "I gave him some antibiotics."

He said, "Good!" and started to work on Tarzan. That's when we found out how sick he really was. Jock was lucky to survive, but it made an old man out of him.

When I got home, I found out the old man was in bad shape, too. John Ford had been vacationing in Europe with his wife and fell down some stairs in Paris. He injured his back. Luana, the kids, and I got in the car and drove out to Bel Air to visit.

I left Luana, Kalai, and June down by the pool with Mrs. Ford and walked upstairs to the old man's bedroom. Ford looked ten years older than the last time I saw him. He couldn't lift himself up to shake my hand. He told me about falling down the stairs; then he asked, "Woody, do you know anything about muscles? I've got all these goddamned knots in my back." I felt his back and the knots in the muscle; the muscle had spasmed.

I said, "Papa, after thirty years of athletics I ought to know something."

"Well then, would you ask Luana if you could stay here a few days and help massage this stuff out of my back?"

Luana gave the okay and I told him, "Papa, I don't care what time it is: if you get to hurting, wake me up and I'll work on you." I sat up in a big arm chair all night, and when the pain woke him up, I went to work.

Finally he said, "Woody, why don't you get comfortable and go lie down in my green room."

"No Papa, I think I'll just make a pallet at the foot of your bed." I got a pillow and a quilt, and I slept on the floor. He had those good old-fashioned rugs that were just like a bed. Sometimes I'd get up at four in the morning and massage his back until he could go back to sleep. I had no idea a few days would turn into four months.

After the first couple of weeks, when he was feeling better, he said, "Woody, would you please go get me a bottle of wine?"

I fetched the wine and the bottle was dry in about fifteen

minutes. At first I tried to drink with him, but I found I was getting drunk all the time. It got so I couldn't keep up, and that escalated until he was really over-drinking. I had to think of a way to keep him from drinking himself into the grave.

One morning he was hanging over pretty bad, and he asked me to go get him a beer. I sat there watching him drink the beer like it was water and I thought, "Bullshit, I'm not going to help pour this man right into the ground." So with the second beer, I poured out half the beer and filled it up with soda water. By the time night came he was cold sober. Mrs. Ford came upstairs to check on him and I figured I'd better tell her what I was doing.

"Mrs. Ford, I've been sitting here watching your husband drink himself to death. I'm not going to sit here and help this great man die. I've been cutting his beer with water."

"Oh my God, Woody, he'll hate you!"

Everybody catered to him, and I decided I wasn't going to be part of that. I figured it was up to me to pull him off the bottle. That night, about midnight, after drinking diluted beer all day, he woke up. He looked at me and said, "Woody, would you please go downstairs and get me a glass full of gin?"

"No sir, I ain't getting none for you!"

He lifted up his eye patch and said, "You cruel son of a bitch, you'll never work in any of my pictures again."

I said, "If you don't like it, why don't you just get out of that bed and try to kick my ass?" I pulled him off the goddamned drinking.

As the weeks turned into months, he got to feeling better. We'd sit together in his green room, read books and talk all day. John Ford had become lonely. John Wayne was involved with his family and his own projects, and everybody else was scattered. I had replaced all those friends. Pat Ford told me, "Woody, you know my father and I don't get along too well. What you're doing for him, I can't provide."

I had a whole different world to tell the old man about. I had all my wrestling stories; that was a strange and fascinating subject to him. We never talked about motion pictures. He wouldn't allow talk about the movies in his house unless we talked about a film he was making. But I always had some dialogue from football or wrestling.

I became his special race horse. As we went along, he watched how I treated my Hawaiian family. He said, "You always have the kids with you."

"Papa, I don't know any other way to be."

Luana and the kids would visit almost every day. The kids would pass the time swimming. They're half-Hawaiian, and swam like fish; their mother taught them. Luana was a great swimmer; she swam like Weissmuller, with her head out of the water, and, boy, she could really motor. I didn't have to worry about anyone drowning. Luana would either be in the pool with the kids or sitting on the sidelines under the umbrella sipping a cool drink with Mrs. Ford.

Well, towards the end of my stay, the old man had just about completely recovered. One day he received a phone call. One of his sisters died. I didn't think I'd have to go to the funeral until Papa said, "You're going."

"I don't have any clothes. I'll have to get Luana to bring me some tomorrow."

He said, "Go into my closet and try on some of my clothes. I've got an old blazer in there; see if you can fit into that thing."

I put on one of his shirts and slipped into a navy blue blazer with shiny gold buttons. It fell on me like it was tailor made. That's when I realized how big he used to be.

Well, by then Pat Ford had heard all the gossip that was floating around Hollywood about me living with his father. I guess people figured I was trying to take advantage of John Ford in his old age. Pat said, "Papa, why don't you let Woody go with me and my two sons? He can sit with us."

"No, he's going with your mother and me." And he dragged me to the big church in Hollywood. Talk about being uncomfortable, imagine me at this funeral sitting next to God in a turtleneck sweater and his head angel. I felt like Gabriel.

I could feel the people staring, and that's when I realized what an awkward situation I had created by staying in John Ford's house. After the funeral Pat Ford said, "Woody, all these people are worrying about what the old man is doing with you. Everyone's asking."

John Ford and I had created a father-son relationship but I began to feel uncomfortable because of the pressure from the outside. I was becoming closer than friends he'd known forty, fifty years. I realized I had gotten too close. I told Luana, "I've got to get out of this man's house. If he dies on me, I'll have a heart attack." Luana didn't put up any resistance; she'd been ready for me to come home four months ago.

I started making some half-assed excuse and was interrupted, "How long you been here, Woody?"

"I was supposed to spend a few days, I've been here four months."

"Oh my God, go home!"

It was a very emotional situation for me because I learned so much from John Ford. He knew American history; in fact, a complete collection of his movies, and he made over one hundred, would tell you everything you need to know about the history of America from the Revolution through the Korean War. His bedroom and green room were libraries. He had a complete history of the Civil War. He made me read a book every week. And I'd watch him read. He'd lift that eye patch up and speed read. He'd read three books to my one. I sat up there and got an education from that old man.

He had a librarian, and she would read all the scripts that were sent to him. She would select the best ones and he would go over those. He became interested in doing a movie that dealt with the relocation of the Cheyenne Indians. He gave me two books to read: *Cheyenne Autumn* by Maria Sandoz, and *The Last Frontier* by Howard Fast. Ford wanted me to tell him which one I liked best because he was going to make the movie. He wanted my opinion because he knew I wouldn't look at the story like an intellectual.

I read *The Last Frontier* first. Howard Fast told about the white officers and what the government's position was. *Cheyenne Autumn* told the Indians' side of the story. I said, "Papa, you'll have to use both books to tell the whole story."

The last of the Cheyenne Indians, 300 warriors, women, and

children, were on the run from the United States government. The government had relocated the Cheyenne 1,500 miles from their homeland, which was in the Yellowstone National Park area. The government put them on a reservation in Missouri or somewhere down in the swamp land. That was very unhealthy for the Cheyenne; they began to die of small pox and tuberculosis, until only 300 were left.

The government knew of the Cheyenne's predicament and promised to send representatives down to work out a solution. When the government representatives didn't show, the Cheyenne leaders, Little Wolf and Dull Knife, decided they would break their agreement with the government and return to their homeland. And the Cheyenne were the proudest, most fierce of all the American Indians.

The Indians fought and retreated. They used trench warfare, the first time that had been used in this country. Here's what the Indians did. Little Wolf, the warrior chief, would sit on a mound smoking a pipe until the army got close and the bullets started to hit all around him. Then he'd slide over backwards into a trench. The cavalry would figure it was safe to move in. When they got close enough, the Indians would pop up out of the trenches and open fire. They'd shoot the horses and kill the soldiers. When night fell, the Indians would build a fire, drag the horses back, cut, cook, eat, and move out.

When the Cheyenne got as far as the Dakotas, winter set in; they were freezing and starving to death. It got so hard on the older people, the women, and the children, that Dull Knife and Little Wolf split up. Little Wolf and most of the warriors continued toward the homeland. Dull Knife took his group to Fort Robinson to try to reach a settlement with the government. The government ordered the Cheyenne to return to the reservation. When Dull Knife refused, the commanding officer locked the Indians in a barn with no food, water, and heat. It was ten degrees below zero.

Well, Dull Knife was prepared to die rather than go back to the reservation. Before he reached the fort, he had his people dismantle all the guns. All of the screws, nuts and bolts they had made into necklaces and hung around the kids' necks. All the heavy

219

stuff was hidden under the hoop skirts of the women. They hid knives in their papoose carriers.

When the government ordered them back to the reservation, Dull Knife made a stand. The Cheyenne assembled the guns and tried to escape. They broke out of the barn and had a skirmish inside the fort. They managed to get the gates opened and they ran, trying to escape.

This was probably the cruelest incident in all the Indian wars. The Cheyenne were slaughtered. Dull Knife's squaw died crossing the river; they gunned her down. Dull Knife managed to escape and met up with Little Wolf 300 miles from the homeland. The cavalry tracked them down, but the government was so embarrassed, because of the slaughter of woman and children at Fort Robinson, that they let the Cheyenne move back to their homeland.

Somewhere I have a picture of Little Wolf; I look just like him. Ford asked me if I wanted to play him in the picture. Well, that was right in my bag. Then the old man got on the phone and called Anthony Quinn. He wanted Tony to play Dull Knife.

I said, "Great. I can do all the fighting; Anthony Quinn can do all the acting."

But again I was walking uphill because Warner Bros. wanted an established name with marquee value to play the part of Little Wolf. About a month away from shooting, John Ford delivered the bad news, "They're going to give the part of Little Wolf to Ricardo Montalban. Gilbert Roland will play Dull Knife. How would you like to be the medicine man?"

"No Papa, you go ahead and make the picture without me."

I couldn't play Little Wolf and I had gotten too close to the character to take any other part. He offered me the medicine man so I wouldn't feel too bad. But for me, Little Wolf was the one. Nobody could do what I could do: ride the horses, shoot arrows, fight. Ricardo couldn't do any of that, not like I could.

I was getting over my disappointment at not getting the part of Little Wolf when I got called in by Columbia Pictures to try out for a part in *Major Dundee* starring Charlton Heston. I would have played one of Chuck's soldiers, but it was a good role for me

220

because it would have kept my progression of western characters going.

I went to Mr. Bressler's office; he was the producer. Sam Peckinpah was there; he was going to direct. Mr. Bressler was sitting behind his desk trying to describe a scene in the picture. "There's a scene, Woody, where you'll be shining this white officer's shoes, and he's got to call you a . . ." He started stumbling over the dialogue because he didn't know how to say "nigger."

Peckinpah, who was standing in the corner, jumped in. "Woody, what he's trying to tell you is that you've got to shine this white officer's shoes and he's got to call you a nigger. But the problem I'm having is that you aren't really a Negro. You're a mongrel." That was his way of telling me I wasn't dark enough for the role.

I dropped my head. I didn't know how to react. All of a sudden a major studio was telling me I wasn't black enough. All they had to say was that I didn't have the look they wanted. But Peckinpah, who was a smart ass anyway, out of the corner of his mouth said, "You're a mongrel." He was a crude man.

My answer to him was, "Mr. Peckinpah, after 400 years we're either half-white or half-Indian. That's the American Negro. We have no control over that."

Major Dundee came out in 1965. Those were the years of the big civil rights movement, the marching and the riots. Now it was "black," you had to be black; not a mixed breed like me. After being colored for fifty years, I wasn't black enough to play a Negro.

When I was back East wrestling in 1962, I was asked to do an interview for a talk show they were taping for the radio. They asked me how my people were doing in Los Angeles. I said, "Well, the colored people . . ."

The interviewer said, "You can't say colored!" Here was a white man telling me what to call myself. I had to ask, "What do I say?"

"Afro-American." They had now established this connection. I remember the days when colored was cordial and polite. That changed to "Negro" and now it's "black." But when you get down to it, I've done just about everything in the world but make money. See, the money is where the Uncle Tommin' comes in, on both sides, white and black. Some white men, like some black men, can't do it. The ones who can bow and scrape, the man says, "Give him a dollar." Those guys are all agents now.

After Peckinpah called me a mongrel, I was insulted and I was going to quit the business. I went to break the news to Sid Gold. He pulled me into his office and slammed the door. He said, "You don't have the guts to stick with it."

I said, "What would you do if they said you weren't Jewish? Go on a Chinese interview?" It became a comedy because that's exactly what happened.

I got a call from Mike Frankovich, who by that time was in charge of all the production coming out of Columbia Pictures. He said, "Woody, I heard what happened. Why didn't you come to see me?"

I said, "Mike, if they don't want you on the ball club there's no reason to try and fight it."

He said, "Do you know Henry Levin?"

"No."

"Well he's getting ready to do a picture called *Genghis Khan,* you'd be perfect for that." We went to see Henry Levin. He looked me over and said, "Yeah, Woody, you'd be perfect. You can play the mute."

Frankovich said, "But Woody can talk."

Henry answered, "Hell, the mute goes all the way through the picture with Omar Sharif. He's his right-hand man."

So I took the part. I play a deaf-mute who befriends guards, and teaches fighting to the young war lord who later becomes Genghis Khan.

It was a $15 million production, and they shot the whole thing in Europe, England, Germany, and Yugoslavia. Henry Levin said, "We'd like to pay for your wife to come with you."

I said, "I can't do that; I have a couple of kids."

"How old are they?"

"Fifteen and seventeen."

"What the hell, we'll take them too."

That's how Kalai and June spent their summer vacation, touring Europe, thanks to Mike Frankovich. It was like the studio telling me, "We're sorry we said you aren't a Negro." So I got the family together, we got on the plane and headed overseas. When we got to Yugoslavia, I saw my picture in the Communist newspaper. Henry Levin fired our publicist over that. He got his job back, and he explained what the commotion was about. He said, "Woody, I don't want you to see the press unless they come through me first."

"What happened?"

"You're getting the headlines and you are not the star of Mr. Levin's picture." The Yugoslavians weren't familiar with Omar Sharif, Telly Savalas, or Stephen Boyd. They couldn't afford the rentals on movies like *Ben Hur* or *Lawrence of Arabia*. They rented John Ford's films because he was a historian. And because of that, John Ford had established my character on the world market. I learned through that experience that the Europeans didn't have any racial hang-ups over the color of my skin.

It took five months to shoot *Genghis Khan,* so Luana and the kids couldn't stay with me the whole time. The kids had to get home and go to school. Kalai had to get ready to be the president of his high school. When we finally finished the picture, I was so exhausted from riding horses and fighting that I decided I would just relax and take the train from West Berlin to France, ferry across the channel, and grab a plane out of London. I sipped whiskey and rode across Europe with my passport stuck in the band of my cowboy hat. Nobody woke me up until it came time to cross the English Channel. That's how they honored the American citizenship in those days.

When I got to New York, I was broke. I wanted to buy Luana some jewelry, so I called my office and asked them to wire me $500. Sid Gold got on the line and said John Ford had put a hold on me. He wanted to use me in his next picture, *Seven Women.*

There were two Chinese leading roles in *Seven Women.* I got one, and Mike Mazurki played the other. He and I fight over a missionary woman and I get killed out of the picture. This time the make-up people put rubber over my eyes and stuck a pigtail on my head. The Chinese musclemen working on the film said, "Woody, you look more Chinese than we do."

I was on the set when Jean Simmons came looking for me. She was an actress who, at that time, was married to Richard Brooks, the director. She said, "My husband is looking for you. He's doing a picture for Columbia called *The Professionals*. He'd like you to come over for an interview."

Well, nobody asked John Ford if they could go on an interview while they were working on one of his pictures. So I asked, "Papa, Richard Brooks wants me to interview over at Columbia."

He said, "You son of a bitch, you haven't finished my picture yet!"

"I'm sorry, Papa."

Later on in the day, Tige Andrews, who was a dear friend of John Ford's, walked up to me on the set. The old man had him do this discreetly. He said, "Yes, you can go."

I still had my Chinese outfit and make-up on when I met Mr. Brooks. He explained the role to me: "Woody, it's about time we show the Negro cowboy in the Old West. The script calls for a Mexican Irish Indian, but I'm going to make him an Indian Negro half-breed." Richard Brooks reached and pulled a book on cowboys from the shelf. I leaned over his desk, and we went through the pictures.

CHAPTER TWENTY-ONE

Star Billing

The Professionals came out in 1966. I played Jacob Sharp, one of the four male leads in the picture. That was the first time I received on-screen star billing. I got my name up there ahead of Burt Lancaster's.

Jacob Sharp is half-Indian, half-Negro. Richard Brooks uses an opening scene to explain the Negro side. Four of us are on a train to rescue Ralph Bellamy's wife, Claudia Cardinale, from Raza the Mexican bandit, played by Jack Palance. Bellamy introduces us to one another. Lee Marvin is the military strategist and small weapons expert. Burt Lancaster is the expert with explosives. Robert Ryan is a wrangler and a veterinarian. I'm an expert with the bow and arrow and a tracker. Ralph Bellamy turns to Lee Marvin and asks, "Do you mind working with a Negro?"

Lee Marvin doesn't miss a beat, "What's the job?"

The movie doesn't make mention of my Indian side. Richard Brooks just stuck a bow in my hand. In an early scene the Mexicans capture Burt Lancaster and hang him upside down by a rope. I come across him; I pull my bow and shoot the Mexicans. I run down to him and cut him loose. He looks at the arrows, picks one up, and says, "I don't know how we beat the Indians!"

Dick Farnsworth, the famous stuntman, taught me how to use

a bow and arrow. He started me off with a fifty-pound bow and twenty-eight inch arrows. I had to graduate to the seventy-pound bow; that's what I use in the picture. A seventy-pound bow and a thirty-four inch arrow will kill anything in the world.

I practiced three hours a day for four months. I got so I could hit a cigarette butt at a hundred feet. I couldn't sight right down the arrow because I have a bad right eye. I had to learn to hold the bow down around my waist and shoot instinctively. You don't pose; you just point and shoot. That's called "live shooting."

I trained out at a horse ranch in the San Fernando Valley. An old cowboy named Jack Carey ran the place, and the studio paid him $400 a week to teach me how to use a rope. I had to learn to throw a sixty-foot rope. I started off roping garbage cans. Once I got good at that, Jack moved me out to the corral. He had some thoroughbreds running out there, and the next step was learning how to catch one.

Now, you don't throw a rope from over your head like you would roping calves. If you try to throw over your head, it'll spook the horses. You hold the rope in your right hand and you drag it on your left side. You cross over like you're reaching for your gun. Well, I could catch the last horse in the pack but I wasn't slick enough to catch the lead horse. When you go after the leader, you've got to loop your rope up in the air so the other horses can run underneath it. I couldn't do that.

After three weeks of practice, I thought I'd see if I could catch the lead horse. Without Jack's permission, I went out to the corral and managed to get my rope around the leader's neck. He took off with me running after, trying to keep up. He got to the end of the corral and slowed down. When the horse gets to that position, you're supposed to sit down and let the rope drag across your pants. Well, I was too excited and had my rope too tight; it was choking that horse. He started rearing and kicking and finally, this beautiful 1,600-pound horse fell to the ground.

Jack came running up hollering. "All right now, loosen up on that rope. Loosen up. LOOSEN UP! Now, just get up and walk away!" When it was over, he said, "You crazy son of a bitch! You want to get me fired?"

I said, "Jack, if I didn't catch that goddamned horse, well then, I ain't got the goddamned guts."

Jack Carey was a hard-nosed cowboy. He was once married to a woman who was part of the Union Oil fortune. He hated the suits so much he had to divorce her. He remarried and his wife told me, "Jack loves you, Woody, and you know he never did like colored people. He wouldn't teach Nat King Cole to ride a horse."

"Well, why does he like me?"

"Because you've got guts."

After four months with Jack, I had become the complete cowboy. Richard Brooks called me into his office for a meeting with all the production people. I stood there and answered technical questions about riding, roping, and shooting. Afterwards I told Jack Carey, "I wish you could have heard me in the office. I sounded like an authority. I looked like a genius, so you must be a genius." I knew everything; Jack had made me a cowboy.

We started shooting the picture in Death Valley. From Death Valley we moved to Las Vegas. Robert Ryan, Lee Marvin, and I made the ride in a limousine. I was riding in the jump seat, and I mixed martinis for 250 miles. By the time we arrived in Las Vegas, we were falling down drunk.

The next day I heard them talking about Lee Marvin like a dog. He got so drunk he thought he was playing the slot machine on a parking meter. But I didn't know how much of a big ass he made of himself because I had set out on my own. The next day, a big muscle-headed guy came to see me at my hotel room.

"Woody Strode?"

"Yes?"

"Do you know what you did the other night?"

"No, what did I do?"

"You went into every nightclub on the Strip, danced, and played guitar. You were at the Follies and danced a hula with all the girls. You went to the Flamingo and got into a fight. You had five security guards on the floor!"

"What?"

I had a little kink in my shoulder and now the memory started to come back. I had an Italian cab driver, and I hired him to take me up and down the Strip. I carried him with me everywhere I went. They wouldn't allow us to come into the Flamingo and I got insulted. I got mad and somebody tried to hammerlock me. When he did, I spun around and that's when the fight started.

So this muscle-head said to me, "Woody, we know you don't want to do anything but have a good time. Why don't you just stay here at the Mint Hotel and have a good time?" They wanted to contain the damage; we were wiping out the town.

That night we had a huge party in my suite. We invited all the Watusi dancers, all the maids, the bartenders, cooks, whoever was off work. We had an open house for them. About three o'clock in the morning everybody was gone and Tony Ebbs, a stuntman who was rooming with me, said, "I can't get no sleep. That goddamned Howdy Podner. I'm going to shoot that son of a bitch."

Now, before I tell this story, I want to quote from this article by Cynthia Lindsay in *Cosmopolitan,* the September, 1966 issue.

ON THOSE MOVIE MEANIES

Marvin's proclivity for drinking has been highly publicized. He refers to his rather extensive intake of alcohol as "juicing it up." The drinking has a peculiar pattern, almost an all or nothing thing. "Once in a while," he says, "when I've been hunting or fishing or skin diving, I get to feeling so good I've got to do something about it."

What he does about it is drink everything in sight. But the remarkable part of his behavior pattern is that he never gets mean. "I just get loose," Marvin says. "The hell he does," says his friend Ty Cabeen. "He gets loud, that's what he gets."

Marvin's clowning has given him such a reputation that he gets the credit whether responsible or not. On the Las Vegas location, he hit the front pages for a caper which occurred when he was sound asleep.

It seems that he and the good guys were juicing it up in his room in the hotel. Meanwhile the mechanism inside a thirty-foot statue across the road at a gambling casino, was croaking, "Howdy Podner." The ghastly noise out of this ghastly figure never ceases, night or day. The display is known as "Vegas Vic" and it is a bona fide atrocity, even for Las Vegas. This particular night, Marvin rose from the group, walked to the window and looked out. "Someday

I'm going to stand here and shoot that s.o.b. Vegas Vic right in the mouth," he said. As he turned away, he added, "And that goes for King Kong, too. Only he gets it between the eyes." (King Kong is a similarly hideous figure of a giant gorilla standing in front of a rival casino.)

Marvin thereupon retired to a blissful sleep. But not the good guys. Their leader's every wish their command. They crawled out on the ledge of the hotel sixteen stories above the ground, carrying the bow and arrows used by Woody Strode in *The Professionals*. Strode drew bead. Vegas Vic got it right in the mouth. The boys then retired and the next morning the papers headlined the stunt as Marvin's latest.

Strode says, "When they came out saying he did it—I tell you, he was ten feet tall he was so pleased.

See, the legend has located the story in Lee's room, but it really took place in mine. It was three o'clock in the morning when Tony Ebbs said, "I can't sleep. I'm going to shoot that son of a bitch." He picked up my bow and said, "Let me test this thing." He shot an arrow at the closet and it went right through the door and stuck in the wall. He said, "Yeah, it works." That seventy-pound bow put the arrow through that door like a hot knife through butter.

Tony took the bow, opened the sliding glass door, and stepped out on the balcony. Right across the street was the California Club, and they had the big gorilla statue out in front. He shot a couple of arrows at it. I figured that was too easy, so I decided I'd try and shoot the orange ball off the top of the Fremont Hotel. I took the bow, but from where we were on the balcony I couldn't get a clean shot.

We went back inside, and I opened the window across from the sliding glass. I still couldn't hit the ball from the window; it was too long a pull. My arrows just skidded across the roof of the Fremont. But from the window I could see Howdy Podner waving.

I decided I was going to hit that goddamned statue. It was a five-foot bow, and I had to crawl out the window to get the angle. The Mint Hotel had ledges and I was sixteen stories up standing on one. I was so drunk, I didn't care if I fell. Tony said, "Wait a second, let me hold you." He reached and grabbed me by the belt at the back of my pants. I found the angle, set, let loose an arrow and hit Howdy Podner right in the mouth. The whole statue started crackling. Sparks were flying everywhere. Then Howdy Podner blacked out and came to a stop.

Right away Tony and I looked at each other, "Cops. Let's get the hell out of here."

Tony pulled me back inside and I said, "I'd better get this bow out of the room." As I was running down the hall, the cops were getting off the elevator. I turned the corner and knocked on Lee Marvin's door. I said, "Lee, don't ask any questions. Just take this bow and hide it. We shot Howdy Podner." Well, that crazy son of a bitch got so excited he fired a shotgun out of his window. The cops came and found the bow in his room. Lee was so proud; it got to be the biggest joke in town.

We had so much fun; if there had been a priest traveling with us we would have corrupted him. Somebody must have told Luana we were going wild because she flew in to keep an eye on me. That was the first time she ever had to chase me down. There was no way for me not to have Luana there because the women kept coming after me. Lee and I screwed up one time and Luana was on the next plane.

After we finished the picture and got back to Los Angeles, Lee Marvin called and asked me to come out to his house in Malibu. Luana and I showed up and Lee said, "You've got to see this letter from Columbia Studios: 'Dear Lee, we want your permission to do this for the sake of the picture. It will have nothing to with the advertising or billboards. We would like to start the film this way: Columbia Pictures' *The Professionals,* starring Lee Marvin and sequence. Starring Robert Ryan and sequence. Starring Woody Strode and sequence.' " Lee stopped right there. He said, "Did you ever think you'd get your name on top of Burt Lancaster's? I'm signing." And without any warning, he leaned over and gave me a kiss right on the lips.

That's how I got my first star billing. The studio had to write letters to all the stars and get their permission on the order of the credits. They put my name ahead of Lancaster's because that worked best visually. They didn't use my name in any of the newspaper ads, and my name didn't appear on the marquees at the Pantages Theater in Hollywood either.

Back when I did *Sergeant Rutledge,* Jeffrey Hunter, Constance Towers, and Billie Burke got the star billing. I was Sergeant Rutledge and I got featured billing. In the newspaper ads there was a little box down in the left-hand corner that said, "Featuring Woody Strode." In Hollywood there's a caste system, and there's always an argument over whose name is going to be first. It was the agent's job to work out the billing process in the contracts.

John Ford told me I should have received an Academy Award nomination for *Sergeant Rutledge*. But who gives a damn? I've never won any blue ribbons. I was a football player, a wrestler. I didn't walk off the street and enter the studio. I had to work my way into the business, slowly.

Awards mean nothing to me. "Oh, here's a medal for you Woody," and every time you come into my house I say, "look at my medal!" All I want to know is that the next time they need somebody, they'd go to get Woody because he's a good worker. He knows how to do the stuff that we need. I never worried about billing. I didn't care if I was last as long as my name was up there somewhere. And I could steal a picture just by having a good moment, as long as the star didn't stand in my light.

CHAPTER TWENTY-TWO

Bene, Grazie, Italia

Well, thank you, Italy. I've spent a lot of time over there, and made a lot of Italian pictures. The first was *Seduto alla sua Destra; Seated at his Right*. From there I went to *C'era una volta il West; Once Upon a Time in the West*. After that, the Italians just beat a path to my door carryin' a big bag full of money. I ended up living in Rome from 1969 through 1971, and in all that time, I never learned to speak Italian. The Italians never cared that I learn their language. But they made a star out of me, and for that I'll always be grateful. For me, Italy was the promised land.

It was 1968 when a director named Valerio Zurlini hired me to star in *Seated at his Right*. Zurlini was a short man with sandy-colored hair from northern Italy. He was an artist and a poet. He'd make a picture every three or four years just like it was a painting or a sculpture.

Seated at his Right is a biblical reference to Christ when he said to the priest Caiaphas, "Hereafter, shall you see the Son of man sitting on the right hand of power, and coming into the clouds of heaven." Originally, the film was supposed to be a forty-minute segment for a five-part film called *Rage in Love*, but Zurlini must have found some extra passion for the story because he blew it up

233

into a full-length feature. It became Italy's official entry at the Cannes Film Festival.

In the movie, I play a Christ-like character who tries to establish peaceful reform within an unnamed African country that's controlled by an overbearing white rule. I travel from village to village preaching to the people. I tell them, "As long as we are united we cannot be defeated, they know this and this is why they will try and infiltrate among you setting brother against brother, and relying on your greed."

The government arrests me for being a revolutionary and orders me to sign papers that would make me forsake my teachings. I refuse. They begin to torture me; I suffer and anguish. They nail my hands to a table. They beat me until I lose my sight. My left side is pierced. The life slowly drains out of me. My face is twisted in pain, and my legs go limp as they drag me from the interrogation room back to my cell. The violence is unbelievable.

Zurlini was trying to show the total devotion to violence of the men who were torturing me, and the horrors of a dictator-style government. For a good third of the film I anguish in pain, and that was probably my most difficult performance ever. The courtroom scene in *Sergeant Rutledge* was probably my most emotional scene, but *Seated at his Right* had the most sustained emotion. And Zurlini was a good director; he got everything out of me.

We shot the film inside an old warehouse in Rome. The Italians are great set designers, and they built everything we needed. Most of the movie takes place in my prison cell, but all the exteriors were also done on stage. It took about ten days to shoot the whole thing, and right after I got finished was when Sergio Leone came after me to star in the opening scene of *Once Upon a Time in the West*.

In this country, Sergio Leone was known as the king of spaghetti westerns. He's the guy that made Clint Eastwood a star. And I remember him telling me, "I'm going to make a star out of Charlie Bronson." That's how he said it, no hemming and hawing. In the United States, Charlie couldn't get arrested, but when the Italians got a hold of him, with his beautiful character face, they made a star out of him.

Sergio Leone knew me through *The Professionals* and the

westerns I had made for John Ford. He offered me $7,500 for fourteen days' work; Sid Gold countered at ten grand. They finally settled at $8,000 because Sid knew that this would be an outstanding film for me.

When I met the production team they were staying at a big hotel about two-and-a-half hours from the location. I wanted to meet Sergio, so I asked the production manager where I could find him. He said, "Mr. Leone is staying in the little town of Guadix," which was about ten minutes from the job.

I said, "That's where my wife and I are going to stay," and they drove us over. We moved into this little joint with Sergio, and he picked up the tab. Sergio, who loved to eat and was pretty big as a result, bought us dinner every night. I remember him asking me in his thick Italian accent why Hollywood had never made me a star. The Italians could never understand why I wasn't a star at home.

I told him, "I don't think they've quite gotten used to me coming off the mountain on a horse with John Wayne by my side." But Sergio saw what I could do, and that was enough for him.

Then he confided in me, "Woody, this is my last western."

"Why?"

"Because they call them spaghetti westerns." Sergio Leone was terribly insulted by that. See, Sergio loved the West just like John Ford. When you see the accuracy of his sets, the costumes and the props, it was classic. And Sergio was a big fan of John Ford, although he wasn't a tough guy like Ford. Sergio was a typical Italian, very warm and emotional. But to show you his respect for John Ford, I found this review of *Once Upon a Time in the West* in the *Hollywood Reporter*.

> [The] Director has stopped playing celluloid "variations" on westerns, and now appears desirous to become a straight oater filmmaker, a sort of Giovanni Ford. This means Leone's own special talent for playing with film ideas gets lost in no man's land of the merely imitative.

Now, there's no sense in explaining the film because Jack Elam and I get gunned down and killed in the opening scene. What happens is, we arrive at a little train station out in the middle of nowhere. The audience doesn't know what we're up to. Jack Elam takes a seat on the platform, and I set up about a hundred yards away under the water tower that feeds the trains. When the train arrives, we regroup. We're standing there and nobody gets off the train. The train pulls out and when it clears the station, it uncovers Charles Bronson standing on the other side. We pull our guns, and Charlie kills us.

When we shot the part where I'm standing under the water tower, it was hot, and I took my hat off to wipe my forehead. When I did, a drop of water fell and hit me. Sergio was standing behind the camera not more than five or six feet away. He had an interpreter with him, because Sergio never tried to completely speak English on the set. As the translator was telling me what Sergio wanted, water from the tower kept dripping, and the camera was picking it up, so Sergio decided to use it.

He directed the scene just like the real-life. I took my hat off, the water dripped and hit me; I wiped and looked up. I put my big, black cowboy hat back on. The camera stayed with it and after a few minutes the brim was full. Then Sergio said, "Woody, drink the water off your hat." I took the hat off, I lifted it, and drank. He said, "Now slowly, put it back on."

Well, that became quite a famous scene, and it was never in the script. It was just an accident because the water happened to drip onto my hat.

Now, at the conclusion of the opening scene—when I get shot and killed—they put a squib under my shirt. That's a bag of blood with a small, explosive charge. Charlie, Jack, and I all pulled our guns and cranked at the same time. When the bullet hit me, I had to fall over backwards. Because of my wrestling experience, I was able to go straight backwards and land on my shoulders. And the blood just burst out.

They had to cut that part from the American version. Just like in *Spartacus* when Olivier sticks me with a knife like a bull. They had a special effects guy crouched behind the railing who shot the blood out of a squirt gun. That was too graphic for the American censors so they cut it out. But *Spartacus* was really graphic, they showed cold turkey what happened; the Italians were the same way.

Once Upon a Time in the West was the only picture I did for Sergio Leone, but he always gave me a good word of mouth, and that helped me a lot in Italy. And he was quite fond of Luana, too. He called her Mama. One night at dinner, he said, "I need an Indian woman to be the scrub woman that runs out of the train station in the opening scene. Why don't you do it, Mama?" So if you ever see the picture, that woman was Luana. Sergio gave Luana a salary plus an extra thousand bucks when it was over.

The first time I saw the film was in Italy, in Italian. When the lights went down, I said to Luana, "Here we go, Mama." The scene with the water was a complete surprise. And the close-ups, I couldn't believe. I never got a close-up in Hollywood. Even in *The Professionals* I had only three close-ups in the entire picture. Sergio Leone framed me on the screen for five minutes. After it was over I said, "That's all I needed."

When I got home and I saw Papa Ford, I told him, "Papa, there's an Italian over there that just loves the West, and he's not going to do another western because they call them spaghetti westerns." I said, "Will you autograph a picture for him?"

Unfortunately, Sergio is dead today, but if you checked with his office, you'd find he has an autographed picture from John Ford. On the picture Ford wrote, "If there's anything I can do to help make Woody a star, I'll do it for free." Those are the little things that make those guys immortal.

While I was home, Euan Lloyd, an English producer, contacted me about being in *Shalako,* a $5 million production for Palomar Pictures International, a subsidiary of the American Broadcasting Company. He'd lined up Sean Connery and Brigitte Bardot to play the starring roles. Lloyd wanted me to play the Indian chief. I said, "No, you've got to get a full-blood Indian to play the role"— because I was fresh off the boat and a little sensitive to the racial situation in America—"There's too much racial stuff going on, and I don't want to get the Indians mad at me."

He said, "Let's try to work something out. I really want you to play the part."

I said, "I'll tell you what I'll do. If you'll hire my Sioux friend, Tug Smith, to play alongside me, then I'll play the chief."

"Woody, Eddie Dmytryk has an Indian who has played in all his pictures. This is Eddie's special person, and he would like this Indian to play your right-hand man."

Eddie Dmytryk had made over forty films, including *The Young Lions* and *The Caine Mutiny*. He also directed westerns and made some great ones like *Broken Lance* and *Warlock*. Eddie had a lot of pull and his special Indian was Rod Redwing, who had the fastest draw in Hollywood. He taught the fast draw to everyone you ever saw. Cecil B. DeMille brought him into the movie business.

So when Euan Lloyd told me Rod Redwing was going to play my right-hand man, I said, "I'm not going to be able to do the job. Every Indian in Los Angeles is looking forward to seeing Tug go overseas with me. If I accept the job, I just don't know how I'll be able to face them."

The Englishman said, "Okay, bring Tug down here and let me take a look at him."

I told Tug, "Put on your Indian outfit because Euan Lloyd's never seen a real Indian."

We went down and met Lloyd at the Copper Skillet, which was right across the street from the studio. Euan Lloyd was wide-eyed as he looked Tug over. Tug was wearing his deerskin suit with the beads and the fringe, a headdress with eagle feathers and moccasins.

I said, "You know, Tug speaks five languages, Cheyenne, Arapaho, everything. Speak some Indian languages, Tug."

The Englishman fell apart, "Oh my God, Woody, he's perfect. He can play your sub-chief, your muscle, and we can take Rod Redwing and let him play your father." So I got the job like that, and I put my wig on.

They shot the film in Almeria, Spain. At that point in my career I was traveling with my own saddle, two 60-foot ropes and an 80-pound bow. Once you reach a certain level, you've got to have your own equipment. I remember there was one scene in *Shalako* where I had to go off-stage and shoot the fire arrows because nobody else could do it. Those are the types of things I had learned after thirty years of action pictures.

And, to go back for a second, in John Ford's *Two Rode Together*, there was a scene where I came riding in with my Indian sub-chiefs. I stepped down off my horse, said something in Indian, hopped back on the horse and let out a war cry. I pulled out with all the Indian warriors on my heels. The horses crossed some light cables; the insulation was cut and the sparks went flying. John Ford got the shot: it was a great scene. I didn't realize how dangerous that run was until I started training for *The Professionals*.

Jack Carey told me, "Woody, I saw you in that goddamned *Two Rode Together*. If your horse had fallen, those Indians would have run right over your ass. Anytime you're ridin' and you're leadin' a pack of horses, the pack has got to split and leave you an alley. That way if your horse falls, the pack runs around you."

That paid off when I got to *Shalako*. I had to make a 1,500 yard run on horseback with all my warriors following me. We ran 1,500 yards right at the camera; the camera panned and we ran 500 more yards up into a canyon. I had a bunch of Spanish Gypsies following me. They didn't look like the European Gypsies, who look more like white people. These Gypsies were real brown; I don't know how they got their color, but they made perfect Apaches.

I told them what I was going to do. "I'm going to run ten yards out in front. I want everybody to split up in two groups, one on either side of me."

The first run-through, my horse fell and I wasn't injured. The second run, I was holding my bow way out in my right hand; we ran right at the camera, turned and ran into the canyon. Probably the greatest horse charge in the history of film. We came back and Eddie Dmytryk said, "We've got to do this scene again."

He had us do it three more times. The third time my horse went wild. I had to take the bow and whip him because he was blowing up, snorting and flaring. I walked back to the camera and Sean Connery, Brigitte Bardot, you can imagine all those high-class actors, said, "Woody, are you crazy? You'll get yourself killed!"

I said, "No actor can do what I just did." And Eddie Dmytryk never used that scene in the film.

At lunchtime, I walked into the tent. A Mr. Giuseppe Colizzi came up to me, "Woody Strode, my name is Colizzi, please, have a cigar.

"I represent an Italian production company. What you did today I have never seen another actor do. I would like you to come to Italy with me and star in my next picture. I can give you $50,000 for ten weeks' work, first class plane tickets for you and your wife, and $500 a week to live on."

First blood.

I told him, "I'm coming, but don't say anything to my agent!"

I got on the phone and called Sid Gold. He said, "Oh Woody, you'll get a bad script." But for $50,000 I would've played Mickey Mouse.

On *Shalako*, I made $1,000 a week, the same as I made on *The Professionals*. I had never made any real money in America. I'd been in some classic pictures and never made a dime. I was never in a position to bargain. Where else was I going to go? I was unique doing just what I had been doing: throwing the spear, playing Indians, slanting my eyes, putting on pigtails. They probably thought they were doing me a favor.

When the Italians saw what I could do, they just flat out made me an offer, and they offered me a star's salary. Mr. Colizzi told me, "You see that white actor over there?"—I won't call his name because I don't want to embarrass him—"He cannot ride a horse and we are paying him $350,000 for one picture."

So I took the part and I flew back to Italy. The picture was titled *Boot Hill* with Bud Spencer, Terence Hill, Victor Buono, and Lionel Stander. They were all starring in their first western. It was an old-fashioned western with a circus in a big top tent. The director told me, "Woody, we want you to put on these tights, climb the trapeze, jump out, grab that rope, and slide down onto this box here on the floor. This stuntman will attack you, and that's when the fight scene starts."

I said, "Goddamn, you finally found someone dumb enough to do it!" But for $50,000 I was going to swing on those ropes.

We were working from six in the morning until ten, eleven o'clock at night. The American actors went by the union rules and that meant twelve hours off between shooting days. They called their agents, and their agents told them to stop working. I told Luana, "Mama, don't say nothing. If this is how the Italians work, then they got themselves a jock strap. It ain't nothing but a little sweat to me."

Nine o'clock one night Mr. Colizzi said to me, "Woody, all the other American actors have quit. We don't want to take advantage of you. Do you want to call your agent?"

I said, "Mr. Colizzi, let me tell you something. You gave me $50,000 to do this job, and I didn't come here to steal your money. What do you want me to do?" He couldn't believe it.

He stopped the production and fired the director. We started up again and Giuseppe Colizzi took over the direction. He gave me an extra $25,000 to finish the picture. I made $75,000, the most money I had ever seen.

I went right from *Boot Hill* to *Ciak Mull, l'uomo della vendetta; The Unholy Four*, directed by Pasquale Squitieri. He was a young director, or as they said in those days, a small oater. I got cash and 25 percent of world sales for that one.

Then Dino De Laurentiis offered me a part in *The Deserters* with Richard Crenna, Ricardo Montalban, and Slim Pickens. Every once in a while you can catch that one on the tube. De Laurentiis gave me another $75,000.

I've often commented on that stage of my life because I didn't know I could just completely live with white people. I was like a zebra with a bunch of lions, and I went right to the trough with them. I learned from that experience that I could live anywhere in the world. I was as comfortable in Italy as I would have been with my own people. I found the Italians to be as simple as the Polynesians. They're the only white group I know that act like natives.

I was paying $120 a month to live a half-block off the Via Veneto in Rome. The Via Veneto was the most famous street name in Rome and one of the most famous streets in the world. That's where all the movie stars lived, like Marcello Mastroianni and Vittorio Gassman. Cafe de Paris was there and Harry's Bar, one of the most famous bars in Europe.

The Via Veneto was like Rodeo Drive in Beverly Hills. You

could buy everything expensive there. I'm glad I mentioned Rodeo Drive, that's probably the best way to describe it. Luana and I lived around the corner on the Via Sardinia. You could drink on my street for fifteen cents; half a block away it would cost you one dollar. There was a Jewish delicatessen across the street; Fellini used to have his coffee there.

Our apartment was six stories up, three bedrooms and a huge living room. The ceilings were painted with cherubs and fat ladies. The windows were like doors, and they opened onto a balcony that ran the entire length of the living room. And we had a flight of stairs to the roof; we could stand up there and look out over the entire city of Rome. If they had treated me like an American, they could have charged me $1,000 a month.

Luana and I were laying up in Rome, kicking back when the telegram arrived. Luana said, "Kenny's sick, Woody!"

I fell out of bed. "How bad is it?"

"Very."

We grabbed the next plane home. I met Kenny at the Cork Room, out on the west side. That's where all our doctors and lawyers used to go. We sat and had a drink. I couldn't believe how skinny he had gotten, and his color was all pasty and ashen. His eyes were sunken in and had dark circles underneath; they'd lost their spark. The veins were sticking out of his hands like a road map. It took all the guts I had to hold the tears back. I felt so guilty; I hadn't talked to him for about two years.

He said, "I've been pretty sick, Woody."

He looked so bad I didn't know how to ask him what was wrong. But I heard he'd spent $35,000 at the UCLA Medical Center.

I wanted to take him back to Rome with me. I made one last pitch. I said, "You've got to come over and see this scene and kick back." Because he had grown up with Italians, and I was glad to pay his way.

I said, "Why don't you come over and we'll sip some wine on the Via Veneto." I didn't know he was going to die in just a few months. And that's the last good conversation we had. I just wasn't prepared for him dying. That was one of the saddest moments and saddest days of my life.

These are the kinds of shocks you get when people you really know get ready to move on. You never think there's going to be an end to the trail. It pissed me off that he could die so easy. It seemed like life should have more to offer the athlete. Some of us are lucky and some of us never get to the wire.

I do think Kenny was happy with the amount of success he achieved. Athletics opened up a lot of doors for him. I guess you've got to feel a little sorry for yourself when you're one of the greatest football players of your day and you don't get a chance to show it. He was twenty-seven years old when he signed with the Rams and his knees were shot. I guess you get a little envious of the guys that are starring today. Guys that are getting a million dollars a year because of you. But Kenny was never bitter.

See, Kenny was really glamorous. People would chase him around. But he always took care of his family. What Kenny did for his family was give them dignity. He made them stars. He made Rocky his business manager; Rocky didn't know it at that time, but when all the deals went down Rocky sat in. I remember when Kenny got $1,000 a game, that was a lot of money. And we thought we were going to play football forever. I guess I'm just not educated to getting old.

Kenny was two months shy of fifty-three years old when he died on June 24, 1971. You've never seen more people at a funeral in your life. All the supervisors from the City of Los Angeles were there. Bill Ackerman, all the UCLA people. I saw the telegram from Richard Nixon. I mean, how many friends do you really have? Well, before Kenny died, we gave him a testimonial dinner at the Paladium in Hollywood and more than 1,000 people showed up.

Everyone was prepared for his passing. It was a lingering type illness. He had a heart condition. They have a name for it, angina or something. The heart itself was good and strong, but the heart's in a sack. His heart sack would fill up with liquid, which would keep his heart from working right. They gave him medication to control the fluid, but then his circulation would screw up. His feet and hands would turn purple. They had a treatment for that, but when they gave him that medication then his heart would flare up. It was like a yo-yo.

They took him to the UCLA Medical Center, and his boss told them not to spare any expense. They made sure he had the best of everything. They even brought heart specialists out from Johns Hopkins. They examined him to see if they could find out what was wrong and they came up empty. They didn't know what to do. In the meantime, the struggle just wore Kenny down. I sat and cried as I watched him getting weaker and weaker because Kenny was always the Big Bad Wolf, the Kingfish.

He died out there at UCLA. Kenny Junior was twenty-nine years old when his daddy died. He told his daddy, "This is the biggest game you've ever played. You've got to decide how far you want to fight it."

Well, he fought it for two-and-a-half years, and he couldn't make it. But Kenny Junior told me when the time grew close Kenny called the family in one at a time and read them the riot act. And the day before he died, and Kenny loved to play the horses, he told Kenny Junior, "I want you to play this and this over there at Hollywood Park." See, Kenny Washington never gave up.

CHAPTER TWENTY-THREE

The Last Hurdle

By 1970, Kalai and June were grown-up people. After June got out of high school, she went to East Los Angeles College, but she wasn't really interested in school and she dropped out. She got her Screen Actors Guild card and messed around with that for a little while.

June is quite pretty; she got all her mother's looks. She visited Luana and me while we were in Spain working on *Shalako*. The locals were so taken by her they asked her to be in a beauty contest and she won. She beat out all the local girls and Brigitte Bardot to win Miss Tourista. That's what really got her interested in acting, but she met a man, got married, had my grandchild, gave up the acting idea, and moved to Honolulu. That's where she is today.

Kalai is the brains of the outfit. He went to UCLA and majored in Asian studies. I remember him begging me to get him a little 100cc motorcycle so he could get around campus, which I did. In his junior year he was invited to attend the International Christian University in Japan; that's where he learned to speak Japanese. He learned it well enough to work as an interpreter for the Japanese gymnastics team. Then he got his master's degree in Asian studies at the University of Hawaii. Now he's talking about getting his doctorate in comparative religion and theology.

Well, with the kids off on their own, Luana and I decided to sell the chicken ranch in Montebello. I bought a house and five acres of land in the foothills of Glendora, California. That's where I live today, about twenty-five miles east of Los Angeles. I had lived there only three months when I moved to Italy. After three years, I came home to see Kenny. After he moved on, I decided I'd stick around and spend some time in America.

Well, by that time, *Seated at his Right* had been sitting on the shelf for three years. A guy named Sig Shore, who produced the film *Superfly,* and also bought and distributed films, bought the rights to the Zurlini film. At that time in America, there was a growing market for black films, and Sig Shore put some money in his pocket behind that. Ron Pennington wrote in the *Hollywood Reporter* on September 22, 1971:

> He [Sig Shore] said he thinks residual values on these pictures are just as good if not better than on other pictures, adding that "television will be delirious to get black pictures, as they are always interested in demographic patterns." Shore also said he feels "airlines will have to start playing these pictures if they expect to attract blacks with their in-flight movie program. They're going to have to come up with a more balanced package," he said.

When Sig Shore called me to say he had bought Zurlini's film, he said, "Woody, I've got it sold in 64 markets. It'll open in New York, and I've given it a new title."

I said, "What will you call it?"

"Black Jesus."

Well, I almost fainted. Because of my Christian background, I'm superstitious. I got back on the phone, *"Black Jesus?"*

He said, "Yes, will you come back to New York to help promote the film?"

I decided not to discuss the religious area. I said, "Okay, I'll come back there." I flew back and met Sig Shore. He set me up on Times Square signing autographs. On the billboard above me was my picture and the lines, "Woody Strode is *Black Jesus.*." And underneath that, "He who ain't with me—is against me," a line I never say in the movie. But Sig Shore was quite a promoter; he was selling an image and a title, not content.

In those years, to compare me with Jesus didn't go over well with distribution, and the movie bombed even though I got some good press. Howard Thompson, film critic with the *New York Times,* wrote:

> "With his keen, lidded eyes and strong, gaunt face, Strode does a perfectly respectable job of portraying an imprisoned, tortured and executed visionary leader in an African country. His gentle spirit of non-violence and agonized endurance under pressure are painfully real."

I don't believe the black press hardly covered it at all. Most of the fans were liberal white people. It was so odd to have a picture like that. The black leaders like Laumuba, that I represented in the picture, were like bandits. The establishment didn't like them. Laumuba was considered a communist, so it was very controversial. Of course, the Italians didn't give a shit; they just didn't like what the white world was doing to the Africans at that time.

Good or bad, I was the star of *Black Jesus,* and the people, the press had to talk about me in those terms. I now had Hollywood thinking about me in those terms.

After the release of *Black Jesus,* Marty Rackin contacted me about being in a picture he was getting ready to make called *The Revengers. The Revengers* stars William Holden, Ernest Borgnine, Susan Hayward, and Woody Strode. Marty was the first one to give me an advertised starring role in an American picture. He paid me $3,500 a week plus free travel and expenses for my wife while we shot in Mexico. That's how the Italians and *Black Jesus* had inflated my value in this country.

That was the last hurdle for me; I had done everything in Hollywood but be a star. Before I went to Italy I always kept my mouth shut and let my agent do the talking. Hollywood took advantage of me because I could either take their offer or not work. But at that time, $1,000 a week was enough money. I just wanted to pay the bills and live comfortably, which I've always been able to do.

I remember when I saw *Yankee Doodle Dandy* with Jimmy Cagney, they showed an all-white New York City. In Hollywood, many of the major studios were being run by Jewish men, but if an actor had a Jewish look he wouldn't make it in the movies. Kirk Douglas didn't admit he was Jewish until ten years after *Spartacus*. Hollywood didn't think anything about integration; they were selling a product.

But Hollywood gave me a certain dignity when they stuck that spear in my hand, because I fought everybody to the death. Here's an example. When I went to the Cannes Film Festival for the screening of *Seated at his Right,* I arrived in my tux. My shirt was open and I had my tie in my pocket. I was a little embarrassed to be there because I was nobody. I started walking down the lane and all of a sudden the photographers' cameras started clicking and flashing. A bunch of kids started shouting my name. I looked out there and waved at them. Then I looked at the producer that had invited me, and I said, "That's from fighting Tarzan." If I had been a waiter, shuffling, doing all that funny stuff, I would have never made it. I was very lucky.

I remember when I was stationed on Guam during the second world war, these raggedy, wild-looking natives were running around calling me "nigga." I went to a USO show and Hattie McDaniel, one of the most famous of our early black entertainers, would perform with a towel wrapped around her head. I became embarrassed and it started with the second world war.

So I had to put things in perspective and look at the progress I'd made. When I was traveling to Mexico to make *The Revengers,* I was on a bus with all the other actors and I saw a drunken Mexican Indian. He was wobbling, thirsty, and water was running down the gutter. He got down, in push-up position, and drank from the gutter. I said, "Well, look at him: 150 years ago we were doing the same thing."

CHAPTER TWENTY-FOUR

An Old Race Horse

After I finished *The Revengers* I went back to Italy and stayed two more years. I came home for good in 1973; that's when John Ford died. I got to his house just before he passed on. His family had moved him to Palm Springs. He had cancer and if you've ever seen a picture of the Jews in the concentration camps, that's how he looked. He couldn't have weighed more than fifty pounds, his hair was all gone, his face looked like a skull. That's what chemotherapy does to you; imagine how cruel it must be. He was propped up in bed having his last drink of whiskey.

I said, "Papa, I just got off the plane. Thanks for the telegram." And I sat there on the side of his bed for six hours, holding his hand until he went into a coma.

He died. His sister and I took an American flag and draped him in it. We got some brandy, toasted him, and broke the glasses in the fireplace. I walked out of that house, and I never looked back. First Kenny, then John Ford: my best friends were dead. I was never close to Mrs. Ford or anyone else in the old man's family. It was just him and me. He was the roughest man I ever worked for. But he directed me so I was never afraid of being in front of a camera. He was so tough I didn't believe he could die. I've never been able to prepare myself for anyone dying.

Luana died in 1980. She had Parkinson's disease. It first showed up in 1975. We were getting off a plane in Portugal. As we were going down the stairs, she stumbled. She said, "Daddy, I'm dizzy." That's how it hit. She started wobbling, but I could handle her. She was like somebody drunk. I took her to a doctor; he found her cholesterol level was way up. He figured it was her circulation.

When we got home I put her through the whole medical scene. They sent her down to a hospital in Santa Monica. They put atomic medicine in her veins, lit up her brain, and took pictures. The doctor told me she had advanced Parkinson's and that it had been lying there dormant for forty years. As she got older and began to deteriorate, it surfaced. The doctor didn't tell me it was hopeless. He didn't tell me there was no cure for Parkinson's disease.

I took her with me to Key West, Florida, where I was doing a picture. After work, we'd go and sit at the bar. She always liked to do that; that was the Hawaiian in her. And that was the last trip we took. I brought her home, and I learned how to cook and clean the house. I had never done that, but I got so you could've hired me to cook Christmas dinner.

She was sixty-four when she died; I was sixty-six. Towards the end she couldn't leave the house. I used to jog stationary, and under the trials and tribulations I got so I could jog two hours straight. I would sip wine and run in place; that's what kept me sane.

A doctor came up to me, a church member, and said, "Woody, this is bad for you. We have places to put Luana. You don't have to do this."

Well, right there I lost respect. As far as my generation was concerned, everybody died in their home. Nobody got farmed out. How can you be with somebody forty years and then shut the door?

I mean, we partied; I had a good life with that woman. The average man went to the pool hall or the golf course. Every time I went out I was with Luana; we'd drink, dance, laugh, and sing all night long. To watch this beautiful Hawaiian woman, this free spirit deteriorate, well, it was more than I could handle. I started sipping that wine all day.

It got so Luana would just mumble; her speech was leaving. Slowly, I watched her disappear. I would sit and play her Hawaiian songs on the guitar. She'd try to sing along, and that'd choke me up so much I couldn't get the words out. I'm glad God gave me the strength, because I was now burying all my people. I held my mother's hand and watched her turn purple. I tried to pull her out of the grave. My brother couldn't do it. I had the guts; some of us have it and some of us don't.

Luana got to that stage after fighting the disease for four years. She was sitting on the brown couch in our living room, and she couldn't swallow. The process had quit; that part of the brain had stopped. I was so panicked; I called the hospital. The emergency ambulance arrived, and they took her to intensive care.

I was down at that hospital four days straight, day and night. I stayed right there in the room with her. I was so scared; I couldn't sleep. Finally the doctor said, "Woody, why don't you go home?"

I told him, "You know, to die by yourself is probably the worst thing in the whole world. I got to be there to hold her hand."

He said, "You'd better get some sleep. I won't let her die."

That's how confident he was. So I went home, and they let her out of intensive care. I took her to the motion picture home, because I just didn't have the know-how to make her comfortable at our home. I was there every day. Just before she died, Kalai and June flew in, and we sang Hawaiian songs to her. It upset the whole hospital.

We finished a song, and when I looked up, she was gone. She had slipped into a coma. Her eyes turned a lighter color, like marble. That's death. I touched her and kissed her good-bye.

I just wish I had been closer to a black church because I believe in miracles. I'd have felt better if they had gotten that old-fashioned prayer going. I felt a little guilty about that. But she was a Mormon, and the Mormons don't believe in a lot of things most churches believe in. They talked about how we would be together in the hereafter. Well, that's the last place I wanted to hear about. I believe in living right here on earth.

And I believe I showed her a good life. If she hadn't married me, she would have probably spent her entire life on the islands. I pulled her all the way into the motion picture industry. Through our traveling, I exposed her to the entire world. By traveling, she got dignity. She was better known than I was overseas. Everybody loved her; I was always second fiddle. I was just there to make some money. They accepted me through her. We'd sing Hawaiian music and Mama would be in the background singing falsetto. She'd say, "Come on, Daddy, let's show these people how to dance." The British, the Italians, we'd just wipe them out. My color would just disappear.

Sometimes we'd have a little too much to drink and she'd do a hula with me on her shoulders. We used to leg fight and I never could beat her. She had a surfboard that weighed 100 pounds, all koa wood, and she would carry that by herself. She showed off her strength until she was forty years old; then I made her stop. She was the last generation of the real Hawaiian people, the sweetest, most beautiful people on the face of the earth.

I give her credit for me being the way I am now. I'm flexible; I don't have the racial hang-ups a lot of my people have. That was from my exposure to the Hawaiian people. Sometimes I have to be careful around my own people because I hang a little too loose, and I'm liable to say something that might make them sensitive.

See, I was always opening doors never knowing what I'd find on the other side. One hundred years from today they'll look at all this and say, "Shit man, this guy did all this stuff before anybody did anything." I never thought of it like that. I was just trying to make a living, just trying to survive in my generation. If I did something outstanding, the press would headline me. They turned me into a celebrity. But for some reason the press never affected us. We were all shy; you were embarrassed if you wanted something.

Some of the kids that come off the street and become big stars, you can't hardly touch them with a ten-foot pole. Because they've never been anything, they're just jumping. But the football and the nine years of wrestling gave me exposure to the crowds, and I became comfortable with it. It was normal for me. And whatever I did, I worked my ass off. When I got to motion pictures, "A phony fight, no more broken bones? Great!" Now they had me riding a horse, playing cowboys and Indians.

Today, the older white men see my cowboy hat and they identify with that. I don't wear boots; I wear moccasins. They see my Indian cheekbones, they accept the moccasins. This is my identity. I don't talk about what I am; I defend myself quietly.

"I'm sorry, boy. You can't get a drink here."

"Well, where can I get a drink?"

"I'll tell you what I'll do. I can't give you a drink over here at the bar. Why don't you sit over there and I'll sell you a bottle?"

I've cut all the corners.

When Kenny and I came along we didn't feel racial prejudice at all. Whether we had blinders on or what, I don't know. Once, Kenny and the Hollywood Bears' ball club sent Luana and me down to a hotel in Arizona where we weren't allowed. We were sitting in the lobby and the white folks were all looking at us. Finally Luana went up to ask to use the bathroom and some white man hit on her and said, "Are you Hawaiian?"

"Yes."

"Well then, put a flower in your hair."

They just assumed I was Hawaiian too. I said, "Those god-damned football players." And when I got to the game, they all laughed. They thought it was a big joke, to send me and Luana there and upset the hotel.

See, when I was growing up, I didn't even know that football wasn't integrated. We never thought about that. Everything we were doing was all brand-new. We knew that baseball had their own Negro league, but out here black guys were playing against white guys. Nobody wrote, "A unique thing is happening in Los Angeles: the blacks are playing the whites."

When I got to UCLA, I had the same rights as any other student. I've got to credit Bill Ackerman for that. We were not ostracized from anything. That freed our minds to listen to Bill Spaulding and Babe Horrell teach us to play football in their system. And a camaraderie developed, because all the kids on the team were from poor families and now they were living high off the hog. If I hadn't had that opportunity, I'd have been a mechanic or a ditch digger; I'd have had a dull life.

For the first five or six years I was acting, I never saw my motion pictures. I wouldn't go to the theater. I was embarrassed; I was in a glamorous business, and I wasn't prepared to be glamorous. I had more of the Joe Louis attitude, and I was confident I had the ability to do anything asked of me. I never thought I was going to get old. I can't believe I'm seventy-four years old. The clock went by so fast.

I don't think I told you, but I was inducted into the Stuntman's Hall of Fame. I'm not a member of the association; I'm an actor, that was just a compliment. All the old-timers know the stuff I've done in the movies.

Yakima Canutt contacted me. He was probably the greatest stuntman who ever lived. In John Ford's *Stagecoach* with John Wayne, he was the guy who fell off the stagecoach; it passed over him and just as it was going by he reached out, grabbed the back and climbed on top. And if you ever saw *Captain Blood* with Errol Flynn, there's a scene where he slides down the full sail on his scabbard. That was Yakima. Well, you got to know how tough that was.

Yakima and I had a good rapport. He first saw me in my infancy in the movies. He walked up to me and said, "I'm Yakima Canutt. You're going to make yourself some money."

He saw I had the ability. He was on the board of directors of the Stuntman's Association. And whoever else was on that board, they voted for me to have my footprints put into the cement out at their hall of fame.

I gave them a photograph of me catching a runaway stagecoach in *The Last Rebel* with Joe Namath. If you ever run across Joe, ask him about how old Woody caught the stagecoach. I made a 200-yard run, jumped from my horse to the runaway horses, and reined in that six-horse team. Joe sat there watching me and couldn't believe it. I was fifty-seven years old and it was the first time I had ever done that.

Well, I'm too old now to catch any stagecoaches. In my last three pictures I've done work that's too hard for me. But I always stay in shape. I don't go to a job out of shape because the man looks at me and wonders, "Can he still do the job?" My camouflage is close fitting T shirts, and I parade in them like an old race horse.

Last Sunday I went fishing with this friend of mine down in Huntington Beach. You don't hardly see any black people at all down there. We went into a hamburger stand to get some cold drinks. A bunch of big-muscled white kids, surfers, discovered me. They said, "Woody Strode, my God, we've watched you all our lives." They talked about my Tarzan film with Jock Mahoney.

I said, "That was over twenty-five years ago."

You know what the kids said? "You were an animal!"

You can imagine the good feeling that gave me. Imagine how that fed my ego. I've done enough films that when I get around a group like that, they admire me just because I've stayed in such good shape. I got all my fans based on this look. I can still attract attention stepping off a plane anywhere in the world. I can still half-ass fight. I can do all that ballet stuff; the only thing I can't do is fall off the horses.

I'm an old man, but life will never make an old man out of me. As long as you look like you can run on Santa Anita's race track, even if you take last, you've still made the field. People see that horse, they wonder what it's doing out there. They don't know it's 100 years old. Well, this is how nature has left me, so it's good.

Woody Strode Filmography

Sundown (1941)
Star Spangled Rhythm (1942)
No Time for Love (1943)
Bride of the Gorilla (1951)
The Lion Hunters (1951)
Androcles and the Lion (1952)
African Treasure (1952)
Caribbean (1952)
City Beneath the Sea (1953)
The Gambler From Natchez (1954)
Jungle Gents (1954)
Demetrius and the Gladiators (1954)
Son of Sinbad (1955)
The Ten Commandments (1956)
Tarzan's Fight for Life (1958)
The Buccaneer (1958)
Pork Chop Hill (1959)
The Last Voyage (1960)
Sergeant Rutledge (1960)
Spartacus (1960)

The Sins of Rachel Cade (1961)

Two Rode Together (1961)

The Man Who Shot Liberty Valance (1962)

Tarzan's Three Challenges (1963)

Genghis Khan (1965)

Seven Women (1966)

The Professionals (1966)

Seduto alla sua Destra/Black Jesus/Seated at His Right (1968)

C'era una volta il West/Once Upon a Time in the West (1968)

Shalako (1968)

Che! (1969)

King Gun (1969)

La collina degli stivali/Boot Hill (1969)

Ciak Mull, l'uomo della vendetta/The Unholy Four (1970)

Tarzan's Deadly Silence (1970)

La spina del dorsale diavolo/The Deserter (1971)

The Last Rebel (1971)

Black Rodeo (narrator) (1972)

The Revengers (1972)

The Gatling Gun (1972)

La mala ordina/The Italian Connection (1973)

Colpo in canna/Stick 'em up, Darlings! (1974)

Loaded Guns (1975)

Keoma/The Violent Breed (1976)

Winterhawk (1976)

Oil (1977)

Kingdom of the Spiders (1977)

Ravagers (1979)

Jaguar Lives! (1979)

Cuba Crossing/Kill Castro/Assignment: Kill Castro (1980)

Scream/The Outing (1983)

Vigilante/Street Gang (1983)

The Black Stallion Returns (1983)
The Final Executioner (1983)
Jungle Warriors (1984)
The Cotton Club (1984)
Lust in the Dust (1985)
Angkor: Cambodia Express (1985)

TV Movies
Breakout (1970)
Key West (1972)
A Gathering of Old Man (1987)

TV Series Appearances
Ramar of the Jungle (1952–53)
Mandrake the Magician (1954)
Jungle Jim (1955)
Soldiers of Fortune (1955)
Thriller (1960)
The Man From Blackhawk (1960)
Rawhide (1961)
The Lieutenant (1964)
The Farmer's Daughter (1964)
Daniel Boone (1966)
Tarzan (1966, 1967, 1968)
Manhunter (1973)
The Quest (1976)

Acknowledgments

The authors gratefully acknowledge the following sources for their contributions to the writing of this book. All photos are from Woody Strode's collection except where noted.

THE LOS ANGELES SENTINEL

THE PITTSBURGH COURIER

THE LOS ANGELES EXAMINER

THE BEST OF GRANTLAND RICE
by Grantland Rice,
selected by Dave Camerer
Publisher: Franklin Watts, Inc.
575 Lexington Avenue
New York, NY

TO ABSENT FRIENDS FROM RED SMITH
by Red Smith
Publisher: Atheneum
New York, NY

THE 100 GREATEST BOXERS OF ALL TIME
by Bert Randolph Sugar
Publisher: A Rutledge Book
New York, NY

261

**CHAMPION: JOE LOUIS: BLACK HERO IN WHITE
AMERICA**
by Chris Mead
Publisher: Charles Scribner's Sons
New York, NY

GRIDIRON

THE LOS ANGELES HERALD-EXAMINER

THE LOS ANGELES TIMES

THE SAN FRANCISCO CHRONICLE

WHATEVER HAPPENED TO GORGEOUS GEORGE?
by Joe Jares
Publisher: Prentice-Hall, Inc.
Englewood Cliffs, NJ

THE SPORTS BEAT
by Wendell Smith

THE DAILY NEWS

THE TORONTO DAILY NEWS

EBONY MAGAZINE

VARIETY

COSMOPOLITAN

THE HOLLYWOOD REPORTER

THE NEW YORK TIMES

A special thanks to Charles Lean, our publisher, and to Tom Wiener, our editor. Their interest, help and support made *Goal Dust* a reality.